James Frederick Chance

Chance of Bromsgrove and of Birmingham

And the Allied Families of Lucas and Homer

James Frederick Chance

Chance of Bromsgrove and of Birmingham
And the Allied Families of Lucas and Homer

ISBN/EAN: 9783744670883

Printed in Europe, USA, Canada, Australia, Japan

Cover: Foto ©ninafisch / pixelio.de

More available books at **www.hansebooks.com**

CHANCE

Of Bromsgrove and of Birmingham

and the allied families of

LUCAS and HOMER.

COMPILED FROM VARIOUS SOURCES

BY

JAMES FREDERICK CHANCE, M.A.

PRINTED FOR PRIVATE CIRCULATION BY
WITHERBY & CO.,
326, HIGH HOLBORN, LONDON, W.C.
1892.

PART I.—FAMILY HISTORY.

§ 1.—DESCENT OF WILLIAM CHANCE OF BIRMINGHAM.
§ 2.—WORCESTERSHIRE CHANCES.
§ 3.—CHANCE OF BROMSGROVE.
§ 4.—SPELLING OF THE NAME.
§ 5.—TILT OF BROMSGROVE.
§ 6.—LUCAS OF ROWINGTON AND HANBURY.
§ 7.—BUTLER AND VERNON OF HANBURY.
§ 8.—HOMER OF ETTINGSHALL AND SUTTON COLDFIELD.
§ 9.—FAMILY HISTORY: 1740—1840.
§ 10.—ARMORIAL BEARINGS.
§ 11.—ON OLD WILLS.

PREFACE.

My reason for this compilation is, that I have found most members of our family quite ignorant as to the names and condition even of their more recent ancestors.

It was the late Mr. Edward Sargant, who first told me about the family monuments in Bromsgrove churchyard, and who roused my interest in the subject by giving me a great amount of information about our relatives of his own and the previous generations. Following up the matter, I have at odd times during the past six years or so frequented Probate Registries and other repositories of ancient records, procured from clergymen extracts from their parish registers, and importuned relatives and connections for information in their possession. The willingness with which these supplied details, which I could not well have obtained otherwise, gave me great encouragement; and I must especially thank for their help Miss Homer, Mr. Thompson Nash, Dr. Frank Chance, and my father Mr. James T. Chance. To these, to Mr. Edward Sargant, and to a mass of papers and correspondence left by my great-uncle, Mr. Henry Chance, who took much interest in the family history, are due most of the details respecting persons who have lived in this century; while for the statements concerning earlier generations I hold myself responsible.

The scope of the work is to trace the ancestry of William Chance, the first of Birmingham, of his wife Sarah Lucas, and of his brother-in-law and partner in business Edward Homer, and to enumerate their offspring; and to give some notice of the persons mentioned. In the Appendix will be found extracts from parish registers, lists of wills, tombstone inscriptions, and other records which I have used; and I have also collected there, and in a great measure put into pedigree form, all the information gathered as to ancient people of the name of Chance, and those especially, who were once so numerous at and about Bromsgrove. Thus much trouble may be saved to any curious person of the future, who may find time and desire to push the investigation further.

CORRIGENDA.

Page 14 note 16 *for* F 4, h *read* F 4, i
,, 19 ,, 41 ,, F No. 25 ,, F No. 22
,, 27 line 11 *read* Appendix F, Nos. 24, 30, 33, 46, &c.
,, ,, ,, 25 *for* 46, 63 *read* 31, 48
,, ,, note 19 ,, 60, 61 ,, 46, 47
,, ,, ,, 22 ,, 14, 24 ,, 11, 21
,, 28 ,, 27 ,, 49 ,, 36
,, ,, ,, 28 ,, 50 ,, 37
,, ,, ,, 29 ,, 30 ,, 26
,, 39 lines 3, 4 *read* Rector of St. Michael's, Sutton Bonnington, Notts.,
          and a Canon and Priest-Vicar of Wells.
,, 74 *for* F. No. 30 *read* F. No. 26
    dele Cp. App. F. No. 37
,, 76 Cp. Appendix F. No. 43
    for F. Nos. 49, 50 *read* F. Nos. 36, 37
,, 91 Rev. Robert Foster, *read as corrected above*.
,, 99 bottom *for* Bentley, Worc. *read* Bentley, Warw.
,, 106 line 20 *for* Oxford *read* Oxford
,, 130 ,, 27 *for* his parents *read* the latter's parents

§ 1. *Descent of* WILLIAM CHANCE *of Birmingham.*

THE grandfather of the present heads of the Chance family was William Chance, of the firm of Chance & Homer, Merchants, of Bread St., Newhall St., Birmingham.[1] His partner, Edward Homer, was also his brother-in-law; he married (1) in 1773 William Chance's only sister Sarah, and (2) in 1778 his sister-in-law Mary Lucas.[2]

William Chance was descended from a family of yeoman degree, which had long been settled at Shepley and Burcott, adjacent hamlets in the parish of Bromsgrove about two miles N.E. of the town. His connection with that family may be proved as follows.

There is in Bromsgrove churchyard, lying flat against the East end of the Church, a tombstone with the following inscription.[3]

Here lieth the Bodies
of WILLIAM CHANCE of
Shepley who died Dec^{br} 26th
1739 Aged 80 Years
and FRANCES his Wife who died
Oct. 25th 1742 Aged 85
WILLIAM their Son who died
March 13th 1743 Aged 61
and ELIZABETH his Wife who
died Oct. 22nd 1765 Aged 64
JOHN the son of WILLIAM and
FRANCES CHANCE who died
Oct. 29. 1771 Aged 84
and SARAH his Wife who died
Augt 19. 1762 Aged 81
THOMAS their Son who died
June 20th 1774 Aged 53

WILLIAM CHANCE
Brother to the aforesaid
THOMAS CHANCE
died May the 2nd 1802
Aged 88

---

[1] So described in the Birmingham Directory for 1781. The firm was started in 1771.
[2] Particulars in § 9.
[3] The Stone was probably placed in the churchyard by the William Chance last mentioned on it, his name, which is in a different style of inscription, being added after his death. When on the

The wills of the Thomas and William Chance last mentioned in the inscription are preserved at the General Probate Registry at Somerset House, London. Executor to the former was William Chance, the brother; while the nephew, William Chance of Birmingham, and Edward Homer were equal legatees. To the latter William Chance of Birmingham, nephew, was executor and residuary legatee, and his inheritance included the lease of the warehouses &c. in Birmingham, occupied by him in partnership with Edward Homer. It follows that William Chance, of the firm of Chance and Homer, was a great-grandson of the William Chance of Shepley (or Burcott) first mentioned in the tombstone inscription.

But who was his father, brother of the two testators? We know that his mother married secondly a Mr. Bell, and that she died[4] at Bromsgrove on the 12th of May 1812, aged 91. It is she, therefore, and her first husband, and his first wife and children, who are commemorated on another tombstone in Bromsgrove churchyard; a stone now placed on the left hand border of the path leading to the West door of the Church.[5] The inscription runs as follows.

In Memory of JOHN CHANCE
who Departed this Life the
13th of Feb. 1750 aged 38 years
Also of Hannah his Wife who
died Feby the 3rd 1746 Aged 34
& of two Daughters MARY died
Feb. yo 2nd 1745 Aged 5 Months
& HANNAH died yo 20th of Augst
1746 Aged 7 months

Also in Memory of
MARY BELL Wife of the
said JOHN CHANCE who
died 12th May 1812 aged 91 Yrs

A Sincere Christian

12th of August 1885 I visited Bromsgrove, the Stone was not to be seen; but subsequently the Parish Clerk, Mr. Rose, found it and some others completely grown over with turf. At my request he cleaned them.

The inscription contains errors in its earlier part, showing that it was not cut till some time after the persons there mentioned died. The errors are as follows. (1) Frances Chance was buried on the 16th Sept. 1742 (Bromsgrove Registers), and so could not have died on Oct. 25th. (2) William Chance her son died not on the 13th of March, but, as appears from the attestations to his will, at about 4.0 a.m. on the 22nd. And he was buried on the 24th. (3) According to the age given in the same William Chance's marriage-bond (Appendix B 1), he was born about 1692; but the inscription makes him 10 years older. Still, the ages given in marriage-bonds are only approximations. (4) William Chance the eldest is described in his will as of Burcott; Burcott however and Shepley are practically the same.

[4] See §9 note 6.

[5] This Stone appears to be older than the other, and the right hand inscription is in a different style to the left hand one. I had on the 12th Aug. 1885 been searching for some time without success, when I noticed some stones near the West door, and pointing with my stick, observed to Mr. E. F. Chance, who was with me, that the stone sought for should be of about their date. Following the line of the stick, my eye caught the very inscription we wanted.

DESCENT OF WILLIAM CHANCE OF BIRMINGHAM.

Mary Bell indeed, William Chance's mother, had survived his father 62 years. Her second marriage, with George Bell of Bromsgrove, took place in 1755, and she had by him two sons and a daughter. Her parents were Joshua and Mary Tilt, of a Bromsgrove family.⁶ The entries in the Bromsgrove Parish Registers connected with inscription No. 2 are as follows :—

1743. Oct. 24. Mar: John Chance & Hannah Hunt both of this Par: by Lycenc.
⁷1744-5. Feb. 4. Bur: Mary Daughter of John Chance.
1745-6. Feb. 5. Bur: Hannah wife of John Chance.
1746. Aug. 22. Bur: Hannah Daughter of John Chance.
1746. Oct. 15. Mar: John Chance & Mary Tilt both of this Par: by Lycenc.
1747. Oct. 12. Born Sarah Daughter of John & Mary Chance.
1749. May 16. Born William son of John & Mary Chance.
⁷1749-50. Feb. 15. Bur: John Chance.
1755. George Bell of this Parish and Mary Chance of this Parish were married in this Church by License this Ninth Day of September.⁸

The bonds for John Chance's two marriage licenses are preserved at Worcester, and may be seen there in the Bishop's Registry. He was the eldest of his family, William came next, and Thomas was the youngest; the intervening children not surviving.⁹

The tracing of the descent of William Chance of Shepley presents difficulties, which are discussed in Part II, Pedigree No. 1. I shall occupy the next section with a general notice of the Worcestershire Chances, and then proceed to those of Bromsgrove; an idea of whose multitude may be gained by inspection of Appendix F 1.

⁶ See § 5, and Part II, Pedigree No. 2.

⁷ Till about 1752, the year was commonly taken to begin on Mar. 25th. Hence what we call Feb. 4th 1745 occurs in the registers as Feb. 4th 1744. And so, while on the tombstone the date of John Chance's death is given in modern style as the 13th Feb. 1750, in the registers his burial is entered as having taken place on the 15th Feb. 1749.

⁸ Witnesses: Joshua and Dorcas Tilt.

⁹ See Part II, Pedigree No. 1. I have their names from a pedigree noted in an old account book of their nephew William Chance.

§ 2. *Worcestershire* CHANCES.

THE name of CHANCE is a singularly local one. There have been for some centuries past plenty of the name in Worcestershire and Gloucestershire, and some of course in the *omnium-gatherum* of London; but I have hardly found it to occur anywhere else.[1] We are only concerned with the Worcestershire families, and will note first, in what parts of the county they lived.

The Worcester Probate Registry received and has preserved wills and administrations from the whole of the old diocese of Worcester, which included Worcestershire and the southern half of Warwickshire. I have searched the calendars in that Registry, and have found 73 wills and administrations in the name of Chance (or Chaunce, Chawnce, &c.) of earlier date than 1750. A similar search at Somerset House, where are preserved many hundreds of thousands of wills and administrations from all the province of Canterbury, shewed only 29 in the name, and of them 10 belonged to Worcestershire, 9 to Gloucestershire and Bristol, and 6 to London and Middlesex.[2] One of the Worcestershire wills being a duplicate of one proved at Worcester, we have in all 82 occurrences for that diocese.

Of this number 25 are of earlier date than 1625. Of them 18 belong to Bromsgrove, 2 to Hadzor (near Droitwich), 2 to Worcester, 1 to Kidderminster, and 1 each to Harvington and Hoblench, in the south-eastern corner of the county; the contents of the two last showing a close connection of the testators with Bromsgrove. Hadzor appears again in 1639[3] and 1649; Kidderminster in 1632; and Bromsgrove and the neighbouring Chaddesley Corbet in 1640, 1648, and 1649. Between 1660 and 1700 Bromsgrove appears 7 times; the neighbouring parishes of Salwarp and Hanbury 3 times; and Worcester, with its suburb Bedwardine, 7 times.

[1] The few early mentions that I have found of Chances, not of Worcestershire, are included in Appendix H.

[2] Of the others, three were of persons dying at sea, while of the fourth I did not enquire.

[3] This is the will of Anne Chaunce, of Upton Snodsbury, who was the widow of Christopher Chaunce of Hadzor.

Of course the wills do not touch the many persons, who for want of means or other reasons did not trouble the officers of the Probate Court ; but the scope of our next source of information is wider.

At the Public Record Office, in London, there are, arranged under counties, an enormous number of rolls containing particulars of the national subsidies granted to the King at different dates; and these rolls often contain the names of the persons taxed. In the earlier times only those contributed to the subsidies, who had a considerable amount of property ; but the impecuniosity of Charles II. produced the tax known as hearth-money, a levy at so much per hearth. The lists therefore of persons who paid hearth-money are practically lists of householders.

As regards Worcestershire, Subsidy Roll No. $^{201}/_{325}$ contains the names, arranged under townships, of more than 8600 persons in that county who paid hearth-money in 1662-3. Another roll, No. $^{201}/_{312}$, appears to be the same list revised for 1667. The two supplement each other's deficiencies, and taking them together, we find as follows :—10 Chances resident at Bromsgrove, 2 at Salwarp, 1 each at Alvechurch, Beoley, Belbroughton, Chaddesley Corbet, Hadzor, Himbleton, Kidderminster, and Bedwardine. All these places except the last, which is a suburb of Worcester, are within 9 miles of Bromsgrove; and in no other part of Worcestershire does in these rolls the name occur.

From the wills then and the hearth-money rolls together it appears, that the Worcestershire Chances in old times were mostly settled in and about Bromsgrove. But already in the 16th century there were several at Worcester, and a few at other places in the county.

The earlier Subsidy Rolls only contain the names of fairly well-to-do persons ; they are interesting to us as indicating their condition and incomes, and whether they were freeholders, assessed in lands, or tenant farmers, assessed in goods.[b] I have searched altogether 36 rolls containing some 30,000 names written in crabbed "courthand," and find that the only family of the name of Chance of any prominence in Worcestershire was settled at Hadzor, and that of the Bromsgrove families, the best-to-do were those of Catshill and Woodcote.

We will leave the Chances of Bromsgrove for a separate section, and begin with those of Hadzor. Among the 4700 persons (or thereabouts) in Worcestershire, who were taxed for the Subsidy of 1523, appears Will'm Chaunce, of

---

[a] I do not understand why the name of Chance does not occur in the Subsidy Rolls relating to Worcester City. Can it be that members of the Clothiers' Guild in that City, to which all the Chances there seem to have belonged, were exempted from contributing to the subsidies ?

[b] See Appendix E. The standard of taxation varies in different years, and with it inversely the number of persons taxed. Thus the only Chance rich enough to contribute under the standard of 1566 was he of Hadzor; while in 1523 six others had to pay their quota.

Hadysor, who had to pay 18d. on an assessment of £3 in goods. I have no further notice of him, but in 1545 a John Chaunce of Hadsor was taxed 3s. 4d. on an assessment of £5 in goods, and in 1566 and 1598 Christopher Chaunce of the same place paid, on the first occasion 6s. 8d. on an assessment of £5, and on the second 14s. on one of £3 10 0, both in land, showing that he had acquired freehold property.[6] The will of John Chaunce of Hadsor, proved in London in 1610, mentions his brother Christofer Chaunce of Hadsor, Gent., and gives the names or number of the latter's children and grandchildren. I am disposed to think that the John Chaunce of 1545 was a son of the William Chaunce of 1523, and father of Christopher and John Chaunce just mentioned.

About this Christopher Chaunce and his descendants I have a certain amount of information. He was in 1563, and before his marriage, as appears from the Chancery proceedings which will shortly be mentioned, possessed of property in Hadzor and Bromsgrove of the value of £60 a year. This is very probably an exaggeration, but whatever it was, he increased it in 1574 by a purchase from Francis Brace, Esq., of 60 a. land, 10 a. meadow, and 4 a. wood, with rights of common pasture, in Hadzor and "Saynt Peter's in Wyche" (Droitwich).[7] Another transaction of his is recorded in the "Feet of Fines"[7] for 1606, and it appears from the said Chancery suit that he on this occasion, with the object of disinheriting his eldest son, put his property into the hands of trustees for the benefit of his other children. One of these trustees was William Chaunce of Bromsgrove, Gent., to whom he seems, through the Barnesleys of Barnesley Hall, to have been closely related.[8]

Christopher Chaunce died in March 1623-4, and was buried at Hadzor. He left a widow and several children. The eldest son, Christopher, at once appealed to the Court of Chancery against the dispositions which his father had made of his landed property, and the "Bill" and "Answer" in these proceedings are preserved at the Record Office.[9] Christopher averred that in 1563 his

[6] Subsidy Rolls—Appendix E. Cp. last note.
[7] Record Office—"Feet of Fines." These documents are official records of transactions in landed property, whether by way of sale, enfeoffment, mortgage, or otherwise. They are abstracts of the deeds proper, and give the names of the parties, and a description of the property, but do not reveal the nature of the transaction. They are arranged by counties and law-terms.
[8] See Appendices C, Nos. 4 and 5, and F Nos. 7-9. For the Barnesleys of Barnesley Hall, Bromsgrove, see § 3 note 15.
[9] Chancery Proceedings temp. Car. I. Chaunce v. Chaunce.
[10] I.e. put into trust. I do not pretend to understand the legal forms, by which the lands were dealt with. In 1606 the process, as regarded part of them, was by "acknowledging and levying one fyne Sur Conusans de Droyt come &c. unto William Chaunce and William Symondes Gent. with proclamation in due form," and for the lands in Bromsgrove, they being of "ancient demesne" and amenable to the customs of that Manor, by having a "wrytt of Right Close" brought against Christopher Chaunce by certain persons in the Manorial Court.

father enfeoffed [10] his lands in Hadzor and Bromsgrove to certain trustees for his own use and that of his heirs in tail, and afterwards married; by which marriage he the complainant was the eldest son. After his father's death therefore in 1623-4 complainant should have had the property; but his brothers Thomas and William, his mother Ann, and certain others,[11] he complains, had occupied the lands, and were in possession of the deeds of feoffment and other documents, and refused to produce them. Defendants in their Answer admitted the recitals, and mentioned the purchase of lands in 1574 above referred to, but they said that complainant had by his course of life displeased his father, and that the latter in 1606 and 1614 had taken steps to cut off the entail, and had put his lands in Hadzor, Hanbury, Droitwich, and Bromsgrove into trust for the benefit of his younger sons. The mother pleaded that she claimed only her dowry, and the other defendants that they were strangers to the suit. Apparently defendants gained the day, as we shortly afterwards (in 1630) find [12] Thomas Chaunce of Hadzor, Gent., fined £10 in lieu of accepting the burden of knighthood; which means that he had an estate worth £40 a year or more.[13]

Four years later, at the Heralds' Visitation of the County, he was found to have usurped armorial bearings, and had to disclaim them. For the subsidy of 1640-1 his assessment was 40s., and for the next year 30s.; on which latter sum he had to pay no less than 12s.[6] As he was assessed in lands, it appears that he was a freeholder. In 1641 we find him [7] purchasing lands in "Gooschill" (Goshull) in Hanbury from John and Johanna Watkins for £100. He died in 1648-9, and his will was proved both at Worcester (1649) and in London (1650). He left his Hadzor property to his eldest son Thomas, and that in Hanbury to his four younger sons, with £125 apiece; and a like sum to each of his four daughters. Thomas we find mentioned in the hearth-money rolls [6] as living in 1662 and 1667 in a house at Hadzor with five hearths, a large house for the times; but the "Feet of Fines"[7] show that

---

[11] Edmond Bercroft, Gent., and William Jones, Clerk. The Rev. Jones was a witness to the will of Christopher Chaunce sen. One of the trustees of 1606 was John Bercrofte of Hanbury, and Humfrye Borcroft, his son, was a trustee under another instrument of 1614.

[12] Grazebrook—"Heraldry of Worcestershire."

[13] By the custom known as "Distraint of Knighthood," all persons possessed of land producing a certain annual income—which income came to be fixed at £40—might be called upon to accept knighthood with its attendant expenses and liabilities, or to pay a fine; and this power was frequently put in force in the 14th and 15th centuries, when the King had exhausted his other sources of supply. Under the Tudors it became the custom to exercise the power only once in each reign, and they only called upon some of the more wealthy of those who were liable; but James I. by his inquisitions and fines caused "grievous vexations," and as these were continued by his son, who fined in Worcestershire alone some 200 persons in sums of from £10 to £40, the custom was abolished by Parliament in 1641. It was in a great measure the indiscriminate multiplication of knights through Stuart impecuniosity that brought the honour of knighthood into disrepute. (See Stubbs, "Constitutional History," and Grazebrook, "Heraldry of Worcestershire.")

he disposed of portions of his property in 1658, 1666, and 1673, so we may conjecture that he did not continue his father's prosperity.

Anne Chaunce, widow of Christopher the elder, died in 1638-9, having passed the latter years of her life at Upton Snodsbury, where her daughter Jane Ganderton was living.

William Chance, her third son, brother of Christopher and Thomas, had received a share of his father's property, and we find him in 1639 [14] and 1642 [6] settled at Newland in the parish of Salwarp, near Droitwich. But I think that William Chance of Newland, who disposed of his property in Hadzor and Droitwich in 1652,[7] and who in 1662 appears in the hearth-money rolls [8] as Constable of Salwarp, and as living there in a two-hearth house, was his son. John Chaunce, who was living there at the same time in a similar house, was probably another son, as Anne Chaunce, widow of William (who died in 1675), mentions in her will (1689) a "brother" of that name. And he was probably the John Chance of Warndon, Yeoman, who died in 1705, and who mentions in his will that he had leasehold property in Salwarp, and desires to be buried there. But we need not trace this family further. Their pedigree will be found set out in Appendix F 3.

In the latter part of the 16th century we find a colony of Chances in the south-eastern corner of Worcestershire, at Hoblench (or Habbelench) and Harrington. The contents of the will (1591) of Nicholas Chaunce of Hoblenche, Yeoman, show that he had property in Bromsgrove and Belbroughton, and that Thomas and William Chance of Woodcote, Bromsgrove, and Christopher and William Chaunce of Harrington were his "cousins."[15] The last-named, who died in 1606, was also a yeoman, possessing besides his farm a shop and a stock of hemp. Both Nicholas and William left widows and children, and the Chances of whom we find a few notices in the 18th century [16] at places in South Worcestershire, may have been some of their descendants.

Nicholas Chance in some Chancery Proceedings of the year 1572 [17] appears as Nicholas Chaunse of Hervington. "In moste humble wyse Compleanynge Shewithe unto yor honorable L. yor poore and daylie orato^r" Roger Wakeman of Bromsgrove, Yeoman, that he was "lawfullye seased in his demesne as of fee of and in one mess' or tenem^t and dyvers Landes medows and pasture" &c., about 30 "Akers," "untyll that nowe of late one Nycholas Chaunse, late of Ryddyche in the County of Warr, yeoman, beinge a verye busye and frawarde

[14] At the date of his mother's will.
[15] "Cousin" in old wills usually means nephew or niece: cousins proper are called "kin."
[16] See Appendix F 4, h.
[17] Record Office. Chancery Proceedings temp. Eliz.—Wakeman v. Chaunse.

p'sonu delyghtingo moore in Trobles and leawde dealings then in honeste Excrcyse or trade of quyet Lyvinge," entered upon his property, cut down trees, &c.; although complainant had repaid certain debts due by him to Nicholas. Against which the latter pleaded, (1) that he had never lived at Redditch (Ryddycho), (2) that the complaint was frivolous, and a matter for common law, (3) that the debts had not been fully paid. Roger in his reply said that he had paid the sum in dispute into the hands of Thomas Chaunce of the City of Worcester, Yeoman, and another. I do not know how the matter ended, but we shall see, in treating of the Chances of Worcester City, that this Thomas Chaunce had an interest in Bromsgrove; and this connection of his with the Harvington Chances, also related to those of Bromsgrove, gives another link between the latter and the Chances of Worcester.

We will now turn our attention to the Chances of Kidderminster. Administration of the goods of Kenelm Chaunce, of that town, was granted in 1557 to his widow Agnes, and again in 1580 to his son John. The latter would be the John Chance, who in 1601, with his wife Margaret, transferred property in " Haberley and Kedermynster" to Nicholas Chaunce, who however got rid of it again next year.[7] But Nicholas had other property in the neighbourhood, as we know from his will (1633), which describes him as of Oldington, Kidderminster, Husbandman. In 1642 Thomas Chauncy, Gent., sold land at Kidderminster[7]; and as this is not a Worcestershire name, it may be a mistake for Chaunce. In 1714 one John Chaunce was a freeholder of Kidderminster[18]; and he in 1694, being then about 54 years of age, married Bridget Clark of Droitwich.[19] They in 1714 and 1719 disposed of property in Kidderminster and elsewhere,[7] on the latter occasion conjointly with Joshua and Mary Tilt (§5). Lastly Richard Chance of Lower Mitton, which is close to Oldington, mentions in his will (1741) his wife Elizabeth and his children Richard and Martha, the former of whom got, among other things, his father's fishing-boat and tackle.

Seven miles west of Bromsgrove are Hartlebury and Elmley Lovett, and at the latter place Henry and Elizabeth Chance and others acquired land in 1581.[7] In 1621 John and Ann Chance disposed of land there; and as persons of the same name disposed of land at Belbroughton in 1599, and in 1636 John Chance sen. and jun. did so in Elmley Lovett, Dodderhill, Upton Warren, and Bromsgrove,[7] we may probably reckon these among the Chances of Bromsgrove. John and William Chaunce disposed of land at Sneedes Green, near Elmley Lovett, in 1636.[7] A Richard Chance of Hartlebury died about 1720.

[18] Prattinton MSS, in the possession of the Society of Antiquaries:—List of freeholders voting in the County Election of 1714.
[19] See Appendix B 1—Marriage Bonds.

Other Worcestershire Chaunces, not of Bromsgrove or Worcester, of whom I find early mention, are :—John Chaunce of Prior's Stoke (Stoke Prior), which is close to Bromsgrove, assessed for the subsidy of 1523 at £2. 0. 8., and taxed 14d.⁶; Roger Chaunce, Prebendary of Clent in 1556[20]; Thomas Chaunce, Patron (by grant from Sir John Lyttelton) of Halesowen Vicarage in 1584[21]; Gilbert Chaunce of Chaddesley Corbet, who died about 1648, and who may very well have been the son of William Chance of Bromsgrove, baptized there in 1606[22]; and Thomas Chaunce of Broughton, Hanbury, who died about 1663. For further particulars I must refer my readers to Appendix F 4.

The importance in English history of the yeoman class, to which these Chaunces belonged, is very great. It is to "the great body of freeholders," says Bishop Stubbs, "the yeomanry of the middle ages, a body which in antiquity of possession and purity of extraction was probably superior to the classes that looked down upon it as ignoble," that we owe in chief measure the maintenance and development of our free institutions. They were the men who constituted the ancient local courts, and mustered in arms under the sheriff. They were the Commons,—*communitas civitatis*,—who from the time of Edward I. sent their representatives to a national parliament; and it was they who, merging into the gentry on one side, and the burghers on the other, linked together in England the interests baronial and mercantile, which on the Continent remained in mutually harmful opposition.[23]

The social condition of farmers of two or three centuries back was not very different from that of the same class at the present day. Then also some were well-to-do, and there was no hard line to be drawn between them and the smaller gentry; while others, from bad farming or want of capital, found it hard to obtain a livelihood. A freeholder with 40s. a year was qualified to vote at elections, or to stand for Parliament himself. With £40 a year, he might be called upon to take on himself the dignity and liabilities of knighthood.[13] Bishop Latimer has left us a picture of a prosperous yeoman's condition in the time of Henry VII. He says:[24] "My father was a Yeoman, and had no lands of his own, only he had a farm of three or four pounds by the year at the utmost, and hereupon he tilled so much as kept half-a-dozen men. He had walk for an hundred sheep; and my mother milked thirty kine. He was able, and did find the King a harness, with himself and his horse, whilst he came to

[20] Nash—"History of Worcestershire"—Appendix, p. xviii.
[21] *Ibid.*—s.v. Halesowen. Perhaps this was Thomas Chaunce of Worcester, mentioned before.
[22] Bromsgrove Parish Registers—Appendix A 1—described in § 3.
[23] See Stubbs' "Constitutional History of England," §§803-806, and elsewhere.
[24] First of Latimer's Lenten sermons preached before the King in 1549.

the place that he should receive the King's wages. I can remember that I buckled his harness when he went to Blackheath field. He kept me to school, or else I had not been able to have preached before the King's Majesty now. He married my sisters[25] with five pounds or twenty nobles apiece; so that he brought them up in godliness and fear of God. He kept hospitality for his poor neighbours; and some alms he gave to the poor. And all this he did of the said farm."

We may get a notion of any particular person's condition from the contents of his will, and especially from the inventory of goods, which is usually attached thereto. For instance, John Chance of Shepley, Bromsgrove, at his death in Feb. 1617-8, was found to possess household goods, and farm stock and implements, which I have summarized as follows. In furniture, he had pots and vessels of brass and pewter, "broch-cobberds,"[26] the ordinary kitchen utensils, "treene[27] wares as barrells skeeles[28] payles wheeles and the like," two large tables and a side-table, two forms, a chair, sundry stools, a cupboard, a chest and three coffers, four bedsteads, three feather-beds and two flock-beds, four feather-bolsters and two flock-bolsters, five feather-pillows, three pillow-"bures" or cases, two canvasses, three coverlets, five pairs of blankets and three single ones, twelve pairs of sheets (two pairs linen, seven "hurden,"[29] and three hempen), seven tablecloths and two dozen linen napkins, five hand-towels, a "herecroth,"[30] a "byble-booke," two pairs of flaxen shoes, twelve ells of hempen and hurden cloth, and a piece of wainscoting. These articles were in the kitchen, the "new parlour," and the "soller[31] over the said parlour"; and there was probably another room upstairs. In the way of provisions and corn he had four cheeses, two gallons of salt butter, eight flitches of bacon, four flitches of "byest,"[32] 12 strike of "mault," and 17 strike of barley; besides rye, "hey," and "corne of the ground." In farm-stock he had seven cows, two steers, two two-year-old and five yearling "beasts," one "weaning calf of the stake,"[33] two mares, and 100 sheep, besides swine, hens, and ducks. In farm implements there were a wain-body,

[25] Latimer had six sisters, but no brother.
[26] Broch, broach, or brauch—a spit; cobberd—a cupboard.
[27] Treene—wooden: made from a tree.
[28] Skeele—any broad shallow wooden vessel.
[29] Hurden—made of a coarse kind of flax.
[30] Herecroth—for "hair-cloth," used for straining.
[31] Soller—an upper room or garret—Germ. söller.
[32] Byest—perhaps "beast," i.e., beef or mutton, as opposed to bacon.
[33] Perhaps a calf tied up for rearing, in opposition to one running by its mother.

two pairs of wheels, a plough plough-share and "coulterne," two pairs of harrows, three yokes, three "towes,"[54] two sets of harness ("horsgores"), and axes and bills. The whole was valued at £136 13s. 4d., showing the very high value of money in those days. Another inventory, that of John Chaunce of Shepley, made in 1670, is given in full in § 11. William Chance of Burcott (or Shepley), who died at the end of 1739 (§§ 1 and 9), left in his kitchen a bed, bedstead, and furniture thereto, a clock, a dresser of drawers, two small tables, three chairs, 10 pewter dishes, 6 plates, 12 spoons, 3 pewter porringers, an iron grate, a warming pan, a frying pan, and fireshovel and tongs; in the back room a chest and trunk; in the buttery three barrels, "tin things and a spit," four brass kettles, two pots, a brass pan, and 10 cwt. of coals; in the chamber over the kitchen a bed, bedstead and furniture, a chest, a coffer, a table and five chairs, a looking-glass, and linen; and in the back chamber two tubs and two benches. Out-of-doors he had only three sheep, but he must have made over his farm stock and implements to his son William some time before his death.

The younger sons of yeomen usually took to a trade, either remaining in the town or village near the ancestral farm, or migrating to some more busy or attractive centre. For the persons whom we are considering, the city of Worcester was the great centre of trade; and it afforded its immigrants the protection of chartered privileges, and the easiest mode of ascent in the social scale. The burghers kept up an intimate connection with the country people who surrounded them, and from whom they were sprung, and took interest in the churches, schools, and charities of their original parishes, sometimes holding property there, or rights of pasture and hunting. For instance, in the case of the Chances of Worcester, we find evidence of the close connection of some of them with Bromsgrove. And doubtless the country cousins on their part gladly fostered a connection which could only benefit them.

The Chances resident at Worcester in the 16th and 17th centuries were mostly engaged in the weaving and dyeing of the woollen cloth, the production of which was then the great English industry. Worcester was one of the chief centres of the trade: it employed there at one time as many as 8000 persons, and at the end of the 16th century 6000 in Worcester itself,[35] and more than twice that number in the neighbouring towns and villages, where the wool was carded and spun; at Bromsgrove, for instance, the bulk of the population were engaged in it or in connected industries. Towards the end of the 17th

---

[54] Towes—(1) ropes of some kind, (2) tools.
[35] Valentine Green—"History of Worcester," i. p. 290. The Clothiers' Guild at Worcester was incorporated in 1510-11, and to encourage their manufacture, already rapidly declining, a

century the manufacture was already almost extinct, and now only survives, in the form of carpet-weaving, at Kidderminster.[36]

The earliest notice I have of a Chance of Worcester [37] is that of Richard Chaunce, Weaver, of All Saints', who died in 1569, leaving a widow and three young daughters. Then we have Thomas Chance "of the cittie of Worcester gent." who some time before 1636 "gave xv^h the int. thereof to be payed to the free schole [of Bromsgrove] yerely for ever" [38]: a gift showing his connection with Bromsgrove. This must have been the Thomas Chance, Gent., who in the years 1578 to 1601 [39] had several transactions in land in St. John's, Bedwardine, and Wick,[40] and in Selly and Northfield, chiefly with persons named Bower and Gower; and whom we find in 1598 [6] taxed 21s. 4d. on property at Wick Episcopi [40] assessed at £8. His wife's name was Rosa.

William Chance of Worcester, Walker and Clothier, whose will was proved there in 1624, is shown by the contents of it to have been a son of William Chance of Bromsgrove, Gent., who died in 1622.[41] Then we have Anthony Chaunce of Worcester, Trowman,[42] who died in 1652 and left a widow. And then John Chaunce of St. John's, Bedwardine, whom we may suppose to have been a near relative of Thomas Chance above. We find him and his wife Elizabeth holding property in St. John's in 1605.[7] And it was probably he, who in 1622 brought a suit in Chancery [43] against one Percivall Johnsons of Worcester,

Charter was granted them by Elizabeth in 1590. The Guild was divided [see the Heralds' Visitation of Worcestershire—1682] into two sections, the "Weavers and Clothiers," and the "Walkers and Clothiers," each with two Wardens. There were also, for the whole Guild, a High Master and a Clerk. The Walker received the cloth from the Weaver, and caused it to be " walked burled and wranglehafted" [Green—*ibid.*—App. p. lxviii]; after which highly technical treatment it was ready for the Dyer. Note that a "Clothier" was a maker of cloth, not of clothes.

[36] The decline and loss of the manufacture are attributed, says Nash [" History of Worcestershire," App. p. cxiv], "partly to the roguery of the manufacturers, who stretched their cloths so much, that when they came to Blackwell-hall, or Turkey [*i.e.*, the markets of the East], they wanted much of their measure, and partly to the workmen's obstinacy, for they persisted in making a thick heavy broad cloth, when the Turks chose rather a thin spungy cloth, which took a brighter dye." A less probable cause, that he also mentions, is "the frequent and expensive oppositions for the election of members of parliament," consequent on the increase in the number of voters ! "Thus," says Green [loc. cit.], " dwindled away by degrees one of the most valuable branches of the commerce of this kingdom, which had distinguished Worcester through every quarter of the globe to which Britain had then extended her trade."

[37] For details about the Chances of Worcester see Appendix F 2. The wills and other sources of my information are there specified.

[38] Nash—" History of Worcestershire "—Appendix—s.v. Bromsgrove.

[39] " Feet of Fines " (see note 7) for the years 1578-82-91-92-96-98 and 1601.

[40] Bedwardine was a suburb of Worcester divided into two parishes, of which St. Michael's lay between the city and the river, and St. John's on the other side of the river. The latter included Wick (or Wyke) " Episcopi."

[41] See § 3, and Appendix F No. 25. "Walker and Clothier," see note 35.

[42] " Trowman "—trough-man, no doubt a technical term in the woollen manufacture.

[43] Record Office—Chancery Proceedings temp. Jas. I.—Chaunce v. Johnsons.

Baker, to recover an obligation which he had given to Johnsons in return for a loan of £40 : which money he claimed to have repaid, but said he could not recover the bond. Johnsons pleaded that he had sold John Chaunce a messuage in "Newport *alias* Ewport St." for £60, its value being £90 (it was usual in these actions to tell lies on both sides), and that being a simple man, and thinking that he could trust John Chaunce by reason of their having married sisters, he had given a quittance, but had not received all the money; and had therefore commenced proceedings at Common Law. The matter was a complicated one, and I am not aware how it ended. John Chaunce's name also appears in the Heralds' Visitation of Worcestershire of 1634 as one of those who on that occasion disclaimed armorial bearings, which, I take it, means, that he had adopted such, though without right; showing that he was a person of some consideration. He probably died in 1662, in the November of which year his widowed daughter Rosa Pillowe entered a "caveat"[4] against administration of his property without her assent; and the administration was only granted to his nephew Thomas Chaunce in 1670. Probably the same John Chaunce was the father of the "William son of Jhon Chaunce of Worcester" baptized at Bromsgrove on the 12th Feb. 1603-4 :[22] another piece of evidence of the connection of the Worcester Chances with that town. In 1662, the probable year of his death, we find[6] that he was occupying a house with four hearths in St. John's, Bedwardine, in common with one John Unett.

Thomas Chaunce, his nephew, died in 1691, and is described in his will as a dyer, of St. Clement's, while the inscription on a monument erected to his memory in St. John's, Bedwardine,[45] states that he was a member of the Common Council of the city. His wife was one Beatrice Ayleway, whom he married in 1663,[19] and who died 15 years before him. No children are mentioned in his will, but he distributes considerable sums to a large number of kinspeople, and among them to his brother-in-law Urban Bowler, to whose son Edward, his own nephew and apprentice, he leaves a quarter of his "dyeing ffats ffurnaces weade dyeing stuffe" &c.

After him we have a Christopher Chaunce of St. Andrew's, Clothier, who died in 1684, leaving a son Christopher, and a daughter married to one John Bowen. Then a Thomas Chance, of St. Clement's, who died about 1688. And then a Richarde Chance of St. Andrew's, Clothier, who died on the 27th Jan. 1687-8, and was buried at St. Andrew's, where there is (or was) a monument to him and to his first wife.[46] He was a Warden in 1682 of the "Walkers and

[44] Bishop's Registry, Worcester. [45] Appendix C—Inscription No. 7.
[46] Appendix C—Inscription No. 6.

Clothiers" section [35] of the Clothiers' Guild. He was twice married,[19] (1) in 1665, to Joane Nicholls, of Worcester, who died in 1684, and (2) early in 1686 to Susanna Hill, of Hollow, who survived him. Other marriages in the 17th century were those of William Chance, of St. Andrew's, in 1666, with a daughter of John Bound, Walker and Clothier, of St. Clement's; and of Warner Chance, also of St. Andrew's, who married (1) in 1667, Elizabeth Jordan, and (2) in 1678, Sarah Brinton, both of All Saints'.[19]

For other Chances of Worcester I must refer to Appendix F 2.

§ 3. *CHANCE of Bromsgrove.*

In Bromsgrove parish there were colonies of Chances at Catshill and Fockbury, two miles north of the town; at Bournheath and Woodcote, three miles north; at Timberhanger, two miles west, and at Shepley and Burcott, two miles north-east; and there were others in the town itself. It was the Chances of Shepley and Burcott, who were our immediate ancestors.

The earliest mention that I have found of a Chance of Bromsgrove, omitting as doubtful a John le Chawne in 1351,[1] is that of Thomas Chawns of Catsulle (Catshill), who in 1352 sold some land in Fockbury.[1] Shortly after him there was a Henry Chaunce there,[2] as appears from a roll of the Manorial Court of Bromsgrove, of date 1504.[3] In this roll is the record of a suit in the Manorial Court between Thomas Tailor and John Chaunce, the gist of which is that these two disputed the ownership of a messuage and 70 acres of land at Catshill, occupied by them in common. John Chaunce gained the cause, at least for the time, by showing that he and one Richard Stokes had by inheritance an equal right to the property,[4] and pleading that as the latter had not been joined with him in the suit, the proceedings were null and void. The interesting part of it to us is, that John Chaunce, to show the joint title of himself and Richard Stokes, traces his pedigree back for five generations, and has it confirmed by a jury; of whose pronouncement, as preserved in the Court Roll, the following is a translation: "They say on their oath that one Roger Loff and Margaret his wife were seised of certain messuages with their appurtenances in Cattishill in the lordship of Bromsgrove in fee tail (talliott), which messuages lands and tenements are now in

[1] Prattinton MSS., in the possession of the Society of Antiquaries. For the spelling of the name see § 4.
[2] This is the spelling of 1504; cp. § 4.
[3] Record Office—Court Rolls (Augmentation Office), Portfolio 5, No. 41.
[4] Perhaps it was this very property that John Chaunce disposed of to John and Joan Stokes in 1593. [Record Office—Feet of Fines.]

the tenure of the aforesaid John Chaunce and Thomas Tailor. Also they say that the aforesaid Roger and Margaret had issue Alice, Margaret, and Agnes. Also they say that the aforesaid Alice took for her husband one Henry Chaunce, and had issue William, which William had issue Henry, which Henry had issue John, which John had issue John, who now seeks this enquiry. Also they say that the aforesaid Margaret took for her husband one John Stokys and had issue Henry, which Henry had issue John, which John had issue Richard, who now survives." Reckoning back from 1504, we must put the Henry Chaunce, who married Alice Loff, in the latter part of the 14th century.

Henry Chaunce, or Chaunse, his grandson, appears as serving on Bromsgrove juries in 1470-1[1] and 1473-4[5]; and a jury, which sat at Bromsgrove on the Wednesday in Whitsun-week in 1474,[5] presented among other things that one Richard ——[6] had "insulted" Henry Chaunce, and that John Chaunce (the son doubtless) had "forestalled" the said Richard and "drawn blood" from him[7]; for which offences Richard and John were each fined 2d. John Chaunce father and son are frequently mentioned in Bromsgrove records of the time of Henry VII.[8]; in 1489 the elder is sub-bailiff of Bromsgrove, and sues John Higges for a debt; in 1491 he purchases land in Bromsgrove from William Pachet of Wolverley[1]; in 1495-6 he serves on Bromsgrove juries; in 1496 John Chaunce jun. has a suit against John Pulter for trespass, and John Chaunce and John Burneford one against Roger Bowdok; in 1498, 1502, and 1504[3] John Chaunce serves on Bromsgrove juries, and in the last year, besides the above-mentioned case of Tailor v. Chaunce, there is a cross-suit between John Chaunce and Richard Baker. In 1507 and 1520[4] John Chawnce witnesses deeds, the former of which is dated at Shepley. In 1529 John Chaunce was Bailiff of Bromsgrove.[1] For the Subsidy of 1523[9] John Chance sen. was taxed 3s. 4d., John Chance jun. 12d., and John Chance, serv[t], 4d., all being of Bromsgrove; and the two former, the elder of whom was probably the John Chaunce jun. of 1496, are no doubt they whose wills were proved at Worcester in 1542.[10] The elder of these left a widow Isabell, who

[5] Brit. Museum—Add. Charter 23855—being a Bromsgrove Court Roll of 1473-4.
[6] Surname illegible.
[7] " Q[d] Ric'us — fec't insult' in Henr' Chaunce Et q[d] Joh'es Chaunce forstallav' p'd' Ric'u' in ... regione ib'm Et q[d] id'm Joh'es Chaunce t'xit sang' nem de p'dicto Ric'o."
[8] Record Office—Court Rolls (Augmentation Office)—Portfolios 5 No. 40, and 34 No. 10.
[9] Subsidy Rolls—Appendix E.
[10] These wills are drawn by the same hand in precisely the same form, and were proved on the same day, 30th Oct. 1542. But that of the elder John is dated 20th April, and that of the younger 10th May in that year. There is nothing in the wills to prove that the two were father

was probably the Isabell Chawnse, whose will was proved in Aug. 1546; a copy of it will be found in §11.

In 1526 we have a William Chaunce, trustee under the will of Hugh Lee, of Bromsgrove.

In 1547 was proved the will of Nicholas Chawnse of Bromsgrove. His name appears in the Court Roll of 1498, when he had to pay a fine of 2d. for not keeping in repair a hedge and ditch of his along a certain road, and he was again fined 4d. in 1502 for taking excessive toll.[8] In the latter year and in 1504[3] we find him serving on Bromsgrove juries, and again in 1546.[11] In 1523 he, "Nycoles Chance," was taxed 12d., and in 1545 3s. 4d. on an assessment of £5 in goods[9]; precisely the same as John Chaunce of Hadzor (p. 12) in the same year. The other of the five Chances of Bromsgrove taxed in 1523 was Thomas Chance, who had to pay 4d.

An Edward Chaunce was executor and probably son to Isabell Chawnse above, and in 1545[11] we find one of the same name suing William Crab for a debt. The name also occurs in Bromsgrove wills[12] about this time, and again later in the century.[13]

The Chances indeed of Bromsgrove now become very numerous, and we cannot stop here to enter into details about all of them, but will reserve that for Appendix F 1. From 1590 we find frequent mention of them in the Bromsgrove Parish Registers.

These Registers begin in 1590, and the first volume of them is in singularly good preservation as far as 1640, but of the latter portion (1640-1652) part is lost, and the rest very loosely kept. The second volume includes the years 1653 to 1719. The entries for 1659-1661 are very defective, and the bulk of 1662-3 is missing; but the remainder is well preserved, though the entries are not so carefully written up as in the earlier part of the first volume.

The latter, according to the search made, contains in the name of Chance 74 entries of baptisms, one being of twins, 36 entries of marriages, and 42 of burials. The second volume contains 58 entries of baptisms, of marriages 31, and of burials 77. In other words, between 1590 and 1640 the baptisms are

and son, but it is highly probable that they were so. The younger had property at Timberhanger. Both left legacies to the building of Bromsgrove Church.

[11] Record Office—Court Rolls (Augmentation Office)—Portfolio 5 No. 42.

[12] In 1546 Edward Chawnse witnessed the will of John Russall. In 1547 Edwarde Chawse witnessed the will of John Bate. In 1554 Edward Chaunce witnessed the wills of Thomas Lynolle and Henry Baker.

[13] See Appendix F, Nos. 11-12.

176 % and the marriages 86 % on the burials, while between 1653 and 1719 the numbers are 75 % and 40 % respectively. It follows that in the latter part of the century by no means all the baptisms or marriages of the parish were entered in the registers, and Nash mentions in his "History of Worcestershire" that there was near the Lickey the supplementary chapel of Chadwick, which was licensed for baptisms and marriages, but was already destroyed in his time (1774). The parish churchyard however remained the sole burying-ground.

I have accordingly been often disappointed in my hopes of finding in the registers entries of baptisms and marriages of persons mentioned in the wills consulted; whereas their burials I have usually found entered. Of course much of the deficiency is due to careless keeping of the books, the entries having been often made in a very haphazard way.

The total number of entries in the name of Chance found in the Bromsgrove Registers between the years 1590 and 1750 amounts to 388; viz. entries of baptisms 157, of marriages 81, and of burials 150. Of the last, there are from 1591 to 1640 inclusive 41 entries, from 1651 to 1700, in which period some years are defective, 50, and from 1701 to 1750 57; one of 1647 and one of uncertain date make up the 150. The increase therefore of the family in numbers in Bromsgrove parish between 1590 and 1750 was not great, but they overflowed into the neighbouring parishes, in which the name becomes continually more common.

I have put in Appendix A the list of extracts from the Bromsgrove Registers *in extenso*, partly to assure the preservation of a work performed for me with admirable care and industry by Mr. J. W. Rose, the Parish Clerk.

In the reign of James I. the most important of the Bromsgrove Chances was the William Chance who died 3rd May 1622.[14] He was connected by descent with the family of Barnesley,[15] and by marriage with that of Dineley.[16] Who was his father does not appear; perhaps it was the William Chaunce to whom, in conjunction with his uncle Gilbert Brandesley (Barnesley), administration of the goods of his brother Gilbert Chaunce was granted in 1570; and who may have been the William Chaunce, administration of whose

[14] Appendix C—Inscription No. 4.

[15] The Barnesleys (also spelt Barndesley, Bardsley, &c.) of Barnesley Hall were an old Bromsgrove family, whose records, says Nash, dated back to Edward III. They entered their pedigree at the Heralds' Visitations of Worcestershire in 1569 and 1634, and bore Arms, Sable a Cross between four Roses Argent barbed and seeded proper. [Grazebrook—"Heraldry of Worcestershire."] Barnesley Hall, a large old mansion-house in the north of Bromsgrove parish, was taken down in 1771, and a large farm-house erected on an eminence near the site. [Prattinton MSS.]

goods was granted to his son William in 1584. The name of Chance also occurs in conjunction with that of Barnesley in the will of Hugh Lee of Bromsgrove before-mentioned, who made (1526) " Nycholas Barnysley of Barnysley gentylma' and Will'm Chaunce " his feoffees (trustees).

The William Chaunce who died in 1622 was certainly he, whom we saw (p. 12) made in 1606 a trustee of Christopher Chaunce of Hadzor. We find him in 1591 acquiring property at Alvechurch, and later at different times at Bromsgrove, Stoke Prior, and Bentley Pauncefote.[16] For the Subsidy of 1598 [9] he was assessed at 40s. in lands, and had to pay 8s.; and in this roll and in the " Feet of Fines" from 1600 [16] he is distinguished by the title of Gent. Two of his sons engaged in the Cloth Manufacture, one at Worcester and one at Bromsgrove; they both died in 1624. The fourth son was named Thomas, and there were four married daughters. I cannot distinguish the eldest son John, nor his eldest son John, among the many of that name of Bromsgrove. He must have been one of the two John Chaunces of Bromsgrove (one of them of Woodcote), who disclaimed Arms at the Heralds' Visitation of 1634. But no fewer than 16 children of John Chances were baptized at Bromsgrove between the years 1605 and 1628, and there were evidently several of the name. In the Subsidy Rolls of 1641 [9] appear the names of John Chance of Catshill, taxed 16s. on an assessment of 40s. in lands, and John Chance and William his son taxed and assessed at half that amount.

It was at Catshill, as we saw, that the first Chances of Bromsgrove resided. Their representative there in the time of James I. was Thomas Chaunce (perhaps the son of William Chaunce lately mentioned), who had in 1600 married Mary Bradlay.[17] He had a son Richard born in 1609,[17] and in 1642 we find Thomas Chance and Richard his son assessed at 30s. in lands and taxed 12s.[9] Thomas was Churchwarden of Bromsgrove in 1622.[17] Richard Chance of Catshill, Yeoman, died in 1686, and was presumably the son of Thomas above-mentioned. He was Churchwarden in 1662,[17] and lived in a house with two hearths.[9] His son Richard was a weaver of Stoke Prior; he died in 1718, and was buried at Bromsgrove. Another family at Catshill was that of John Chance previously mentioned, whose son was Nicholas Chance of Catshill, Yeoman and Alderman, baptized at Bromsgrove in 1617, and buried there in 1682.[17] He occupied a house with four hearths,[9] and was no doubt a

---

[16] Record Office—" Feet of Fines," see § 2 note 7. In 1591 he acquired property at Alvechurch; in 1594, 1598, twice in 1600, and in 1612 property at Bromsgrove; and in 1601 property at Stoke Prior and Bentley Pauncefote.

[17] Bromsgrove Parish Registers.

man of considerable means. His eldest son John succeeded him at Catshill, and must have been the father of William and Thomas Chance, Gents., the former of whom is commemorated by the "Chance Monument" in Bromsgrove Churchyard,[18] while the latter married a Vernon of Hanbury, and was the ancestor of the 18th century Chances of Upton-on-Severn.[19]

Nicholas Chance's second surviving son was named after him; he was a yeoman of Bournheath, married in 1681 Lydia Dewce, and died in 1709. His son was John Chance of Bournheath, Yeoman, who died in 1724.[20] He had also a daughter Elizabeth, who lived for many years unmarried at Belbroughton; where also lived two of her married sisters. But for details about these Catshill Chances I must refer to Appendix F, Nos. 27, 42, 45, 49-52, 60.

Anthony Chance of Bournheath, Yeoman, who died in 1711, was probably a brother of Nicholas Chance the elder, since their children are called in the wills kinsmen, which usually means cousins. And the father's name in both cases was John. Anthony was just ten years younger than Nicholas, having been baptized in Feb. 1626-7.[17] His father was a tanner, and when we find [21] that John Chance of Bromsgrove, Tanner, married in 1661, at the age of 80, a widow of 60, we may suppose him to have been the same person. Anthony's eldest son John succeeded to the farm at Bournheath, while the second son William also lived there, following the trade of a weaver. John died in 1711, and William early in 1705, the latter apparently unmarried. A third son was Anthony Chance of Bromsgrove, Skinner, who died in 1717, having married in 1694 Mary Nash, and leaving several children. We find him and his wife Mary and others disposing of land in Holloway field, Hanbury, in 1701.[16] For details of this family see Appendix F, Nos. 46, 63.

Of Bournheath Chances of the 16th century we have Richard Chance, who died in 1576, and John Chance, Yeoman, who died in Jan. 1614-15,[17] and was probably the John Chance assessed in 1598 at £3 in goods, and taxed 8s.[9] He had a son Hugh, and several grandchildren.[22]

We come lastly to the Chances of Shepley, whose line of descent is traced and discussed in Part II., Pedigree No. 1. How Elianor Chaunce of Shepley, who died in 1585-6, and her son John were connected with the earlier Chances, I have nothing to show. It is curious that in 1592 Elianor Chaunce, widow, and John Chance her son and heir acquired property at

[18] See Appendix C—Inscription No. 10.
[19] *Ibid.*—Inscription No. 11, and Appendix F, Nos. 60, 61.
[20] *Ibid.*—Inscription No. 9.
[21] Marriage Bonds—Bishop's Registry, Worcester—Appendix B 1.
[22] See Appendix F—Nos. 14, 24.

Bromsgrove[16]; and it is hardly to be supposed that they were the same persons as those first mentioned. There were certainly in the next reign two distinct John Chaunces of Shepley, each of them with a son named William. That one of them, whom I have concluded to be our ancestor,[23] has already been mentioned in §2 (p. 17), where I gave the inventory of the goods left by him at his death. He was a mason — "freemason" he is called in the inventory—by trade, and some extracts[24] from an old memorandum book of Sir Edward Pytts, of Kyre Park, Worcestershire, show that he was employed in 1588 and the following years as chief mason in the building of the Manor House there. Of his son and grandchildren, one of whom I believe[23] to have been the John Chaunce of Shepley, Yeoman,[25] who died in 1669-70, I have nothing to say; and so we come to William Chance, son of the last-named. He was in 1660 settled in Belbroughton, a parish adjoining that of Bromsgrove, having married in 1655-6[26] a widow named Elizabeth Perkes, who appears to have had property in Belbroughton; and in 1667 he was occupying a one-hearth house there.* Perhaps he had migrated to Belbroughton on his marriage. Very soon after his father's death we find (in 1670) William Chance and Elizabeth his wife and John Perkes (a trustee perhaps) disposing of property in Belbroughton[16]; the former doubtless intending to occupy the paternal farm at Shepley. It is uncertain in what year this William Chance died. In a Poll-Tax assessment of 1690 we find at Shepley John Chance and William Chance, each with a wife and three or more children[27]; and in 1700 William and Henry Chance rented land there.[28] But as the John Chance who died in 1669-70 had other sons Henry and John, and these had children with the usual names, and there was another Henry[29] (and others perhaps) descended from the other William Chaunce of Shepley of James I.'s reign, it is impossible to identify or distinguish. The Bromsgrove Parish Registers record burials of William Chances of Shepley

[23] See Part II., Pedigree No. 1.

[24] Printed in the "Antiquary" for 1890, Vols. 21, 22. "The building of the Manor House of Kyre Park, Worcestershire, 1588-1618." One of the extracts runs: "Bargayned with John Chaunce of Bromsgrove Freemason the 24 of February 1611 not being Shrovetide to be my cheiff mason workman and survey'r of the work and workmen for repayring & newe building Kier house for the wages of £10 yearly meet drink lodging & washing till the work be finished God will." Kyre Park is not far from Tenbury.

[22] The inventory attached to his will is appended in full to § 11.

[26] See Appendix A 1, a b, and Part II., Pedigree No. 1, where certain difficulties which arise in this connection are discussed.

[27] Appendix F, No. 49.

[28] Ibid., No. 50.

[29] Ibid., No. 30. His widow Elianor acquired land in Shepley in 1668, dying some 14 months later. She occupied a one-hearth house in Bromsgrove. [Feet of Fines, and Appendix E.]

in 1666-7 and 1723; but if the latter was the one who married Elizabeth Perkes, he must have lived to well past 90. He and his wife were alive in 1706, as in that year [16] we find William and Elizabeth Chance, John Perkes sen. and jun., and Wheeler Perkes,[20] disposing of property in Belbroughton. In 1700 William Chance of Shepley, the same presumably, rented a small holding in the Manor of Dyers (in Bromsgrove parish),[28] besides the property he held at Shepley; and in 1709 William Chance the younger received under the will of his kinsman William Lowe of Padstones, Bromsgrove, the reversion of two houses in Dyers " near the Crebbmill farm "; which property he came into on the death of the widow Lowe in 1717.[31]

William, son of William Chance and Elizabeth Perkes, was baptized at Belbroughton in 1660, and I have little doubt[25] that he was the William Chance who died at Christmas, 1739, "aged 80," as is recorded in the tombstone inscription (p. 7). Whether it was he or his son William, who was the legatee of William Lowe just mentioned I cannot say; nor have I any further information about him. The inventory of his goods was given on p. 18. We will take up the history of his descendants in § 9.

Wheeler Perkes was the name of Elizabeth Chance's first husband, and this Wheeler Perkes may very well have been her son by that marriage.

[31] Will of William Lowe proved at Worcester 20th June 1709; that of his widow Dorothy 31st Jan. 1716-7. The matter is also mentioned in the Bromsgrove Manorial Records, under the year 1711.

§ 4. *Spelling of the Name.*

WE, who are familiar with a fixed orthography, are apt to forget the difficulties which presented themselves in old times to anyone who wished to represent in letters the sound of a spoken word. And if the forms assumed by common words were uncertain, still more arbitrary and various was the rendering of proper names, which men wrote, indeed, in any way that occurred to them at the moment.

The name of Chance has been less subject to variation than many, and yet, apart from its regular development, we find a number of eccentric modes of representing it. The present mode has been the rule for about two centuries, and I have found instances of it even in the 16th century; but the usual spelling before the 18th was Chaunce. In more than one will that I have examined the two spellings, Chance and Chaunce, occur together, and I have even found the same person's name spelt both ways in the same will. The oldest spelling, that I have met with, is Chawns,[1] which occurs in a Bromsgrove deed of 1352,[2] and this mode appears again later; viz. as Chawnse, in three wills of 1542 and 1547; as Chawse, in another will of the latter year; and as Chawnce, in Bromsgrove deeds of 1491 and 1507,[2] in a will of 1546 (together with Chaunce), and on a Hadzor tombstone with date 1625. Chaunse I have found under dates 1473[3] and 1572.[4] But Chaunce was the common spelling already in the 15th century, and does not disappear from the Bromsgrove Parish Registers till 1684; on a Bromsgrove tombstone it occurs as late as 1759.[5]

[1] Cp. p. 22. In a deed of the previous year occurs Le Chawne, which may possibly be connected with Chawns.
[2] Prattinton MSS., in the possession of the Society of Antiquaries.
[3] Bromsgrove Court Rolls.
[4] § 2, note 17.
[5] Appendix C—Inscription No. 9. Perhaps the name was so spelt to agree with the others of earlier date on the same stone.

Eccentric or accidental variations are: Chanch in two wills of 1572 and 1573; Chaunche in a will of 1591 (though in the rest of the document the name is spelt Chaunce); Chanes in the Parish Register under date 1664, and on a tombstone with date 1742 (the person in the latter case being entered in the Burial Register as Chance); Chanch again and Chonce in the Registers under dates 1704 and 1736 respectively. It is curious that Chanch and Chawse, so unlike each other, should be variations of the same name.

It is improbable that the Chances have anything to do with the well-known families of Chauncy and Chauncey of the Eastern counties.

I am unable to suggest any probable derivation of the name, but note that Chawnes and Chawnos occur in the Roll of Battle Abbey.

§ 5. *TILT of Bromsgrove.*

MARY TILT, mother of William Chance of Birmingham, came of a family of Bromsgrove townspeople, millers, maltsters, &c., who extended their business to Kidderminster. I have been able to trace her descent straight back to Henry Tylte of Bromsgrove, who died in 1606; but have only found earlier mentions of the name in two wills of 1585 and 1586. Possibly there was a connection with John Tyllett "seneor of Kethermyster," whose will was proved at Worcester in 1575.

Besides the Tilts who were connected with the corn-trade, there was in the time of Charles I. "John Tilt, a very honest man of Bromsgrove, who was skilful in making mortar-pieces and ordnance."[1] And Mary Tilt's father and brother were in the leather trade.

Joshua Tilt, her father, did not apparently live in Bromsgrove, at least none of his three marriages took place, nor were his children baptized there; yet those of the latter who died young were brought thither for burial. Tradition says that Mary Tilt came from Stourbridge[2]; but if Joshua lived there, the required entries ought to be in the Parish Registers of Oldswinford, which they are not; excepting that of his second marriage. At the time of his death he had a work-shop in Bromsgrove on Spadesbourne brook, and he had previously under his mother's will inherited an acre of land on "Sauntridge," Bromsgrove, together with other property devised to her by his father Caleb Tilt.

The last-named was evidently the first of the three Tilts, Caleb, Henry, and William, who were freeholders of Bromsgrove in 1703-4.[3] He had

---

[1] Nathaniel Nye, "Art of Gunnery &c.," 1647. Quoted by Noake, "Worcestershire Nuggets," p. 298.

[2] William Tilt of Stourbridge voted as a freeholder of Bromsgrove in the County Election of 1741. [Prattinton MSS.] Perhaps the tradition arose through him.

[3] Grazebrook—"Heraldry of Worcestershire"—List of freeholders of that county in 1703-4 : ages 21 to 70, and minimum value of holdings £10.

considerable property there, which he divided at his death among his wife and younger sons. John and Joshua, the two eldest, were already provided for; the former of them holding, for instance, some property known as Slideslowe, or Slightslow, which had belonged to his grandfather William Tilt. Caleb had also a house and garden in Mill St., Kidderminster. He died in 1727, and his widow Dorcas in 1733. Further particulars of the family will be found in Part II., Pedigree No. 2.

The only one of Mary Tilt's female ancestors, whose maiden name I have obtained, was Alice Hill, her great-grandmother, who was a daughter of Henry Hill of Bromsgrove and Stoke Prior, Yeoman. His descent I have not been able to determine; there were a large number of Hills at Bromsgrove from early times, and some of them were no doubt his ancestors. He had a son John Hill, and one of his daughters was Hannah, wife of Edward Harris; and as John Hill, Rector of Upton Warren, who died in 1699, had a "brother" named Edward Harris, it is probable that this was the John Hill in question.

Mary Tilt lived to the great age of 91, and it is probably to her in a great measure that the Chances of Birmingham owe their constitutional vigour. By her second marriage with George Bell she had two sons and a daughter. From the last were descended the Cranes of Birmingham (see Part II., Pedigree No. 2, and p. 50).

Neither of the sons married. The elder, John, died in 1814, and the other, Joshua, in 1840.

§ 6. *LUCAS of Rowington and Hanbury.*

FAMILIES bearing the name of Lucas have long existed in most English counties and in Ireland, the principal family of the name in old times belonging to Essex. It is one of those surnames which are taken from Christian names, Lucas being the Latin form of Luke or Lukes.[1]

The particular family, to which belonged Sarah and Mary Lucas, wives respectively of William Chance and Edward Homer, may be traced back to certain yeomen of Warwickshire. They were daughters of Robert Lucas of Bristol, the youngest, or youngest but one, of the ten children of Clement Lucas of Feckenham Park, Hanbury, a parish in Worcestershire only separated from Bromsgrove by that of Stoke Prior. The names of eight of these children appear in Clement Lucas' will, proved at Worcester in Dec. 1757; and three of these, Thomas, Margaret, and Robert, and a fourth named Joseph, were baptized at Hanbury in the years 1700-1705. But before the year 1700 the name is not to be found in the Hanbury Parish Registers.

However we have a clue to Clement Lucas' place of origin, as we learn from his will that he had freehold property at Rowington, near Warwick; and on consulting the registers of that parish, we find under the years 1692-1696 the baptisms of Elizabeth, Clement, William, and John, children of Clement Lucas jun.; and these are the names of four of the other children mentioned in the will. Of the eighth there mentioned, Samuel, and of another son, Benjamin, buried at Hanbury in 1716, I have not found the baptismal entries, and we may assume that they were born between 1696 and 1700, and baptized at some place where Clement Lucas was residing in that interval.

Clement Lucas, as appears from the age given in his marriage bond,[2] was born about 1663, or 1668. He was no doubt the son of one of the same

---

[1] Compare the names Matthews, Marks, and Johns.

[2] Bishop's Registry, Worcester, 22nd May, 1691—Appendix B 3. The figures giving his age are blurred, and may be 23 or 28.

name, who was buried at Rowington in 1702; and in the Rowington registers he is accordingly described as "Ju." I have not obtained the entry of his baptism, but a daughter of Clement and Dorothy Lucas was baptized at Rowington in 1665, and would be his sister.

Clement Lucas, his father, was baptized at Rowington 30th Dec. 1638, and was the son of William Lucas of that parish, Yeoman, who was buried there in April 1679. The Rowington parish registers only commence in 1638, but we can get back a step further by means of the will of another Clement Lucas, of Stratford-on-Avon, proved at Worcester in that same year. This testator desires to be buried at Rowington, and mentions his father Clement, still living, and his brother William, who would be the William Lucas of Rowington above-mentioned. Who this last Clement Lucas was, I cannot say. His family may have been long settled at Rowington, or may have migrated thither. There were several families of the name in Warwickshire, but they were not of station sufficiently high to appear in the Subsidy Rolls (p. 11), that is, to pay their quota to the national taxes. The oldest wills in the name preserved at Worcester belong to Rouslench and Brailes.

Clement Lucas of Hanbury married in 1691 Elizabeth, daughter of John Tibbatts of Rowington.[3] I have not been able to distinguish her family among several of the name in that parish. As the marriage bond[2] puts her age at 27, she may have been the child baptized at Rowington 10th May 1663.[3]

The elder children of Clement and Elizabeth Lucas were baptized, as above said, at Rowington, but the family must have left there about 1697, and not long afterwards have settled at Hanbury, where the younger children were baptized. Clement Lucas' will is dated 30th May 1749, but was not proved till 1757.

His eldest child, Elizabeth, was in 1749 unmarried, and I dare say remained so. She received under the will £50, besides £14 a year from the Rowington property. The eldest son, Clement, received £50, and each of his children a like sum. He married firstly, in 1721, Anne, daughter of William Lilly of Hanbury, and in the marriage bond[4] he is described as of Hadzor, Yeoman, and it was there that his eldest child Dorothy was baptized. But his younger children were baptized at Hanbury, and he was living there, at "the Pumphouse," in 1751.[3] His wife died in Nov. 1738, and in Feb. 1741 he married Anne, widow of Robert Penrice; but she died six weeks later.[3] He seems to have married a third time, as a certain Sarah, wife of Clement

[3] See Appendix A 4, 5.
[4] See Appendix B 3.

Lucas, was buried at Hanbury 21st Nov. 1753. But this may have been a step-mother, or perhaps his daughter-in-law. There were also a Clement and Mary Lucas of Tardebigg, who had two children baptized and one buried at Hanbury in 1748 and 1754[3]: and this may have been his eldest son Clement, born in 1726. Particulars of this branch of the family will be found in Part II., Pedigree No. 3 A.

The second son, William Lucas, received under his father's will £300. He is described in his will, proved at Worcester in 1777, as of Hanbury, Gent. He left a widow Dorothy, but not apparently any children.

The last of the children of Clement Lucas baptized at Rowington was John. He inherited from his father the property at Rowington known as Squadge (or Squagg) Hills, and Great Pool Meadow; and by his will, proved in the Hanbury "Peculiar" Court in 1765, he left the same to his brother Clement. He also had property at Stock and Bradley, which he left to his cousin Mary, daughter of Thomas Tibbatts of Rowington. His will describes him as of Hanbury, Yeoman. It is strange that he does not mention therein his daughter Mary, or any of her children. She married John Saunders of Grafton Lodge, Bromsgrove, and by origin of Gloucester, of which city his eldest brother Abraham[5] was Sheriff in 1759. Mary Saunders' daughter Elizabeth was in 1780 a legatee under the will of Elizabeth Lucas, widow of Robert Lucas. She married Robert Smith of the Grove, Edgbaston, and her daughter married William Bartleet.[6]

After John Lucas came two sons, Samuel and Benjamin (unless the latter was the youngest of the family). From the former are descended some of the present Lucas' of Bristol. He had sons Samuel and William,[7] the latter of whom was no doubt that nephew of Robert Lucas, who was partner with him in his cooperage business at Bristol.[8] Samuel Lucas the elder received under his father's will £400. He was living in 1776.[7] Benjamin his brother was buried at Hanbury in 1716.[3]

We now come to those children of Clement Lucas who were baptized at Hanbury, and firstly to Thomas, whose legacy from his father was £150, besides £50 to each of his sons, William and Thomas, when 21. He died in

---

[5] Probably the Abraham Saunders, Alderman of Gloucester, whose will was proved in London in 1793.

[6] These particulars about Mary Saunders and her descendants were obtained by Mr. Edward Sargant from Mrs. Bartleet. Mary was known as "Pretty Polly Saunders." Mr. R. L. Chance has photographs of her and her husband, taken from silhouettes, and others of Mr. and Mrs. Robert Smith, from portraits painted in 1822.

[7] Will of William Lucas, their uncle above-mentioned.

[8] Will of Robert Lucas (below).

1776, and his will describes him as of Ipsley, Redditch, Gentleman. His two sons survived him, and the Redditch property passed to William. Thomas engaged in business at Bristol as a Cooper, or "Hooper," of Lucas' Hall, Marsh St.[9]; the similar business of his uncle Robert Lucas being in Nicholas St. As he left sons Robert, Thomas, and William, I assume that it was the two latter who were "Hoopers" of Marsh St., Bristol, about 1810.[10] He had also a daughter Elizabeth, unmarried in 1780, and this must have been the Elizabeth, daughter of Thomas Lucas "of Hanbury," who in 1783 married Richard Pearsall of Bristol, and became the mother of Robert Lucas Pearsall.[11]

William Lucas of Redditch, Gent., brother of Thomas, died between 1782 and 1786. He left a daughter Catherine, who some time between these dates married George Silvester. There was also a "daughter-in-law" Catherine James, at the date of the will (1782) unmarried and under age, so that the term perhaps means step-daughter, or possibly adopted daughter.

Returning to the children of Clement Lucas, the next was named Joseph, and probably died young; and then came Margaret, who became the wife of Jonathan Nash, younger son of Goodwin Nash of Bromsgrove. They had four sons and four daughters, and one of the former, Jonathan, married his cousin Frances Lucas (below). The will of Jonathan Nash of Arbor's Gate, Stoke Prior, and Prior's Field, Upton Warren, whose wife's name was Margaret, was proved at Worcester in 1767, and this may have been Clement Lucas' son-in-law; but there were several families of the name in Worcestershire. Several of the children were born before 1749, and received legacies under the wills of their grandfather and of their uncles William and John Lucas, and it is from these wills that I have obtained their names (see Part II., Pedigree No. 3 E). Jonathan and Frances Nash also had several children, but the only surviving son was Jonathan Nash of Bristol, who died in 1845; he married Frances, daughter of David and Mary Onion, and among their children are Mr. Thompson Nash, Miss Anne Nash, and Mrs. William Sargant.

[9] See his will, proved in London in 1784, but dated 1780.
[10] Holden's Directory of Bristol, 1809-11.
[11] Burke's "Landed Gentry"—1868. The Pearsalls appear to have elaborated their pedigree (see the "Herald and Genealogist," vii. 270); and this would account for their describing Thomas Lucas as of Hanbury instead of Bristol. Richard Pearsall was the third son of John Pearsall of Willsbridge, Glouc., and his widow (he died in 1813) bought that property from his eldest brother. On her death in 1836 Willsbridge passed to Robert Lucas Pearsall, who further bought Wartensee Castle, near St. Gall, in Switzerland, at which place he died in 1856. He was a man of some distinction. His son Robert entered the Austrian 4th Uhlans, a regiment officered solely by nobility (for which reason perhaps the pedigree); and his elder daughter, Elizabeth Still Pearsall, became 7th Countess of Harrington. The younger, Philippa Swinnerton, married John Hughes, Barrister-at-law.

Lastly we come to Robert Lucas, whose daughters married William Chance and Edward Homer. He was baptized at Hanbury 28th Mar. 1705, and was already at Bristol, engaged in business as a Cooper, in 1739, in which year he married Elizabeth Butler of Hanbury⁴ (§ 7). In 1741 he held freehold property at Bromsgrove, voting with that qualification in the County Election of that year.¹² He received £100 under his father's will, besides 200 guineas invested in a mortgage on the property of one Thomas Butler of Feckenham, which brought in 10 guineas a year.¹³

The cooperage business was located in Nicholas St., Bristol. It prospered, and Robert Lucas extended his ventures to the manufacture of glass bottles, which, with other partners, he carried on near the Limckiln Dock, in the parish of St. Augustine. From this his son went on to the manufacture of window-glass at Nailsea, as we shall see in § 9.

Robert Lucas died on the 18th Apr. 1775, at the age of 70. He left to his wife his three freehold houses at Kingsdown, in one of which he had resided, and the bulk of his property. The half of his interest in the cooperage business went to his only surviving son, John Robert Lucas, who was not yet of age; his share was valued at £1000. As he further had the reversion of the property left to his mother, he had a good start in life. Besides him, Robert Lucas had four sons and seven daughters, but all the former, and the eldest daughter, died in infancy; nor did Margaret, the sixth daughter, survive her father. Of the others, Frances, who married her cousin Jonathan Nash, has already been noticed.

The next daughter, Elizabeth, married James Lockier, "Upholder," of Bristol, and had nine children, all daughters. One of them, Frances, married George Gee, a ~~relative, I suppose,~~ [brother] of Mrs. J. E. Homer (p. 53). She and an unmarried sister (Sarah, I believe) kept for some years a school at Hendon. Another sister, Sophia, married Henry Cooke, a merchant in London, and a brother of Isaac Cooke, the family solicitor at Bristol, with whom Henry Chance was placed (p. 54). A fourth sister, Harriet, married Daniel Prince¹⁴ of Hendon. The sisters were very intimate with their Chance cousins (§ 9), often staying in Birmingham, and seeing much of Robert Lucas Chance's family at Highgate. More than one of the Chances were at the school at Hendon.

[12] Prattinton MSS., in the possession of the Society of Antiquaries.

[13] Wills of Clement Lucas, 1757, and of Thomas Butler of Feckenham, 1725. Feckenham is 4 miles S.E. of Hanbury.

[14] Daniel Prince was also a merchant. I conjecture that he and Henry Cooke were partners in the firm of Cooke, Prince, & Co., of London, with whom Robert Lucas Chance had dealings.

The fourth daughter, Ann, was twice married, (1) to Thomas Manley, and (2) in 1784 to Henry Pater. By the former marriage she had one daughter Elizabeth, who married the Rev. Robert Foster, Vicar of Wells and of Sutton Bonnington, Notts.; and by the second she had a son, who died unmarried at Naples at the age of 45, and two daughters, the elder of whom married George Watson Pritchett, and the younger Admiral William Robertson; they spent the latter years of their lives at Bath, and attained the ages of 80 and 85 respectively.

Notice of the other surviving children of Robert Lucas I must defer to § 9.

§ 7. BUTLER and VERNON of Hanbury.

ELIZABETH BUTLER, wife of Robert Lucas (§ 6), was the eldest of the three daughters of John Butler, of Hanbury, by his marriage with Elizabeth Vernon, also of Hanbury, solemnized at Bromsgrove on the 22nd June 1714.[1] The other two daughters were named Mary and Frances. Who this John Butler was, I have not discovered. There were at Hanbury a John Butler in 1560, and a William Butler, Gent., in 1566, both of them assessed at £5 a year in lands,[2] and therefore well-to-do freeholding yeomen; and though in the Hearthmoney Rolls[3] of a century later, which include the names of a very much larger number of persons, the name as regards Hanbury does not appear, there was then (in 1668) a Robert Butler, Husbandman, living in the parish,[1] who may have been John Butler's grandfather. In the neighbouring parishes of Bromsgrove and Feckenham there were plenty of Butlers, and of these, Gilbert Butler of Bromsgrove married in 1682 Elizabeth Crab,[1] and had an eldest son named John[4]; while John Butler of Feckenham had a son John who was not of age in 1690[5]; so that, as far as dates go, John Butler of Hanbury, who was born about 1686,[1] may have been either of these. But I have not been able to obtain identifying proof. The fact, that his marriage took place at Bromsgrove, seems to indicate a connection with that place. And therefore I may remark, that the Butlers were one of the old yeoman families of the Manor of Bromsgrove, and were already in the 16th century dignified by the title of Gent. (They intermarried with the Shepley Chances in 1599—see Part II., Pedigree No. 1.)

Family tradition has it that John Butler was connected with Samuel

[1] Appendix B 5—Marriage Bonds.
[2] Record Office—Subsidy Rolls Nos. 200/190 and 200/197. See p. 11.
[3] See p. 11.
[4] Will of Gilbert Butler, proved at Worcester 29th Oct. 1722.
[5] Will of John Butler, proved at Worcester 23rd Mar. 1690-1.

Butler, the author of "Hudibras." I have no means of proving or disproving this. Samuel Butler was born at Strensham, in the extreme south of the county, in 1612, but married and lived the latter portion of his life in London· There was a John Butler at Defford, which is close to Strensham, in the reign of Charles II.[6]

Turning now to John Butler's wife, we find that there was in the 17th century an important family named Vernon at Hanbury, who claimed descent from, and used the Arms of the great Vernon family, whose headquarters were in Cheshire.[7] The first of this family at Hanbury was Richard Vernon, Rector of the parish from 1581 to 1627. He purchased land there at various times,[8] and his eldest son Edward, a Cavalier, bought the Manor and Advowson. His fourth son John succeeded him as Rector of Hanbury from 1627 to 1681 (so that they covered between them just a century), and he had eleven other children, and grandchildren in great profusion and of various distinction.

On meeting therefore with the name of Elizabeth Vernon of Hanbury as an ancestress, I certainly supposed that she was a member of this family; but it is not so. One of the persons, from whom Richard Vernon obtained land in 1591, was a Robert Vernon, and from him the Hanbury Parish Registers show that Elizabeth Vernon was lineally descended.

She was the second of twelve children of Robert Vernon of Hanbury, Yeoman, who in 1674 married Elizabeth Smith of Stoke Prior.[1] She and the four next children, one of whom was her twin, were baptized in the years 1676 to 1681 at Hadzor, near Droitwich, showing that her father was then residing there; but on the death of his father he returned to Hanbury, and it was there that his other children were baptized. In 1703-4 we find him a freeholder of Hanbury.[9] His father was occupying about 1660, as under-tenant to Richard Vernon (a grandson of the old Rector), some land known as Broadmeadow, "contayning by estimation foure dayes Math," and Moorecroftes (9 acres), in Hanbury [10]; and perhaps this was the land which he got from Richard Vernon in 1647.[11] But he no doubt had freehold land as well. His descent will be found set out in Part II., Pedigree No. 4.

[6] Hearthmoney Rolls.
[7] See Nash, "History of Worcestershire," s.v. Hanbury, and Appendix of Arms.
[8] Record Office—"Feet of Fines"—1591, 1592, 1601, 1611, 1612. Cp. § 2, note 7.
[9] Grazebrook, "Heraldry of Worcestershire"; cp. § 5, note 3.
[10] Wills of Richard Vernon, of Hanbury (Worcester—1661), and of Margaret Vernon, his widow (Worcester—1675).
[11] Record Office—"Feet of Fines."

F

Elizabeth Vernon was married at Bromsgrove, as above stated, to John Butler of Hanbury, on the 22nd June 1714. On her father's death, in 1720, she received certain houses in Bromsgrove, held on a lease of 2000 years.[12] I have not ascertained when she or her husband died. Their three daughters, the eldest of whom married Robert Lucas, I have mentioned above.

[12] Will of Robert Vernon of Hanbury, 1720.

§ 8. *HOMER of Ettingshall and Sutton Coldfield.*

EDWARD HOMER, partner in business with William Chance of Birmingham, and brother-in-law both to him and to John Robert Lucas, came of a family domiciled for four generations at Sutton Coldfield, and for centuries before that at Ettingshall in Staffordshire. His grandfather, father, and elder brother were solicitors, and held the office of Deputy Steward to the Corporation of Sutton Coldfield; and his uncle was the well-known Henry Homer, Rector of Birdingbury.

Of Edward Homer's maternal descent I am not informed; his paternal grandmother was one of the Bracebridges of Atherstone, a well-known Warwickshire family, and her mother was heiress to the Ludfords of Ansley; while his other paternal great-grandmother was Elizabeth, daughter of William Sadler of Castle Bromwich, of a family long settled in that neighbourhood.

His great-grandfather, Thomas Homer, first of the family at Sutton Coldfield, came thither from Ettingshall, where in 1710, at the date of his will, he still possessed inherited property. As his ten children were baptized (in the years 1674-1687) at Water Orton,[1] it is probable that he resided there before settling at Sutton Coldfield; and his father-in-law was close by at Castle Bromwich. The Ettingshall property was still held in 1745 by Edward Homer, eldest son of Thomas; but of him below. A brother of Thomas Homer, named Edward, was still living at Ettingshall in 1710, as is mentioned in the will.

To trace Thomas Homer's descent, we must have recourse to the registers of Sedgley parish, in which Ettingshall was formerly included. These are preserved from 1558, and have been searched; and the only baptism of a Thomas Homer found of suitable date (bearing in mind that his eldest child was baptized in 1674, and that he died about 1711) was that of Thomas, son of Edward and Elizabeth Holmer (*sic*), in 1637. This Thomas had brothers and

---

[1] Parish Registers of Water Orton, preserved at Aston.

Elizabeth Vernon was married at Bromsgrove, as above stated, to John Butler of Hanbury, on the 22nd June 1714. On her father's death, in 1720, she received certain houses in Bromsgrove, held on a lease of 2000 years.[12] I have not ascertained when she or her husband died. Their three daughters, the eldest of whom married Robert Lucas, I have mentioned above.

[12] Will of Robert Vernon of Hanbury, 1720.

4d.[7] In 158—[8] William Holmer of Sedgeley, yeoman, brought an action in Chancery against Ralph Tuncks, executor to "Johan" Bromall, late of Walsall, "wyddowe." Joan was mother-in-law to William, and the action was about some property at Walsall left by her to his children, John, Margaret, and Joan (Johan),[9] which property Tuncks would not surrender, claiming debts due to him from William Holmer. I do not know how the suit ended.

For the latter half of the 16th century we have the aid of the Sedgley Parish Registers, which begin in 1558. A complete search for the name of Homer (Holmer) has been made in them for the first 50 years, and the results are set forth in Appendix A 7. The entries however are only genealogically useful from 1580, as before that date the names of the parents of the children baptized are not given. From the registers, with some aid from the Court rolls, I have constructed the earlier part of Pedigree No. 5, in Part II.

There were other Holmers and Homers in early times, besides those of Sedgley. About 1280 we find Holemeres occupying lands in Oxfordshire, near Wallingford[10]; and in 1338 a Thomas de Homere received lands in Dorsetshire from John Mautravers the elder.[11] (There are still Homers in that county). There was also an Andrew Homer (see § 10) in the time of Edward III., who used the same armorial bearings that were afterwards used by the Homers of Ettingshall and Sutton Coldfield, and are now used by their Somersetshire descendants. In the 16th century there were many Homers in North Worcestershire and South Staffordshire: e.g. in 1582 a marriage license was granted at Worcester for Simon Pitt, and Frances Holmer of Kidderminster[12]; in 1598 the will of William Homer of Worcester was proved there; and in 1600 a marriage license was granted to Richard Holmer of Rowley Regis,[18] one of whose bondsmen[13] was Edward Homer of Halesowen. In the "Feet of Fines"[14] Richard Homer appears in 1589, 1608, 1632, and 1638 as a landholder at Dudley and Cradley; Leonard Holmer in 1622 at Yardley; and Thomas Holmer in 1626, 1629, and 1637 at Dudley; and in more modern

---

[7] Record Office—Subsidy Rolls—Nos. 177/96 and 177/120.
[8] Record Office—Chancery Proceedings, temp. Elizabeth: Holmer v. Tuncks.
[9] Probably the children baptized at Sedgley in 1571, 1570, and 1573; [see Appendix A 7 a.]
[10] Record Office—Hundred Rolls—see the printed Index to them.
[11] Brit: Museum—Harl: Charters 53 D 26. See also the "Collectanea Topographica et Genealogica," VI. 349-352.
[12] Marriage Bonds—Bishop's Registry—Worcester.
[13] See § 11, note 1.
[14] See § 2, note 7.

times the name frequently occurs in the country between Dudley and Halesowen, and about Hanbury.[15] But withal the name must be considered to be decidedly uncommon and local.

There were also Homers in early times in Somersetshire, of which county one Thomas Homer was a Deputy-Lieutenant in the time of James I.[16]

An American family of the name, of Boston, supposed themselves to be descended from the Homers of Ettingshall, through a Captain John Homer, said to have been born there in 1647. But I have not obtained from the Sedgley registers any notice of his baptism. The subject was investigated some 30 years ago, by Mr. Benjamin Homer Dixon, of Boston. He elicited from a Mr. Benjamin Homer, of Bilston, the tradition that the Staffordshire Homers were descended from those of Dorsetshire (p. 45), but did little further.

These are all the notices of Homers of the 17th century and earlier that I have collected, and we may return to the Homers of Sutton Coldfield. Thomas Homer died in 1711-2, leaving his property at Ettingshall and his books, manuscripts, &c., to his eldest son Edward; his son Henry getting £150, and his unmarried daughters, Mary and Dorothy, £300 apiece. The property at Water Orton and Sutton Coldfield appears to have been settled on his wife, but to have come to Edward Homer on her death, as this Edward died in 1745 possessed of property in Sutton, Minworth, Water Orton, Curdworth, and Coleshill.[17] The bulk of this passed to his eldest son Thomas, but he died the next year, and it presumably then went to the next son, Edward, who succeeded his father as Solicitor and Deputy Steward of Sutton Coldfield.[18] The Ettingshall property went to the youngest son Henry, then or afterwards Rector of Birdingbury; it was part copyhold and part freehold, and was saddled with £250 for Henry's sister Katharine, who not long afterwards married the Rev. Thomas Dadley, Vicar of Budbrooke, and Master of Temple Balsall Hospital.

The Rev. Henry Homer[19] was a man of mark. He was born in

---

[15] See the Calendars of Wills in the Worcester Probate Registry.

[16] Brit: Museum, Add. MS. 5496, Correspondence of the Earl of Hertford, Lord Lieut. of Somersetshire, about 1610.

[17] The last four places are from 3½ to 7 miles to the S.E. of Sutton Coldfield.

[18] This Edward Homer, with Joseph Duncomb, made in 1759 Blackroot Pool in Sutton Park.

[19] These notes about Henry Homer and his sons are mainly taken from Colvile's "Worthies of Warwickshire"; see also the "Gentleman's Magazine" for 1791, pp. 492, 685. Colvile gives his name as Henry Sacheverell Homer, but this is doubtful. He was a godson of the famous Henry Sacheverell.

1719, and obtained in due time a Fellowship at Magdalen College, Oxford, becoming later Vicar of Willoughby and Rector of Birdingbury; and he was also at one time Vicar of Ansley.[20] As a man of noted integrity, and combining with his scholarly attainments great business ability, he assisted largely in the management of his patron's and of other gentlemen's estates, and among other things wrote a treatise on road-making, which Macadam quotes as the only useful work that he had met with on the subject. He died suddenly while returning from his hayfield, or according to another account while walking back from Willoughby to Birdingbury, on the 14th July 1791, and was found sitting as if asleep against a tree.

His eldest son, the Rev. Henry Homer, was born at Warwick, entered Rugby School at 7, and at 14 was head boy, afterwards becoming a Fellow of Emmanuel College, Cambridge. He was a chief friend of the famous Dr. Samuel Parr,[21] with whom he was constantly in correspondence on literary and other matters, and indeed he was "one of the most accomplished scholars of his day." He died of a rapid decline at his father's house at Birdingbury on the 4th May 1791, having previously resigned his Fellowship on account of religious scruples. The Variorum edition of Horace on which he was engaged was completed after his death by Dr. Combe.

The fourth son, the Rev. Arthur Homer, D.D., was educated at Rugby and at Magdalen College, Oxford. He was for five years an Assistant Master at Rugby School, and afterwards Rector of Standlake, Oxon. He was a "friend and companion of Burke, Fox, and other leading politicians of the day."

The tenth son, Philip Bracebridge Homer, was also educated at Rugby and Magdalen, and was an Assistant Master at Rugby for 37 years. He was not much of a disciplinarian, but a most elegant scholar, and wrote much both in prose and poetry.

Richard Homer, the third son, was a Clerk in the India House, where he distinguished himself by auditing all the accounts from the commencement.

The second Edward Homer of Sutton Coldfield died on the 10th June 1763,[22] having lost his wife six years before. He left two sons and a daughter, and divided his property among them, including various articles of silver and old china. His law books and papers he left to his elder son William,

---

[20] A dispensation was granted him for this purpose in 1774 ["Gentleman's Magazine," XLIV., p. 143]. He was then Chaplain to Edward Lord Leigh.

[21] See Johnstone's "Memoirs of Samuel Parr," chaps. III., V., VI., VIII., and Parr's "Answer to the Statement of Dr. Combe." Samuel Parr was also an Emmanuel man.

[22] "Gentleman's Magazine," XXXIII., p. 314. His will is at Somerset House (1764).

whom accordingly we find later—at the date of the will (1758) he was not of age—filling his father's place as Solicitor and Deputy Steward of Sutton Coldfield. William maintained the family reputation for integrity. He died about 1807, and in his will (dated in 1790, and left incomplete) he alludes to great troubles which he had gone through, and leaves the bulk of his property to his housekeeper as a reward for the help she had been to him during those troubles. There is no mention of wife or children.

Of the second son, Edward Homer, we shall treat in the next section. Of the female lines of his ancestry I have embodied such information, as was to hand in print, in Part II., Pedigrees Nos. 5 to 7.

§ 9. *Family History—1740 to 1840.*

WILLIAM CHANCE first mentioned on the Bromsgrove tombstone (§ 1) was, like his ancestors (§ 3), a yeoman farmer, and owned freehold and copyhold land at Shepley and Burcott, adjacent portions of Bromsgrove parish. For the sake of distinction we will call him William Chance No. 1. The land passed at his death to his elder son William, who paid heriot on the copyhold portion in May 1740,[1] and who appears, as noted in § 2 (p. 18) in connection with the inventory of his father's goods, to have carried on the farm for some time previously. All the property detailed in the inventory was left to the widow, Frances Chance; and the will also mentions a son-in-law William Brooke, and a daughter Hannah Albutt; the latter was baptized at Bromsgrove on the 6th Oct. 1698.

William Chance No. 1 died at Christmas 1739, aged 80, and his widow in 1742; she was buried at Bromsgrove on Sept. 16th in that year. She left her property to her son and executor William Chance, and her other son John, her son-in-law William Brooke, and her grandson William Albutt[2] are also mentioned in the will.

William Chance No. 2 died after a few hours' illness on the 22nd Mar. 1743. His unsigned will, attested by his attorney and others, was proved by his widow Elizabeth a week later; and she also then proved his mother's will, which he had not done. He left nine children, all under age, but I have not investigated their history, and so, noting only the significant names of the two youngest, Joseph and Benjamin, we will leave this the elder branch of the family.

[1] Bromsgrove Court Rolls. Heriot was a payment made to the Lord of the Manor, on the death of a copyholder, by the successor to the copyhold. It usually took the form of the best beast of any kind in the copyholder's possession; but on some manors the best piece of plate, jewellery, or other property was exacted.

[2] Probably this was William Albutt of Finstal Heath, Stoke Prior, who died about 1770, leaving a widow Mary, who died in 1773. He had relations with his cousin William Chance.

John Chance, the younger of the two sons of William Chance No. 1, survived his brother nearly 30 years, following the trade of a cordwainer[3] in Bromsgrove. He had six children, but only three of them, John, William, and Thomas, survived their infancy.

The eldest son John, born the 6th Oct. 1711, followed his father's trade. He married 24th Oct. 1743 Hannah Hunt, a woman of his own age, daughter of Thomas and Hannah Hunt of Bromsgrove. But she and her two infants died within three years, and John Chance only waited eight months to marry a second wife, Mary, daughter of Joshua and Mary Tilt of Bromsgrove (§ 5). This marriage is said to have displeased John Chance the elder; but why, does not appear.

Mary Tilt and Hannah Hunt may have been relatives, as the latter's mother was a Tilt. John Chance jun. had by his second marriage a daughter and a son, but died on the 13th Feb. 1750, when the latter was not quite nine months old. A week after John Chance's death, his father made a will leaving the widow 1s. only[4]; and this will remained unrevoked at the time of his death 21 years later.

Mary Chance married secondly, on the 9th Sept. 1755, another cordwainer of Bromsgrove, named George Bell, and had by him issue as detailed in Part II., Pedigree No. 2 B. One of her grandsons, George Crane, was for a short time (1815-6) a partner in the firm of his half-uncle William Chance, of Birmingham (see below). Later he engaged in iron-smelting at the Yniscedwin Iron-Works, near Swansea, and here he introduced his process for the use of anthracite coal in smelting in conjunction with the hot blast; a process by which he "conferred an invaluable benefit upon the district, the extensive stone coalfields of which were, previously to the discovery, of comparatively little value."[5] His patent for this is No. 7195, dated the 28th Sept. 1836. He died on the 10th Jan. 1846 from having taken poison in mistake for medicine.[5]

Mary Bell lived to the age of 91, and repaid her father-in-law's dislike, if that story be true, by resuscitating his almost extinguished branch of the family; for her son, his only grandson, inherited her strong constitution, lived

[3] Cordwainer, a shoemaker. Properly, a worker in *Cordovan* leather, *i.e.* in goat's, as opposed to neat's leather. "Cordwain" is an old word for goat's leather.

[4] This is not necessarily a mark of displeasure. If she was already provided for, it would be following the usual practice to put her name in the will, in order to bar any subsequent claim on the ground of inadvertent omission.

[5] From a Welsh newspaper—the "Cambrian" I believe—of Jan. 1846.

to the age of 78, and had 13 children. When she died, she was buried⁶ with her first husband, deceased 62 years before.

John Chance the elder died on the 29th Oct. 1771, his wife having been dead 9 years. His will, referred to above, was not proved till 1774.

William Chance No. 3, his second son, born in 1713, inherited his father's property. He was first a saddler, but afterwards traded in iron, and by combined economy and enterprise acquired considerable wealth. He brought up his nephew William Chance, and aided him to begin business in Birmingham as an iron factor⁷; and dying in 1802, he made him his executor and residuary legatee. The property thus left to William Chance No. 4 in Bromsgrove, Birmingham, and elsewhere was estimated in 1817 for purposes of stamp duty at £7054. Besides this, £2000 were left on trust for testator's great-niece, Sarah Homer.

Thomas Chance, the third surviving son of John Chance the elder, born on the 9th Feb. 1721, is stated to have been the captain of a merchant vessel trading to Jamaica. At Bromsgrove he certainly engaged in mercantile pursuits, doing business with, among others, the Lucas' of Bristol, and making "adventures" to the West Indies and other parts of the world. In 1773 he purchased the remainder of a lease of 97 years of a piece of land in Ring Close, Birmingham, and had built thereon two houses, afterwards Nos. 17 and 18 Newhall St., and a warehouse and stable opening into what was afterwards Bread St. The lease was to expire in 1867. The next year (20th June 1774) Thomas Chance died. He left to his nephew, William Chance, and to his niece's husband, Edward Homer, £300 apiece, and the rest of his property passed to his brother William.

We now come to the closely connected William Chance No. 4, the first of Birmingham, and Edward Homer (§ 8). These two were at school together at a red-brick house at Winson Green, close to Summerfield, and they were apprenticed afterwards to Messrs. Male and Rock, Factors,⁷ of Birmingham. In 1771 they started business as iron factors on their own account, each providing a capital of £700: they traded first at premises in Church St., and afterwards rented from William Chance of Bromsgrove (No. 3) the new houses and warehouse in Newhall St. and Bread St. above-mentioned. In 1773

---

⁶ Her son writes in a MS. book, from which his son Henry Chance preserved some extracts; "My mother departed this life May 12, 1812, about a quarter of an hour before four o'clock in the morning, at Bromsgrove, aged 91, and was buried there methinks May 16 in the same grave as my father was buried in, her first husband. I and one of my sons (Edward) and some of the Craces attended the funeral."

⁷ A Factor was a merchant who confined himself to inland trading.

Edward Homer married William Chance's sister Sarah; and they lived in No. 17 Newhall St., while William Chance occupied No. 18.

Sarah Homer did not long survive her marriage. She died on the 14th Sept. 1776, leaving a daughter Sarah, born the 16th Dec. 1775, who grew up and married her father's cousin, the Rev. William Homer, a master at Appleby Grammar School in Leicestershire. He was the 11th son of the Rev. Henry Homer of Birdingbury (p. 47). After his death in 1838 his widow lived at Rugby, where she died on the 4th Apr. 1863, aged 87.

The tie between the brothers-in-law was soon renewed by their marriages on the 30th of June 1778 with the two sisters, Mary and Sarah Lucas, daughters of Robert Lucas of Bristol[e] (§ 6). The double marriage is noticed in Aris' Birmingham Gazette for Monday, 6th July 1778, as follows:—" Married ..... Tuesday, at Bristol, Mr. Homer, Merchant of this Place, to Miss Lucas, of Bristol. At the same Time and Place, Mr. Chance, Merchant of this Town, to Miss Sally Lucas, of Bristol." Not long after this—30th Mar. 1780—William Chance received the freedom of the City of Bristol.

Now John Robert Lucas, only surviving son of Robert Lucas, had bought some Glass Works at Wick, near Bristol. Whether through difficulties, as the story goes, with the Excise, or merely desiring to extend his business, he entered into partnership with William Chance and Edward Homer, who had become his brothers-in-law; and they brought into the business, it is said, £10,000; a fourth partner being William Coathupe of Bristol. This partnership was already existing in 1793, as appears from a deed renewing it in 1807 after a 14-years' term; and it included the Crown Glass Works at Nailsea; but I am not certain whether these important works were built by the above partners, or by John Robert Lucas previously to the formation of the partnership. The warehouses were in Nicholas St., Bristol, where the cooperage premises mentioned in § 6 were also situated. In 1807 John Robert Lucas owned more than half of the capital, William Coathupe one-sixth, and William Chance and Edward Homer each about one-seventh.

It was, I suppose, in consequence of this partnership that Edward Homer, in 1794 or thereabouts, left Birmingham and went to reside at West Town, Backwell, not far from Nailsea. The Birmingham partnership had been renewed for 21 years in 1778, and at the expiry of this term was again extended for five years; after which Robert Lucas Chance (of whom below)

---

[e] It is said that the families became acquainted with each other through the medium of Thomas Chance, who, as above noted, had business relations with the Lucas[f] of Bristol. But Robert Lucas was himself a freeholder of Bromsgrove (§ 6, note 12).

became a third partner (1 Jan. 1804). The business had greatly prospered under the management of the last-named, and each of the two partners had been drawing out from £500 to £750 a year, besides largely increasing the stocks. In Jan. 1805 William Chance's estate was estimated at £18,600, and Edward Homer's at £16,350. Of the former, the Birmingham business accounted for £3800, the Nailsea Works for £8000, and Canal Shares for £6800. When in 1802 William Chance No. 3 died, he left the lease of No. 18, Newhall St., and of the warehouse, to his nephew, and to Edward Homer the lease of No. 17 for life. The latter finally retired from the business in 1807, disposing of his interest in the house to William Chance towards the end of 1808. Continuing to reside at West Town, he remained a partner in the Nailsea Works till his death in 1825. He left by his second wife a son and three daughters (see Pedigree No. 5, E). The son, James Edward Homer, married Miss Harriet Gee[9] of Bristol, and resided first at Brockley Court, and afterwards at Wraxall, Som. He too became a partner in the Nailsea Works, and still held a share in 1844.

John Robert Lucas was very successful in business. He married Miss Anna Adams, and lived in great style at the house which he built on Backwell Hill. He died in 1828, and only one of his children, Emma, wife of Reginald Henry Bean, of West Stoke, under Hambden, survived him. Mr. Bean inherited further property from an uncle, William Rodbard, whose name he adopted, as also did his elder son, John Rodbard Rodbard. The share of John Robert Lucas in the Nailsea Glass Works passed to his two grandsons, John Rodbard Rodbard and Henry Lucas Bean. For further particulars of this family see Pedigree No. 3, F. Mrs. Emma Rodbard lived in later life at Clifton.

William Chance No. 4 ceased his connection with Nailsea in 1821. On the 21st Mar. 1828 he died. Himself an only son, and an only grandson, he had 13 children, of whom 8 survived him.[10]

Robert Lucas Chance, the eldest surviving son, born 8th Oct. 1782, was a man of very great mental capacity, and of a passion for work, which his strong constitution and temperate habits enabled him to indulge to the utmost.

---

[9] She was the daughter of Thomas Gee, a merchant of Bristol. He had died before her marriage, and his widow had married 2ndly John Covell, Esq., of Margate.

[10] His wife had been dead nearly 20 years. He notes in his MS. book (see note 6):— "1809. September 7. My wife (Sarah) departed this life between seven and eight of the clock in the morning, aged fifty-three. She was buried Septr. 13 at St. Paul's Chapel—mourners our five sons and also our son Sargant, also poll-bearers with hat-bands scarfs and kid-gloves, and two clergymen, Mr. Young and Kennedy, and Dr. John Johnson. Myself not attended for want of methinks fortitude."

He entered his father's business at the age of 12, and by the time he was 14 was able to manage it, and was known as "the little master in the jacket." He became a partner on the 1st Jan. 1804, and continued to manage the business for about seven years. In 1810 it seems to have been thought that help was required at the Nailsea Works, which were not at that time very prosperous, and that William Chance should send thither one of his sons. His youngest son Henry had been intended for this, and in the autumn of 1810 he went down to Bristol with his brother Lucas, and actually spent a few weeks in the office in Nicholas St. But whether it was that experienced help was wanted, or from some other cause, Robert Lucas Chance decided to take up the work at Nailsea himself, and he and Mr. Coathupe strongly advised that Henry Chance should give up the idea of business, and avail himself of what they considered an exceptional opening offered to him in the office of Messrs. Cooke and Sons, Solicitors.[11] This was at length decided on, and Robert Lucas Chance commenced work at Nailsea early in 1811.

He had another object in his visit to the West in 1810, and that was his suit for the hand of his cousin Louisa, youngest daughter of Edward Homer. His offer was accepted, and the marriage took place on the 7th May 1811.[12] The married pair resided at the house at Wraxall, where afterwards lived James Edward Homer.[13]

Robert Lucas Chance soon made his influence felt at Nailsea. In 1812 he brought thither from Dumbarton John Hartley, who was thought to know more about the manufacture of Crown Glass than anyone else in the country; and he writes of him in December of that year as a great success. Yet he did not remain there much longer, but early in 1815 set up as a Glass Merchant in London, residing first at 14, Upper Gower St., and afterwards in a house with a large garden at the top of Highgate Hill.[14] His business premises were at St. Paul's Wharf, in Upper Thames St.; but in 1816, desiring to separate his

---

[11] One of the advantages put forward was the excellent moral influence of Messrs. Cooke's office. The other apprentice there was a youth of great steadiness, and "Mr. Cooke's hours," writes Robert Lucas Chance, "nine till nine, give young men very little opportunity of being wicked, should they be so disposed."

[12] It is an illustration of what was thought proper at the time, that Robert Lucas Chance in one of his letters urgently desires the company of his sister Elizabeth Sargant on his wedding trip.

[13] Miss Homer writes :—"My grandfather [Edward Homer] rented what was afterwards our house [at Wraxall], part of the property inherited by my mother from her father. Our uncle and aunt Chance also rented the same place before they moved to London, and with my father's approval he made the first addition to the house in the same style that was afterwards carried out by my father. Some of the trees he planted are still standing."

[14] At Highgate his literary tastes brought him into intimate acquaintance with, among others, the poet Coleridge, who was then residing there.

export from his inland trade, he opened a warehouse at 55, Skinner St., Snow Hill. To manage this, he obtained the help of Evan Rees, who had been employed in the Birmingham business, and was the son of an old family friend, Jonathan Rees of Neath. In the same year, requiring all his capital in London, he sold the few shares which he held in the Nailsea firm. In 1824 he bought from the British Crown Glass Co., then represented by Messrs. Palmer and Stock, the Crown Glass Works at Spon Lane, near Birmingham, which had apparently been built some 10 or 12 years before.[15] Hither in 1827 he brought John Hartley to conduct the glass-making, much to the disgust of the Nailsea firm. He continued himself to reside at Highgate.

In 1831-2 changes took place at Spon Lane. Robert Lucas Chance was joined in the undertaking by his brother William, who supplied capital and advice, attending the board meetings, but not taking further part in the management. Now also was carried out the great work of the introduction of the Sheet Glass manufacture into England. An inferior kind of glass, known as spread or broad glass, had, it is true, been made by the cylindrical method in England before this date, but its surface was rough, uneven, and defective in brilliancy, and it was quite unfit to compete with the English crown glass, the manufacture of which had been brought to great perfection. The advantages of sheet glass properly made, as in France and Germany, were forced on Robert Lucas Chance's attention on the occasion of a visit to M. Bontemps' works at Choisy-le-Roi in 1830. The valuable co-operation of M. Bontemps having been secured, the next step was to induce a sufficient number of French and Belgian workmen to come over; a difficult thing to do, on account of the exclusive restrictions in force among them. This, however, and other great difficulties were successfully overcome, and the first sheet glass furnace was started at Spon Lane in the autumn of 1832.[16] In the summer of the same year Robert Lucas Chance enabled himself to superintend the business more directly, by leaving London, and taking up his residence at New Inn Hall, Handsworth; here he lived for seven years, and then removed to Summerfield House.

Old John Hartley died on the 15th Aug. 1833, and his place was taken by his two sons, James and John Hartley, who became partners in 1834, when the name of the firm was changed to Chances and Hartleys. This partnership however only lasted till 1836, when the Hartleys retired to Sunderland, and the firm received its present title of Chance Brothers & Co. Shortly afterwards

[15] These works then consisted of three Crown Glass houses and appurtenant buildings on the Old (or Upper) Canal, close to Spon Lane. The rest of the site covered by the present works was then open country, with a house and some cottages.

[16] See "Reports of the Juries"—Exhibition of 1851—p. 526.

James Timmins Chance, the last-named, William Chance's eldest son, who had just taken high honours at Cambridge as a wrangler, abandoning his intention of entering the legal profession, joined his uncle and father at Spon Lane; and from the 1st Jan. 1839 these three were the partners.

Robert Lucas Chance continued his headship of the firm till he died, full of years and honour, on the 7th March 1865, while visiting a friend at Northfleet House, Gravesend. The following sentences are taken from the obituary notice of him published in the "Birmingham Daily Post" for the 9th of that month. "We shall not be wrong in saying, that to his remarkable ability, farsighted enterprise, sound judgment, and unwearied industry, the progress of that House [C. B. & Co.] is greatly due. Partly on account of deafness, and partly from his habit of mind, Mr. Chance avoided all public business. But there was one great public duty, which few men have more thoroughly or unostentatiously discharged; on a settled principle of benevolence, and as a point of conscience, he acted rather as the steward than as the owner of his well-earned wealth. His public munificence, great as it was, relatively bore a small proportion to his private beneficence. . . . . . Mr. Chance, by natural gifts and acquirements, was eminently fitted for a high place among public men. . . . . . He had read much, and thought deeply."

The next surviving of William Chance's sons was William, born on the 29th Aug. 1788. He entered the business of Chance and Homer about 1801, became a partner early in 1810, and managed the business after his brother Lucas' retirement to Nailsea. In 1814 trade with America, with which country peace was expected to be shortly made, began to be thought of in the Chance family; and in 1815, in the spring of which year the peace was ratified, William Chance jun. (No. 5) and his brother George set up independently as American Merchants in Great Charles St. The requirements of this business caused George Chance to reside in the United States, while William conducted affairs in Birmingham. The partnership was renewed for 14 years from the 1st Jan. 1822: but after that term George Chance retired from it, and the business was carried on as William Chance, Son & Co.; the son being William Chance No. 6.

At Birmingham William Chance No. 5 devoted himself mainly to public business and works of philanthropy. He had all his elder brother's intellectual power, but lacked his energetic temperament. He had married on the 6th Aug. 1811 Phœbe (Phebe), daughter of James Timmins, of the firm of Jas. and Geo. Timmins, of Mount St.; and he resided first in Newhall St., next door to his father, afterwards in George St., Edgbaston, and lastly at

Spring Grove, Ladywood, whither he removed in the spring of 1832. He served as Constable of Birmingham in 1817-8, and as High Bailiff in 1829-30, an eventful year, which saw the visits to Birmingham of the Princess Victoria, our present Queen, and of the Duke of Wellington and Sir Robert Peel. The former event took place on Aug. 9th, 1830, and it fell to the High Bailiff to conduct the Princess about the town; while the Duke and Sir Robert came on Sept. 23rd. Among the places of interest visited on the latter occasion were the Glass Works at Spon Lane, whither the distinguished visitors went by one of the Canal Co.'s passenger barges, returning by road. William Chance, as High Bailiff, afterwards entertained them and some 700 others at dinner; on which occasion the windows of the Royal Hotel, where they were dining, were broken by the mob, the Duke being then at the height of his unpopularity. In the same year, in January, William Chance declined to call a Town's Meeting in furtherance of the objects of the celebrated Birmingham Political Union, founded in this year by Messrs. Attwood and Scholefield. But though not approving of their views and methods, he was no bigoted Tory, and it was part of his design, in arranging the Duke's visit, that the latter should see for himself that Birmingham was a town of sufficient importance to demand representation in Parliament. And he was always zealous for the furtherance of undertakings for the improvement of the people; for instance, in the matter of education, his firm were among the first to establish, of their own resources, schools for the children of working-men; schools which, opened at Spon Lane in 1845, and at Oldbury in 1851, have continued ever since to be among the most successful in the country, and models of their kind.

William Chance's busy life ended in 1856, when the following obituary notice appeared in the "Birmingham Daily Press" (Monday, 11th Feb. 1856): "In the death of William Chance, which took place on Friday last, Birmingham has lost a man who was universally respected, whose kindness endeared him to many, and whose charity was felt in all directions. He had not lately taken any active part in politics, either local or general, but during the earlier part of his life he had held many of those public offices, the election to which showed the estimation in which he was held by his fellow-townsmen...... He was a magistrate for the borough, and the counties of Warwick and Worcester...... Mr. Chance was an earnest and zealous member of the Church of England, the lay offices of which he often filled. His life was like that of the good men of all parties, and by the good men of all parties his loss will be deplored."

George Chance, the next brother, born on the 26th July 1790, was apprenticed at the age of 15 to Ames Hellicar jun., of Bristol. In 1809 he had begun work for his father's firm, and was made a partner in it in Jan. 1814. In the following year, as we saw, he set up in business with his brother William, and left England for the United States. He was at this time engaged to be married to Mary Timmins, sister of his brother William's wife, and her death in Aug. 1816 caused him a great grief. Nearly nine years later he married, on the 19th May 1825, Cornelia Maria de Peyster, of one of the most distinguished families of New York.[18] He returned to England before 1840, and resided at Edgbaston, having retired, as above said, from the business of William and George Chance. He died at Edgbaston on the 16th Sept. 1861.

Edward Chance, the fourth surviving brother, was born on the 19th May 1792. He served an apprenticeship with Robert Bunney the elder, of Coventry, and then, like his brothers, joined his father's firm, becoming a partner in Jan. 1814. He managed the business after his brothers had left it, and though in 1817 Robert Lucas Chance advised that it should be given up, Edward and his father in 1819 entered into a new partnership for five years. Subsequently the business was transferred to other hands, and before 1830 Edward Chance became a publisher, trading as a partner in the firm of Thos. Hurst, Edward Chance, & Co., booksellers and publishers, of 65 St. Paul's Churchyard. In 1834 Thos. Hurst's name alone represents this firm in the London directories; and in 1836 Edward Chance is described in them as a Hardware and General Commission Merchant, of 2 Coleman St. Buildings. He never married, and died on the 4th Nov. 1866.

William Chance's youngest son Henry was born on Michaelmas Day 1794. He was, as we saw, intended for business, but instead thereof went into the office of Messrs. Cooke and Sons, the family solicitors at Bristol. Subsequently he became a barrister of Lincoln's Inn, where he chiefly practised conveyancing, and distinguished himself as one of the first draftsmen of the day. Thus his father's will, drawn by him, is given as a model in Martin's "Practice of Conveyancing," Vol. v, p. 54, form 5. (Yet his own will was complicated, and burdened with seven codicils.) He was the author

[18] The de Peyster family, at the time of the Massacre of St. Bartholomew in 1572, were resident in France. Being Huguenots, they fled to Holland, and John de Peyster left Haarlem for New York early in the next century. His descendant, Col. Arent Schuyler de Peyster, was of leading service in the conquest of Canada from the French.

Mrs. George Chance's uncle was the celebrated General Alexander Macomb, whose "distinguished and gallant conduct in defeating the enemy at Plattsburg" obtained the thanks of Congress, and a commemorative Medal. He received a State Funeral in 1841, when the General Orders issued from the War Office recorded "his advancement to the highest military rank known to the laws."

[D. F. Valentine's "Manual of the Corporation of the City of New York," 1861.]

of "Chance on Powers," a standard work. He was remarkable for the great care and caution with which he safeguarded his clients' interests. He was exceedingly industrious, but as he did all his work himself, got through it but slowly, and the volume of it was not what it might have been. But what he did was done thoroughly well. He married in 1836 Ann Maria, daughter of William Evans of Wolverhampton: we remember her as Mrs. Henry Chance of Leamington, where she died on the 7th May 1887. In his latter years, Henry Chance suffered much from loss of eyesight and general ill-health. He had never been very strong, and had had a very severe illness in London in 1815. He lived however till the 10th Feb. 1876. He left a mass of papers relating to the family, and I have been deeply indebted to them for information on various points of detail.

We will now turn to William Chance's daughters. His eldest child, Elizabeth, was born in 1769, and educated at "Weston." She married in 1799 William Sargant, son of William and Sarah Sargant of Birmingham, and grandson of Isaac Sargant, who was the second son of William Sargant of King's Norton. There the Sargants had long been settled, and I have frequently met with their name in old records. Elizabeth Sargant died in 1850, having survived her husband nearly 30 years.

The only other married daughter of William Chance was Sarah, who became in 1832 the wife of Jonah Smith Wells jun., of the firm of Jonah Smith Wells and Son, Stockbrokers, of Lothbury, E.C. She died within three years of her marriage, and neither of her two children (who, I believe, were twins) survived their infancy. The marriage was against her brothers' wishes, and there were great difficulties in regard to the settlements; indeed after her death her brother Henry (chief trustee) and her husband had a quarrel which lasted a quarter of a century. The latter married secondly, in 1840, Eliza, daughter of Thomas Southey, of Islington; and after that again a third time. He died in 1876. Sarah Wells was no less than 21 years younger than her sister Elizabeth Sargant.

Of Miss Maria Chance, youngest of William Chance's thirteen children, my memory is still fresh. Born in 1803, she was two years younger than her niece Sarah Sargant, who however survived her by three years. She died unmarried at the age of 78.

William Chance's other children did not survive him. Their names, &c., and those of his 39 grandchildren, will be found on pp. 79-84; and of the latter it is not part of my plan to write here. I will therefore conclude by remarking on the longevity displayed by the Chance family. Of eight persons mentioned in tomb-stone inscription No. 1 (p. 7), five lived to be 80 or over, and the whole eight average 74½; of William Chance's children seven averaged the age of 75; while their grandmother, Mary Bell, lived to the age of 91, and William Chance himself to 78. Taking only those who were Chances by birth, we have 13 persons, whose ages attain the high average of 74½.

§ 10. *Armorial Bearings.*

WILLIAM CHANCE, the first of Birmingham, appears, from a memorandum of his of which I have a copy, to have used Arms already in 1773. He states that he got them from the Heralds' Office in London, but no grant of them is to be found in the Registers of the College of Arms. The Arms are described in Robson's "British Heraldry" (1830) as "gu. on a saltire betw. three towers and a sword erect in base a fleurdelis. Crest a demi-lion ramp. holding between both paws a sword erect." William Chance's sons used these Arms quartered with those of Lucas (below).

In 1845 William Chance, son of the last-named, investigated the matter, and found that there was no proper grant of Arms; and the College then granted to him and his descendants and to the other descendants of his father William Chance the following Arms, modified from those above described:—" Gules a Saltire Vair between two Fleurs de lis in pale and as many Towers in fesse Argent, and for the Crest, On a Wreath of the Colours A demi Lion rampant Gules semé of Annulets Or holding between the paws a Sword erect entwined by a wreath of Oak all proper."

The Heralds do not now, as I understand, take cognizance of Mottoes. The

Chance Motto now in use is "Deo non Fortuna"; the older one was "It's a Chance Try."

The date of the Grant of Arms is 12th May 1845.

John Robert Lucas used the following Arms:—Argent a chevron gules between three pellets, on a chief azure a moorcock of the field between two crosses crosslet fitchée or.[1] With these he quartered, for his mother's family the three Covered Cups of Butler, and for his grandmother's the "On a Fesse three Garbes" of Vernon.

The Homers have long used the Arms "Ermine a Fesse" (I believe gules). These are figured in a large collection of Armorial Bearings known as "Philpot's Ordinary," made early in the 17th century, and preserved at the College of Arms. To the figure is appended the note, "Ex sigillo Andrei Homer dat a° 38 E 3," which means that it was taken from a seal of one Andrew Homer attached to a document of date 38 Edw. III. (1364). Who this Andrew Homer was, I do not know, but the same Arms were used by the Homers of Ettingshall and Sutton Coldfield, and are on the seals attached to some of their wills (see p. 44, note 2); and the presumption is therefore that these Homers were descendants of Andrew Homer, or of a common ancestor. The present Homers have then an ancient right to these Arms.

[1] These are the Arms of Lucas of Fenton, Lincolnshire.

§ 11. *On Old Wills.*

I THINK I may say something about the wills, which have been the chief source of my genealogical information. Of families entitled to bear Arms the Heralds have been careful to preserve records true or fictitious, but the genealogist, who interests himself in the descent of families which had not that distinction, would make little progress, but for the information preserved for him in the Metropolitan and Diocesan Probate Registries; information which is, from its nature, entirely authentic.

Most of my work in examining wills has been in the Worcester Probate Registry, where I have met with the utmost kindness and attention. I have consulted all the Chance wills that I could find there of earlier date than 1750, and some of later date; also many others in the names of Butler, Hill, Lucas, Tilt, Tibbatts, Vernon, &c. The *Chance* and *Tilt* wills were numerous, without being so much so as to forbid their examination; but those of *Tibbatts* were few, and did not connect themselves together, while those of *Hill* were too many, and I could not find the right ones. Of the many *Lucas* wills, I was able to distinguish those which concerned our family, and similarly those of Robert and Elizabeth *Vernon*. For the *Homers* the work lay at Lichfield, and considerable success was met with. I have also examined many wills at the General Probate Registry at Somerset House; and altogether have consulted wills and administrations to about the number of 235.

It is quite a lottery whether a will, when procured, will give any information. The best wills for genealogical purposes are those of wealthy bachelors or spinsters, who will name every relative they can think of, if only to disinherit them. The worst are those, where a trustful husband leaves everything to his wife, sometimes even omitting to mention her Christian name. Where wills fail one, is in not giving the wife's maiden name; in one or two cases I have obtained this information from the mention of the woman's father or brother, but this is very rare. Here comes in the genealogical value of marriage-licenses,[1] and of entries of marriages in Parish Registers; but the former are few, and for the latter one cannot always tell where to look. And so I have been obliged to leave too many of the female descents in the pedigrees blank.

The terminology of relationship in old wills is vague. "Son" and "daughter" often mean son-in-law and daughter-in-law; while "brother" may extend as far as wife's brother-in-law. Nephews and nieces are usually called "cousins" ("cozen," "cosin," "cussen," &c.); while cousins proper, and "unckles" and "auntes" sometimes, are denominated "kin." I have even found "cousin" applied to a grandson. Where two or three wills are connected, they supply each other's deficiencies in this respect, but in single cases one is left in uncertainty.

The literature of wills is not as a rule enlivening, but in some, and especially in the older ones, one comes across quaint bits of spelling and expression. The usual things specified are articles of furniture or dress; as, a "Rugg Gowne," "the biggeſt Braſſe Potte"; "the great Table in the hall, the great hanging Preſſe, the great Joyned Chaire, & the great Bible"; "brewing and backing furnaces"; pots, pans, pewter dishes, &c.; or out-door things, as, "all materialls I have belonging to Horsgeares";[2] "3 strike of mault to buy sheep"; &c. In 1591 Gilbert Barnesley leaves to his son Roger, "my Spaniſhe ierkin and my fine puke[3] ierkin"; to his son Richard "my ſeconde mandilione[4] beinge hus-wife's medlye"; and to his son Walter "my beſt gowne my beſt mandilione my two beſt paire of hose my two velvett nightcappes my croſſebow and my lute." In 1624 Nicholas Hill leaves to his son John his "Waynes Tumbrelles[5] Plowes Harrowes Bowes Towes[6] and all implements whatſoever belonginge or app'teyninge unto huſbandrye." In 1586 Elizabeth Lucas comes in for a grand legacy from her father, John Lucas of Brailes: "a cobbard and a coffer & iiij pewter platters & a broch[7] a payor

---

[1] I have no acquaintance with the modern practice in marriage-licenses. Formerly two "bondsmen," one of whom might be the bridegroom, were required to make affidavit that there was no lawful impediment to the marriage. At least as late as the reign of James I. the bondsmen were bound in a sum of money, and hence the name. The bonds give the names and ages of the parties, and one or more churches are appointed, in which the marriage may be solemnized. See Appendix B.

[2] Harness, &c.   [3] Puce—a dark-brown colour.

[4] A kind of sleeveless cloak, app. of Italian origin. "Housewife's medley" probably means that it was made of patchwork.

[5] Tumbrils—a kind of cart.

[6] Towes = tools. Bowes: curved irons passed over the back of the shaft-horse and fastened to the shafts; or, the part of an ox-yoke through which the neck passes; hence simply an ox-yoke.

[7] A spit.

of cobbardes a doubel Twylle cloth a boulſter two payer of ſhettes[8] a dobnet[9] and a litell cauthan[10] a pickforck[11] & a tablecloth a tabell bord a bench and a forme a payer of Treſtelles & a bedſted a payer of potthockes & linckes a table bord & a great weyt." Her sister Anne gets a similar lot, including a "shefpeck."[12]

The following is a copy of a will of 1546; that of Isabell Chawnce of Bromsgrove :—

"IN THE NAME of god Amen the vj day of November the xxxvij of the Raygne of o' ſou'aygne lorde kyng Henry the viij by the grace of god of Englande France & Ireland kyng defende' of the faythe & in erthe ſup'"me hed of the churche of England & Ireland I Iſabell Chawnce ſike in body & hole in mynde make my teſtament in this wyſe firſt I bequethe my ſoule unto Almyghty god & my body to be buryed in the churche yarde of Bromeſgrove Itm I bequethe to the hie Ault' there iiij^d Itm to the cluth' churche of Wigorne iiij^d Itm to pore people xx^d Itm to Margarete chaunſe a pott a pa'ne[13] a coofer[14] a peyer of moggey[15] ſhets a bordecloth[16] a towell vj peſes of peut' and a candſtike[17] Itm Elizabethe chaunſe a ſpice morter & ij ſilv' ſpones The Reſidue of my goods my detts & funerall expenſ' payde & this my p'ſent teſtament fulfilled I bequethe to Edwarde chaunce wch edwarde I make myne Executor & Richard Higgins ou'ſear These witneſſe Will'm Bawle & Rychard Tommys w^t other moo written the day & yere above ſpecified."

I wish I could reproduce the writing also. It is known as Courthand, and many of the characters are quite different from our modern ones, and more like the German. To read the old writing at all requires considerable practice.

To the wills are attached inventories of the goods of which the testators were possessed at their decease. I have given two examples of these in § 2,

[8] Sheets.
[9] Dobnet—not explained.
[10] Probably for cauldron (caulthron).
[11] Pitchfork.
[12] Sheaf-pick, another word for a pitchfork. The word "sheppeck" is still used in this sense in Worcestershire.
[13] Pan.
[14] Coffer.
[15] Moggey, perhaps the same as "mutchy," dark-coloured, but more probably for "noggey" (noggen), i.e. made of "nogs," a coarse refuse of flax or hemp.
[16] Board-cloth, i.e. tablecloth.
[17] Candlestick.

in illustration of the social condition of the yeomen farmers; and the following is a copy of a third,[18] that of our ancestor John Chaunce of Shepley, who died about New Year's Day 1670 (modern style).

	£	s.	d.
"Money and wearing apparill	5	0	0
one tablebord one forme one cubberd	1	6	8
one grat too peare of linkes one peare of tungs one peare of belos[19] & one gridjarne[20]		2	6
one gine[21] chare three gine ſtooles & other ſtoles		4	0
one peale[22] one pedel ſtaff[23] a axx & bill		2	0
one gine[21] bedſtid & one fetherbed to fether bolſters & to pillowers & one peeare of ſheetes & to blankits one cofferlit one other bolſter in the parler	3	10	0
too trunkes		16	0
too quoſſers[24]		12	0
too bibles & too other bookes		16	0
three ſiluer ſpoones & one & twenty ſiluer buttons		16	0
one peare of ſhetes & one tablecloth	1	6	8
to toweles & too pillowes beares[25] fower napkins	1	3	4
one peare of gine bedſtides	1	10	0
one fetherbed & one flockbed one flock bolſter one peare of ſhetes too blankets on couerlite	3	2	6
one worming pann		6	0
the Chamber ore the hall—one fetherbed one flockbolſter one little pillow one peare of ſheets & three blankets	1	13	0
one chafe bed[26] one flock pillow one little fetherpillow one ſhitt tow blankets		10	0
one gine table & a gine fourme		10	0

[18] The spelling in this inventory is more of an illiterate than of an archaic character; and in the former respect is no worse than some modern specimens that I have met with, e.g., "one bught youst for tar" (one bucket used for tar).

[19] Bellows.

[20] "Jarne" for "iron" throughout.

[21] Joined.

[22] A baker's shovel.

[23] A stick armed with a "paddle," i.e. a hoe or spud, used for breaking up clods, and for other purposes.

[24] Coffers.

[25] Pillow-cases, usually spelt "-bures."

[26] Chaff-bed : a mattress stuffed with chaff.

ON OLD WILLS.

	£	s.	d.
8 diſhes of pewter to little ſauſers to ſalts & one faggon [27] one candelſtick	1	6	8
30 elle of new Cloth	1	10	0
3 ſheetes		14	0
8 napkins		4	0
one ſheet & one bordcloth one pillow beare		10	0
one bagg of hoppes		8	0
three ſcore & 4 of cheeſes	1	10	0
one pott of butter of milck & on of lard & on pott of lard and other licker		8	0
one parrell of tarre		2	0
to rangers [28] & other ould Jarne		3	4
to truſles & other plankes		2	0
one ſikle & a pale		3	0
one ſteele & heeters [29]			8
8 ſtrick [30] of moŭt [31]		16	0
4 ſtrick of oates		4	0
5 bagges		2	6
one great wheele & to little ons		4	0
a panell & bride & gearth [32]		1	0
one cheeſepreſs one coffer one ſtrick [33] & one fourme		8	4
to tubes [34] & a bred ſkeele [35]		8	0
one paile & one gaune [36]			10
one brauch & cobbrts [37]		3	4

[27] Probably for "flagon."

[28] Chimney-racks, i.e. iron frames, with hooks attached, fixed inside the chimney, or perhaps bacon-racks fixed against the ceiling.

[29] Steel and heaters: for what purpose does not appear. Or possibly still and heaters, a distilling apparatus.

[30] Strike: a measure of quantity.

[31] Malt: usually spelt "mault."

[32] Panell, bridle, and girth. The first, a saddle-cloth or pad, Fr. "panneau." Now used for the stuffed cushion forming the under part of a saddle.

[33] Strike: here the measuring jar. The word is also still used for a flat piece of wood used to strike off the top corn from the jar, to make it even.

[34] Tubs.

[35] Skeel; any broad shallow wooden vessel.

[36] A wooden pail, one of whose staves is left longer than the others, so as to form a handle. A "lade-gaun" is a long-handled ladle for pigwash, &c.

[37] "Brauch," usually spelt "broch" or "broach," a spit. "Brauch-cobbrts," spit-cupboards or cases.

	£	s.	d.
to ſheppoxs [38] & one bill		1	0
one pott & pott hooxs [39]		10	0
foure Cettls one braſen candelſtick one bras baſting ſpoone	1	3	4
6 ſhelves		4	0
one friingpan		1	0
too barrills one Chearne & chearne ſtaf & cheſe lather [40]		8	0
one halfe hodghat [41] of warjes [42]		10	0
to hodgg [41] of baken & other offoll meat & the fouarme [43] that they lie upon	3	0	0
one barrill & baſket		2	0
the corne peaſe oates and hay	3	10	0
the plow & powciarnes [44]		1	0
the tumberel which & drafts [45] & whilborrow		5	0
the Cart		10	0
6 cowes too caues [46] and a horſe	17	0	0
one acker of corne growing & muck	1	5	0
the coles		3	0
the cockes & hens		4	0
33 ſhepe	8	0	0
hoppepoles & a grindillſton [47]		3	4
ſundries		3	4
	[48] £70	6	4

---

[38] "Sheppecks," see note 12.

[39] Hooks: evidently pronounced by the writer "hookses."

[40] "Cheese-ladder": a lattice-work arrangement for drying cheese.

[41] Hogshead: still pronounced in the Midlands "hawkshut" or "hotchut."

[42] Verjuice: crab cider.

[43] An elaborate way of spelling "form."

[44] Plough irons (plowiarnes) must be intended.

[45] Which; a moveable box placed upon the "tumbril" to hold materials such as could not be carried otherwise, as manure. Another word for it is "crone." From the combination of which and tumbril has developed the modern cart.

Drafts: moveable side-rails for extending the capacity of the tumbril.

[46] Calves.

[47] Grinding-stone.

[48] I make the sum 6s. less: perhaps there is a mistake in the copying. The numerals in the original are Roman.

PART II.—PEDIGREES.

No. 1.—CHANCE OF SHEPLEY (BROMSGROVE), AND OF BIRMINGHAM.

No. 2.—TILT OF BROMSGROVE.

No. 3.—LUCAS OF ROWINGTON, HANBURY, AND BRISTOL.

No. 4.—BUTLER AND VERNON (ROBERT) OF HANBURY.

No. 5.—HOMER OF ETTINGSHALL, SUTTON COLDFIELD, AND WEST TOWN.

No. 6.—BRACEBRIDGE OF ATHERSTONE.

No. 7.—LUDFORD OF ANSLEY.

General Pedigree.

- William Chance of Bromsgrove = Frances
  - John Chance of Bromsgrove
  - Sarah
    - John Chance of Bromsgrove
- Caleb Tilt of Bromsgrove = Dorcas
  - Joshua Tilt of Bromsgrove
  - Mary
    - Mary Tilt (who m. 2ndly George Bell of Bromsgrove)
      - William Chance of Birmingham

- Clement Lucas of Rowington = Dorothy
  - Clement Lucas of Feckenham Park, Hanbury
- John Tibbatts of Rowington
  - Elizabeth Tibbatts of Rowington
    - Robert Lucas of Bristol
      - Sarah Lucas of Bristol
      - John Robert Lucas of Backwell Hill, Somersetshire.
      - Mary Lucas of Bristol
- Butler
  - John Butler of Hanbury
- Robert Vernon of Hanbury = Elizabeth Smith of Stoke Prior
  - Elizabeth Vernon of Hanbury
    - Elizabeth Butler of Hanbury

- Thomas Homer of Sutton Coldfield = Elizabeth Sadler of Castle Bromwich
  - Edward Homer of Sutton Coldfield
- Thomas Bracebridge of Atherstone (Vicar of Abkettleby) = Jane Ludford of Ansley
  - Katherine Bracebridge
    - Edward Homer of Sutton Coldfield
    - Jane
      - Edward Homer of West Town, Som. (His first wife was Sarah Chance, only sister of William Chance above.)

Pedigree No. 1.   CHANCE of Shepley, Bromsgrove.

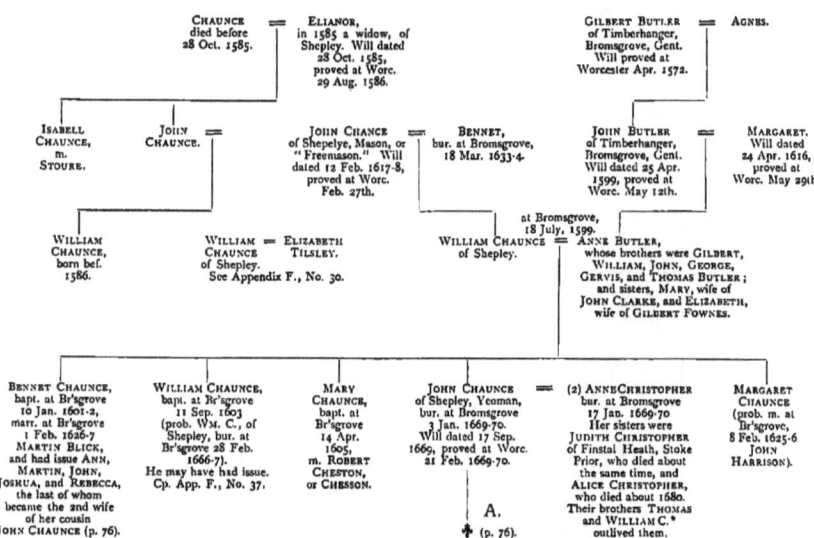

PEDIGREE No. 1.—CHANCE OF SHEPLEY, BROMSGROVE.

The construction of the Pedigree just given is to a certain extent conjectural. The following are our fixed data.

1. Elianor Chaunce had a grandson William, son of her son John.
2. John Chance, of Shepley (will 1617-8), left a widow, named ‡ Bennet. Of his five grandchildren, the eldest, he states, was William; they were children of his son William.
3. John Chaunce, of Shepley (will 1669-70), had three sisters living in 1669; Bennet, Mary, and Margaret.
4. Margaret Butler (will 1616) mentions Margaret, daughter of her daughter Anne Chaunce. William Chaunce was one of the overseers to her will.
5. The Bromsgrove Register has :—

MARRIAGES.	BAPTISMS OF CHILDREN OF WILLIAM CHAUNCE.	
	20 June 1593.	Thomas.
	5 Oct. 1595.	William.
18 July 1599. William Chaunce and Anne Butler.	15 Dec. 1599.	William.
	*10 Jan. 1601-2.	Benet.
	*11 Sep. 1603.	William.
	*14 Apr. 1605.	Mary.
	3 Dec. 1606.	Gilbert.
28 Nov. 1611. William Chaunce and Elizabeth Tilsley.	18 Aug. 1611.	Elizabeth.
	*15 May 1613.	Henry.
27 July 1614. William Chaunce, Gent., and Jane Lillie.	1 Feb. 1613-4.	Anne.
	*18 Dec. 1614.	Gyles.
	†21 Sep. 1615.	Elizabeth.
	* 8 June 1616.	Mary.

It follows from these Register entries that there were two William Chaunces of Shepley, contemporary, and that each of them had at least three children, the one series baptized in the years following 1601, the other in those following 1612. The first series would be the issue of the marriage of William Chaunce and Anne Butler, and the second that of the marriage of William Chaunce and Elizabeth Tilsley. That these two William Chaunces were not the same person, is shown by the fact that Anne Chaunce was living in 1616, at the date of her mother Margaret Butler's will. Which of the two was grandson to Elianor Chaunce, of Shepley, I cannot say.

* These six are specified as children of William Chaunce of Shepley.
† Daughter of William Chaunce, Glover. She was buried 30 Nov. following.
‡ Anglicized from 'Benedicta.'

PEDIGREE No. 1.—CHANCE OF SHEPLEY, BROMSGROVE.

We may conclude from her name, that Bennet, daughter of William Chaunce of Shepley, was a granddaughter of John and Bennet Chance (or Chaunce) of Shepley. We see from the Register entries that she had a brother William, and a sister Mary; and if, as we may also suppose from them, she was a daughter of William Chaunce and Anne Butler, we know from Margaret Butler's will that she had also a sister Margaret. But Bennet, Mary, and Margaret were the names of the three sisters of John Chaunce of Shepley, who were living in 1669, and it would be very strange if these were not the same persons as those before mentioned. If they were the same, we have the names of the first John Chaunce's five grandchildren. That the baptisms of John and Margaret are not entered in the Register is no objection, as the entries may not have been made, or the children may have been baptized elsewhere. And William's name would naturally not appear in his brother John's will, if, as is probable, he was the "Wm. Chance of Shply" who was buried at Bromsgrove 28 Feb. 1666-7.

The difficulty is, that John Chaunce in his will (1617-8) speaks of William his grandchild, and the four younger children of his son William. But he may easily have made a slip, forgetting that William was only the eldest son; or he may have purposely excluded Bennet, and there may have been four children younger than William.

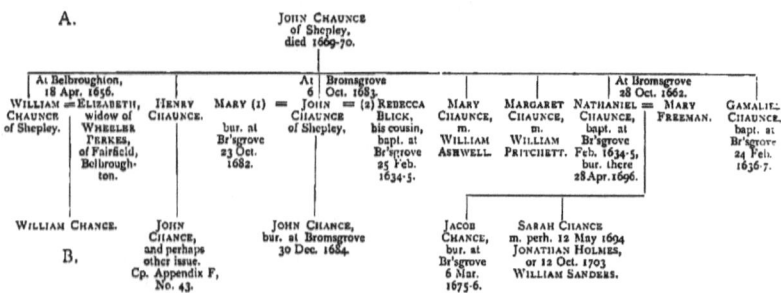

Note that John and William Chance, each with a wife and three children, were living at Shepley in 1690; and Henry, William, and another Chance were living there in 1700. (Appendix F, Nos. 49, 50.)

Elizabeth wife of William Chance was buried at Bromsgrove 14 Sept. 1723, and William Chance of Shepley 3 Oct. 1723.

PEDIGREE No. 1.—CHANCE OF SHEPLEY, BROMSGROVE.

I have alluded (§ 3—note 26) to difficulties in connection with the marriage of William Chance and Elizabeth Perkes. They are as follows.

The Bromsgrove Register has, under date 18 March 1655-6,

"The same day pub: the third time an intended marriage between William son of John Chance of Sheply yield yeo: & Elizabeth Perkes of Forfield, widowe, married the 19th of June following."

(Forfield or Fairfield is a part of Belbroughton parish.)

The Belbroughton Register has, under date 1656,

"William Chance and Elizabeth Perkes were maryed the eighteenth of Aprill."

Three possible solutions of the difficulty suggest themselves:

1. That there were two couples of the same names and parishes married within three months. This is of course possible.
2. That the same parties were married twice over.
3. That one of the entries is erroneous.

This third explanation seems probable, as regards the last words of the Bromsgrove entry. This portion of the Register was made up from some older documents; the entries are classified for each month into births, burials, and publications of banns, and are signed in batches. And the signatory is not John Spilsbury, then Vicar of Bromsgrove, but Thomas Milwarde, or Richard Vernon. Under these circumstances an error may easily have crept in. Besides, (1) three months is a long time to elapse between banns and marriage, (2) the custom was then, as now, for the marriage by banns to take place in the bride's parish.

But my private opinion is, that the second solution of the difficulty is the true one; that the last words of the Bromsgrove entry refer to a civil marriage; and that Thomas Milwarde and Richard Vernon were not clergymen but magistrates. An instance of such a civil marriage in this very year, (and note that it is in the time of the Commonwealth), will be found on p. 120.

Whichever of the three explanations be adopted, I am still of opinion that the child of William and Elizabeth Chance, baptized at Belbroughton 4th Oct. 1660, (p. 114), was the William Chance of Burcott first mentioned in the Bromsgrove tombstone inscription (p. 7).

PEDIGREE No. 1.—CHANCE OF SHEPLEY, BROMSGROVE.

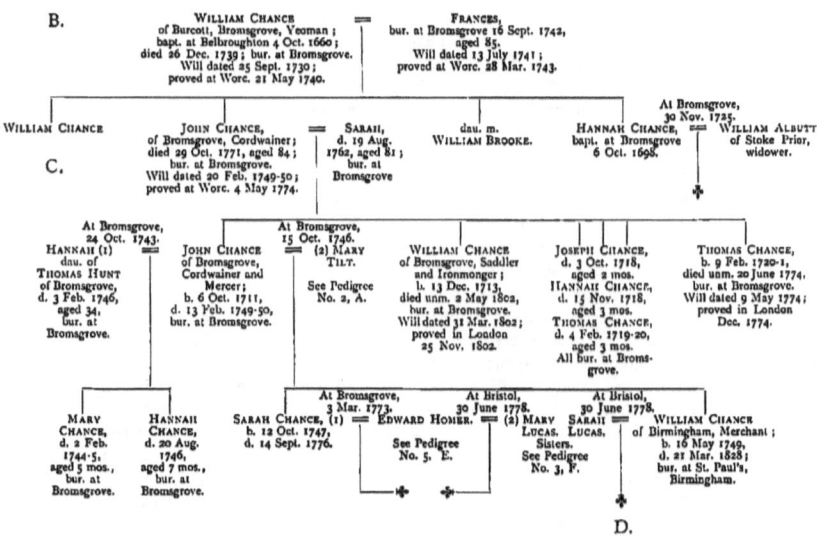

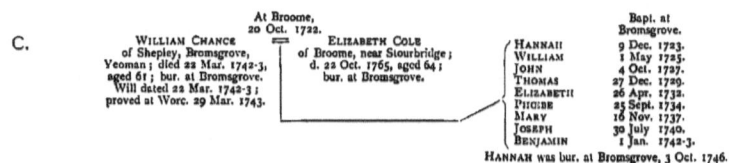

PEDIGREE No. 1.—CHANCE OF SHEPLEY, BROMSGROVE.

D. *Children of* WILLIAM CHANCE *of Birmingham.*

(NOTE.—The particulars given in inverted commas are from a MS. book of William Chance, extracts from which were preserved by his son Henry.)

1. ELIZABETH, "born April 26th 1779. Was christened at St. Philip's Church, Birmingham. May 29th 1779, and registered. Sponsors, Mother[1] Elizabeth Lucas,—Cousin Mary Saunders,[2] & Brother James Lockier.[3]" Educated at "Weston School." "Confirmed at Church, May 4. 1797, and Married Octr. 15. 1799."

She married on that date at St. Martin's, Birmingham, William Sargant, of Birmingham. He died on the 7th Mar. 1821, aged 52, and she on the 6th Nov. 1850. Both were buried at St. Paul's, Birmingham.

2. WILLIAM, "born October 11th 1780. Was christened at St. Philip's Church, November 8th 1780, and registered. Sponsors, Sister Ann Manly,[4]—Brother Edward Homer, & Thomas Bingham . . . . . . He died September 6, 1787 of the scarlet fever & putrid sore throat after an illness of a week. He was buried at St. Paul's Chapel by Mr. Young, attended by his father and Mr. John Dadley[5] as mourners, and the bearers were Master John Cope, Joseph Rock,[6] George Eyre Lee, & James Welch, upon the 8th September."

3. ROBERT LUCAS, "born October 8. 1782, was privately baptized November 1st by Mr. Shipley. Was christened at St. Philip's Church January 7. 1783 by Mr. Shipley, and registered. Sponsors, Aunt Dorothy Woodcock, Brother Edward Homer, and James Woolley . . . . . . Confirmed at Church May 4. 1797. Married May 7th 1811 to Louisa Homer his first cousin."

She was the third daughter of Edward Homer, and the marriage took place at Backwell. She was born Nov. 3rd 1787, and died Dec. 24th 1873,

---

[1] *I.e.*, mother-in-law. So "brother," "sister," are used throughout for "brother-in-law," "sister-in-law."

[2] Dau. of John Lucas, uncle of Wm. Chance's wife. She was known as "Pretty Polly Saunders."

[3] Brother-in-law of Wm. Chance's wife.

[4] *I.e.*, Ann Manley, Wm. Chance's sister-in-law.

[5] First cousin of Edward Homer. He died in 1807, and was the father of Mr. Wm. Bowes Dadley. *A Joseph Rock (p.56)*

[6] ~~Presumably he, who afterwards~~ married Wm. Chance's granddaughter, Ann Sargant.

her husband having died Mar. 7th 1865. Both were buried at the General Cemetery, Birmingham.

4. JOHN, "born March 23. 1784. Was christened at St. Philip's Church, Birmingham, May 13. 1784, and registered. Sponsors, Cousin John Sanders,[7] Brother Edward Homer, and Sister Mary Homer[8] . . . . . . Died May 26. 1792 of the scarlet fever and sore throat after an illness of about a week. And was buried at St. Paul's Chapel by the Revd. Dr. Croft, attended by his father and his uncle Homer as mourners,—and the bearers were Mr. Robert Felton,[9] a young Mr. Ward or Lardner, Master Joseph Townshend and Master Charles Cope, upon the 29th May."

5. MARY ANN, "born March 21st 1786. Was christened at St. Philip's Church, Birmingham, May 23. 1786, and registered. Sponsors, Brother Henry Pater, Sister Mary Homer, and Sister Ann Pater,[10] wife to the former. . . . . . Died April 4th 1787 of an inflammation of the lungs after an illness of about a week. She was buried at St. Paul's Chapel upon the 7th by Mr. Young."

6. WILLIAM, "(the second), ... was born August 20th 1788, a few minutes before six of the clock in the morning. Was privately baptized by Mr. Clutton September 5, at home. Was christened at St. Philip's Church, Birmingham, & registered, by Mr. James. Sponsors, Brother Ed. Homer, John Saunders, and Mary Saunders, wife to the latter. . . . . . . Was confirmed at St. Philip's Church August 5. 1801. Married Phœbe Timmins August 6. 1811."

She was the daughter of James Timmins, of Birmingham, and the marriage took place at St. Martin's.

She was born July 2nd 1790, and died Apr. 15th 1865, her husband having died Feb. 8th 1856. Both were buried at the Church of England Cemetery, Warstone Lane.

7. GEORGE, "born July 26. 1790 about 10 minutes past 8 of the clock in the morning. Was christened at St. Philip's Church September 15 and registered by Mr. Laurence. Sponsors, Brother Edward Homer, Mr. John Dadley, and Sister Mary Homer. . . . . . . Was confirmed at the College, Bristol, by Dr. Luxmore, then Bishop of Bristol."

He married, May 19th 1825, at Gracechurch, New York, Cornelia Maria, daughter of Arent Schuyler de Peyster, of that city. She was born Feb. 20th

[7] Properly Saunders. He was the husband of Mary Saunders, above.
[8] Wife of Edward Homer, and Wm. Chance's sister-in-law.
[9] William Homer, brother of Edward, had a nephew of this name.
[10] Formerly Ann Manley (see p. 91).

1806, and died Dec. 30th 1881, her husband having died Sept. 16th 1861. Both were buried at the Church of England Cemetery, Warstone Lane.

8. EDWARD, " born May 19. 1792 about ¼ before 1 o'clock, morning. Was baptized at St. Philip's Church June 18, by Mr. James. Was christened [11] December 7 at St. Philip's Church by Mr. James, and registered. Sponsors, Brother Edwd. Homer, Mr. John Cope, Mrs. Homer (sister), and Miss Elizabeth Saunders.[12] . . . . . . Was confirmed at St. Philip's June 6. 1806."

He died unmarried Nov. 4th 1866, and was buried at the Church of England Cemetery, Warstone Lane.

9. HENRY, " born 1794 September 29 about half past two of the clock in the morning. Was christened at St. Philip's, Birmingham, by Mr. Laurence, and registered, December 19. 1794. Sponsors, Mrs. (Revd.) Cooke, Brother Edwd. Homer, & Mr. Robert Smith.[13] . . . . . . Was confirmed June 2, 1810 at Birmingham p methinks Bishop Cornwallis."

He married in April 1836, at Yardley, Ann Maria, daughter of William Evans, of Wolverhampton. He died Feb. 16th 1876, and she, at Leamington, 7th May 1887, aged 79. They were buried at Highgate Cemetery.

10. CHARLOTTE, " born May 25. 1796 about eleven of the clock in the morning. Was christened at St. Philip's Church, Birmingham, by Mr. Vale. Sponsors, Mrs. John Cope, Cousin Mary Saunders, Brother Edwd. Homer, (Mrs. Saunders represented by Nurse Ball, the Sponsor being too late coming to church). . . . . . . Was confirmed June 7. 1809 at Grantham, p the Bishop of Lincoln."

She died unmarried June 2nd 1827, and was buried at St. Paul's, Birmingham.

11. CAROLINE, " born May 20, 1798, about half past one of the clock in the morning. Was privately baptized by Mr. (Revd.) Dales at St. Philip's Church, June 25th. Was christened March 15. 1799 by Mr. Madan at St. Philip's Church. Sponsors, Sister Mary Homer, Brother Edwd. Homer, and my daughter Elizabeth Chance. . . . . . . Was confirmed by the Archbishop of Canterbury April 15. 1813, at Bow Church, London."

" 1818 February 4. My daughter Caroline departed this life about two of the clock in the morning after an illness about twenty-one weeks.—Nervous fever &c. She was buried at St. Paul's Chapel by Mr. (Reverend) Ran

---

[11] This distinction between baptism (in church) and christening is new to me.
[12] Daughter of John and Mary Saunders above-mentioned.
[13] He married Elizabeth Saunders just mentioned.

Kennedy, February 10. Mourners, R. L. Chance, William Chance, Edward Chance, and William Sargant, her Brothers, and pall bearers six."

12. SARAH, " born May 14th 1800 about half past five of the clock in the morning. Was privately baptized by the Revd. Mr. Woodcock May 23rd, And was christened Septr. 9th at St. Philip's by Mr. Woodcock, Sponsors, Mrs. George Wilson, Mrs. Wm. Sargant (her sister),[14] Brother Edwd. Homer, and Mr. William Sargant. . . . . . . Confirmed by the Archbishop of Canterbury at Bow Church, London, say March 23. 1815."

She married, March 20th 1832, at St. Pancras' Church, London, Jonah Smith Wells (see p. 59). He was born Apr. 15th 1796, and died May 27th 1876. His wife died Feb. 3rd 1835, and was buried at Kensal Green Cemetery.

13. MARIA, " was born 1803, April 1, about two of the clock, day. Was privately baptized May 9th p Mr. (Revd.) Woodcock at my house. Was christened Jany. 11. 1805 at St. Philip's Church p Revd. Mr. Maule. Sponsors, Mrs. Cope, High Street, as representative of my daughter Sargant, my niece Sarah Homer,[15] and Brother Edwd. Homer."

She died unmarried May 2nd, 1881, and was buried at the General Cemetery, Birmingham.

E. *Grandchildren of* WILLIAM CHANCE *of Birmingham.*

1. Children of Robert Lucas and Louisa Chance.
    Sons : Edward, died in infancy.
        Robert Lucas, married Fanny Elizabeth, eldest dau. of Abel Peyton, of Birmingham, and had issue.
        Edward Homer, died in infancy.
        Frank, married Jane Susan Katharine, 2nd dau. of James Brewster, of Huntingdon and Brampton, and had issue.
        John Homer, married (1) his cousin Cornelia de Peyster Chance, (2) his cousin Frances Maria, 4th dau. of James Edward Homer, of Wraxall, Som. Issue by the first marriage.

[14] *I.e.*, sister of the infant.
[15] Daughter of Edward Homer by his first wife, Sarah Chance.

PEDIGREE No. 1.—CHANCE OF SHEPLEY, BROMSGROVE.

Daughters: Sarah Louisa, unmarried, died in her 32nd year.
Mary Anne, unmarried, died in her 34th year.
Emily, died in her 13th year.
Caroline, married her cousin, Edward Homer Sargant, and had issue.
Sophia, died in infancy.

2. Children of William and Phœbe Chance.

Sons: James Timmins, married Elizabeth, 4th dau. of George Ferguson, of Houghton Hall, Carlisle, and had issue.
William, married Mary Elizabeth, dau. of Joseph Frederick Ledsam, of Birmingham, and had issue.
George, married Mary, 2nd dau. of Revd. George Richard Downward, of Whitchurch, Salop, and had issue.
Frederick, unmarried, died in his 21st year.
Edward, married Maria Isabella, 3rd dau. of Joseph Ferguson, M.P., of Carlisle, and had issue.
Henry, married Mary Letitia, eldest dau. of George Latham Bennett, of Glenefy, Co. Tipperary, and had issue.

Daughters: Eliza, 2nd wife of John Unett, of Birmingham. No issue.
"Eliza daughter of William Chance Junr. and Phœbe Chance was christened at St. Mary's Chapel by Revd. Mr. Burne, February 18. 1813. Sponsors viz:—myself, William Chance Senr., my daughter Sargant, and Miss Timmins."
Sarah, 1st wife of Charles Rogers Cope, of Metchley, Harborne. Had issue.
Phœbe Louisa, married Revd. Richard Ferguson, 2nd son of George Ferguson above-mentioned. No issue.

3. Children of George and Cornelia Maria Chance.

Sons: George, died in infancy.
George, died in infancy.
Arent de Peyster, married Maria, eldest dau. of his cousin William Lucas Sargant, and had issue.
William Edward, married Laura, 4th dau. of T. Thorneycroft Kesteven, and had issue.

PEDIGREE No. 1.—CHANCE OF SHEPLEY, BROMSGROVE.

Alexander Macomb, married Florence, oldest dau. of Major Arthur Hill Hasted Mercer, formerly of the 60th Rifles, and had issue.

Daughters: Cornelia de Peyster, married her cousin John Homer Chance, and had issue.
Henrietta Louisa, died in childhood.
Sarah Lucas, married Robert Power, and had issue.
Maria Louisa, married Revd. Henry Cave-Browne-Cave, Vicar of Edington, Wilts., and had issue.

4. Children of William and Elizabeth Sargant.
Sons: William, died in infancy.
William Lucas, married (1) Maria, dau. of William Redfern, of Birmingham, (2) his second cousin Theodosia, dau. of Jonathan Nash, and had issue by both marriages.
George, died in infancy.
Henry, married Catherine Emma, only dau. of Samuel Beale, of Russell Square, London, and had issue.
Edward Homer, married his cousin Caroline Chance, and had issue.

Daughters: Sarah, unmarried, died in her 84th year.
"1801 July 21. Myself and wife were Sponsors to our daughter's child, Sarah Sargant, who was christened by Mr. Woodcock at St. Philip's Church this day,— the other Sponsor was Mrs. Sargant the elder, her grandmother."
Elizabeth, unmarried, died in her 60th year.
Ann, married Joseph Rock, of Birmingham, and had issue.
Louisa, died in infancy.

5. Children of Jonah and Sarah Wells.
Two, who died in infancy.

20 of these grandchildren of William and Sarah Chance had children, in number more than 80; and the children of these amount already (1892) to at least 54. The total number therefore of descendants of William and Sarah Chance is, up to the present date (1892), more than 186, and of them at least 130 are living.

Pedigree No. 2. **TILT of Bromsgrove.**

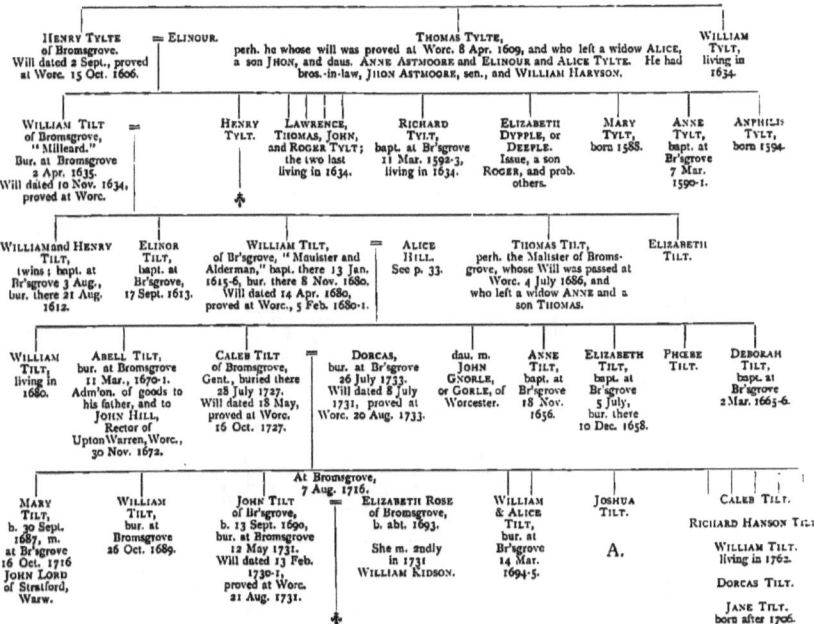

PEDIGREE No. 2.—TILT OF BROMSGROVE.

A.

JOSHUA TILT of Bromsgrove, Skinner and Glover. Will dated 27 Oct. 1762, proved at Worc. 14 Oct. 1766. = (1) **MARY** (2) at Oldswinford, 15 Mar. 1721-2, **THEODOSIA WALDRON**, widow. (3) **HESTER** who survived him.

Children:

- **WILLIAM TILT** of Kidderminster, Skinner. Will dated 10 Nov. 1770, proved at Worc. 27 Sept. 1771. = (1) **ANN WRIGHT**, dau. of JOHN WRIGHT, Timber Merchant. (2) **MARY** Will dated 30 Nov. 1775, proved at Worc. 8 Jan. 1780.
  - **JOHN WRIGHT TILT.**

- **JOHN (1) CHANCE** At Bromsgrove, 15 Oct. 1746. See Pedigree No. 1, B. = **MARY TILT** d. 12 May 1812 aged 91. Bur. at Bromsgrove with her first husband. At Bromsgrove, 9 Sept. 1755. = (2) **GEORGE BELL** of Bromsgrove, Cordwainer. Will dated 28 July 1782, proved at Worc. 18 Feb. 1791. Son of CHRISTOPHER BELL of Br'sgrove.

* The other children of JOSHUA TILT were: ANN BARBER, DORCAS WILLINGTON, THEODOSIA BACHE, and four others, SARAH, ANN, JOHN, and "THEADO :," buried at Bromsgrove. (See p. 116.)

I cannot tell which of these children were by which wife. But Mary, our ancestress, was certainly by the first wife, as she was born before the second marriage took place. I have a notice of Joshua and Mary Tilt as man and wife in 1719 [Feet of Fines].

- **ELIZABETH BELL** b. 11 Feb. 1757. = **JOHN CRANE** of Bromsgrove, d. 17 Dec. 1836, aged 82.
- **JOHN BELL** of Bromsgrove, b. 11 June 1760, d. 26 July 1814. Will dated 17 Nov. 1813, proved in London 21 June 1815.
- **JOSHUA BELL** of Bromsgrove, Cordwainer, b. 2 Jan. 1762, d. 31 Mar. 1840. Will dated 16 Feb. 1839, proved at Worc. 11 Apr. 1840.

Children of Elizabeth Bell and John Crane:

- **JOHN BELL CRANE**, Currier, d. 4 Jan. 1839, aged 54. = **ELIZABETH GREENING**
- **GEORGE CRANE** of Yniscedwin Ironworks, near Swansea, died unm. Jan. 1846. See p. 50.
- **JOSHUA CRANE**, m. a Miss CARPENTER, and died without issue bef. 1840.
- **WILLIAM CRANE**, Linen Weaver, m. **CATHERINE BULLARD** of Worcester.
- **ELIZABETH CRANE**, d. 2 Apr. 1863; m. (1) Revd. EVANS, (2) Jan. 1832 JOHN CROFT HARDY of Birmingham, Manufacturer.

Pedigree No. 3. LUCAS of Rowington, Hanbury and Bristol.

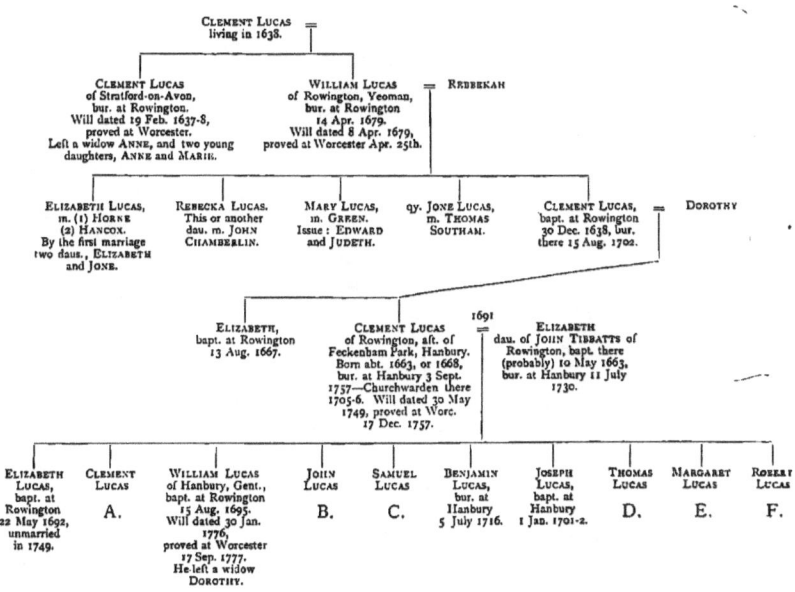

88   PEDIGREE No. 3.—LUCAS OF ROWINGTON, HANBURY, AND BRISTOL.

A.

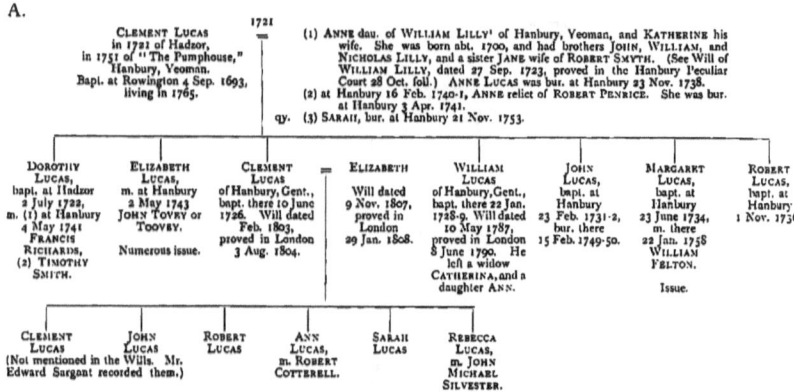

* Nash ("Worcestershire," s. v. Hanbury) quotes a monumental inscription at Hanbury to WILLIAM LILLY, late of Wichbold, Gent., who died 29 Sep. 1723, and was a son of NICHOLAS LILLY, of Wichbold, and grandson of GILBERT KIMBERLEY, of Bromsgrove, Gent. He was aged 80 at his death. His daughter ANNE LUCAS is described in her marriage license as of Dodderhill, which is close to Wichbold.

B.

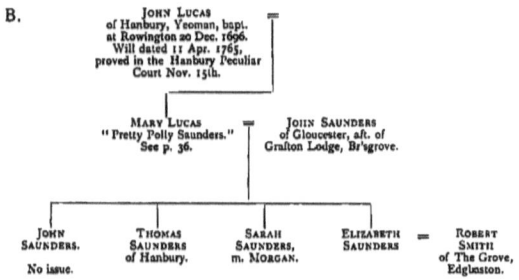

PEDIGREE No. 3.—LUCAS OF ROWINGTON, HANBURY, AND BRISTOL   80

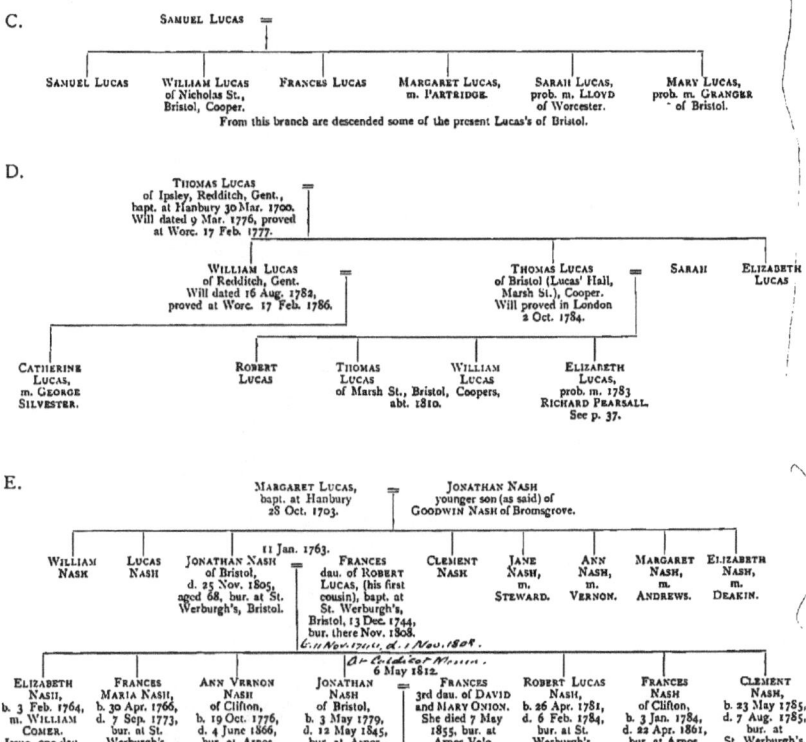

PEDIGREE No. 3.—LUCAS OF ROWINGTON, HANBURY, AND BRISTOL.

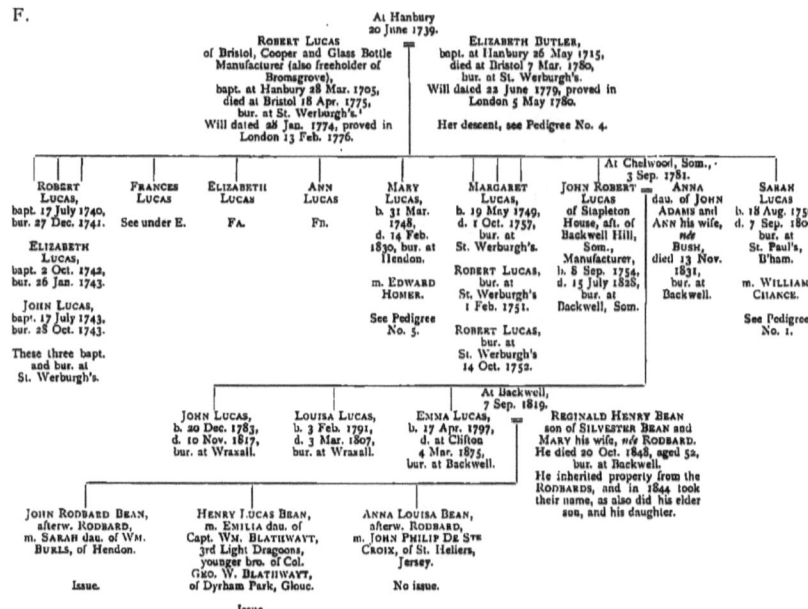

[1] In 1877 St. Werburgh's Church was pulled down and re-erected with the old materials near Montpelier, outside the city of Bristol. The contents of the Lucas vault were removed to the new church.

PEDIGREE No. 3.—LUCAS OF ROWINGTON, HANBURY, AND BRISTOL. 91

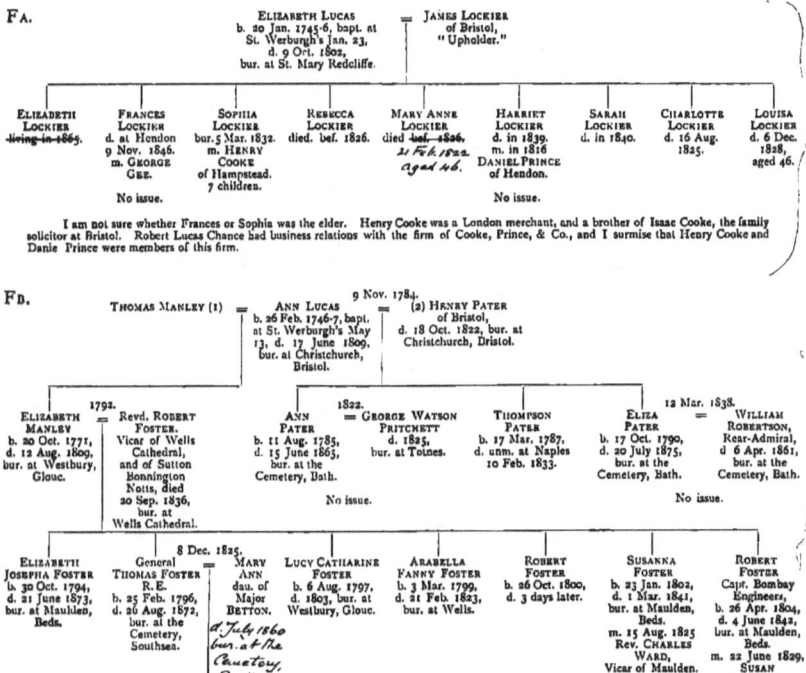

Pedigree No. 4.   VERNON (ROBERT) and BUTLER of Hanbury.

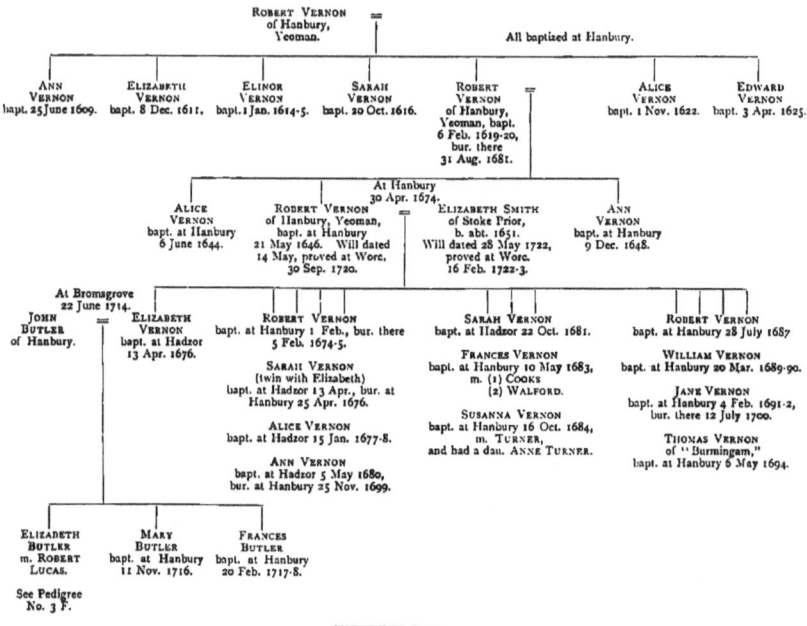

Pedigree No. 5. HOMER (otherwise HOLMER) of Ettingshall and Sutton Coldfield.

(Note that Ettingshall was in Sedgley parish.)

Early mentions see p. 44.

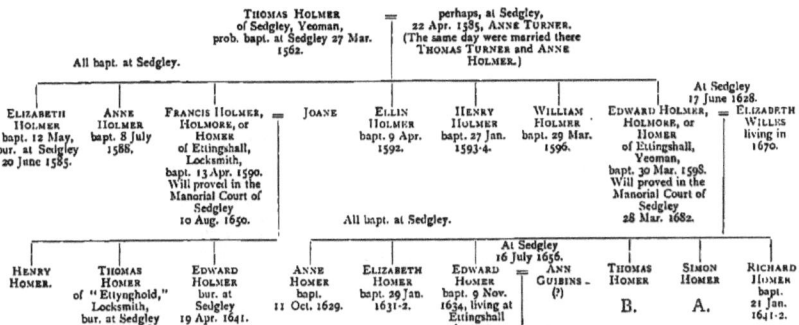

A. SIMON HOMER of Walsall, Tanner, bapt. at Sedgley 24 Mar. 1638-9 (Will dated 31 Dec. 1680, proved at Lichfield 14 Feb. 1680-1), left a widow, ANN, and issue, EDWARD HOMER of Walsall, Tanner (Will dated 16 June 1713, proved at Lichfield 2 Nov. 1715), and five others.

PEDIGREE No. 5.—HOMER OF ETTINGSHALL AND SUTTON COLDFIELD.

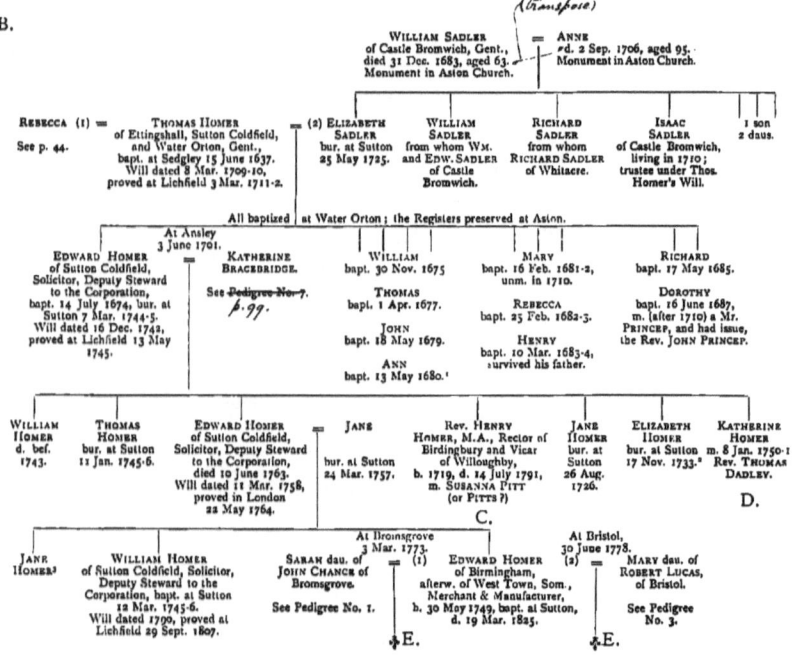

[1] In the Castle Bromwich Register is an entry of the baptism of ANN dau. of THOMAS HOMER—7 June 1681.
[2] Other entries of burials in the Sutton Registers are :—
   1740. Apr. 19. A child of Mr. RICHARD HOMER named MARY.
   1750. Mr. EDWARD HOMER jun.
   1760. Miss CATHERINE MARY HOMER, Spinster.
   These were probably grandchildren of THOMAS HOMER.
[3] JANE HOMER I suppose to have been the mother of WILLIAM HOMER's nephews EDWARD and ROBERT FELTON, mentioned in his will.

C. *Children of the Rev. HENRY HOMER, Rector of Birdingbury and Vicar of Willoughby.*

1. HENRY, b. 10 Nov. 1751, d. at Birdingbury 4 May 1791.
2. EDWARD, b. 4 Mar. 1753, d. at Hockley, B'ham, 24 Dec. 1826.
3. SUSANNA, b. 10 June 1754, d. 23 Sept. 1830, m. Revd. JOSEPH HUTCHINS, Vicar of Ansley, Warw., and had 8 children, one of whom was Revd. HENRY HUTCHINS, of Teignmouth.
4. RICHARD, Clerk in the India House, b. 21 Oct. 1755: his sons were GEORGE HOMER, and ARTHUR ASTON HOMER, of Solihull.
5. CATHERINE, b. 16 Mar. 1757, d. in London 2 Dec. 1764.
6. ARTHUR, Rector of Standlake, Oxon., b. 8 July 1758, d. at Standlake 2 July 1806.
7. JOHN, b. 22 Sept. 1759, d. at Birdingbury 10 Apr. 1760.
8. THOMAS, b. 27 Mar. 1761, of Coventry, Solicitor, then Wine-Merchant. His son was Dr. HENRY HOMER, of Leamington.
9. ELIZABETH, b. 10 June 1762, d. at Attleborough Sept. 1804.
10. WILLIAM } twins, b. 15 Aug. 1763, both d. at Birdingbury.
11. JOHN
12. CHARLES, b. 25 Nov. 1764, d. at Bristol Hot Wells, 6 May 1799.
13. PHILIP BRACEBRIDGE, of Rugby School, b. 22 Feb. 1766, d. Apr. 1838.
    m. (1) C. ADAMSON, died Feb. 1815 leaving 6 children, one of whom was ELIZABETH (BESSIE), who m. her cousin Revd. HENRY HUTCHINS of Teignmouth (above);
    (2) LUCY LAWRENCE, by whom a son, Revd. HENRY HOMER, of Burlestone.
14. CATHERINE, b. 29 Apr. 1767, d. at Birdingbury 9 Mar. 1768.
15. WILLIAM, of the Grammar School, Appleby, Leic.; b. 11 June 1768, d. June 1838; m. SARAH HOMER (E).
16. JANE, b. 18 July 1769, d. at Birdingbury 3 Sept. 1769.
17. DOROTHY, b. 5 Jan. 1771, m. Rev^{d.} Mr. COBBOLD.

D. The Revd. THOMAS DADLEY, who married as his 2nd wife KATHERINE HOMER, (B), was Master of Temple Balsall Hospital, and Vicar of Budbrook, Warw., and a son of WILLIAM DADLEY, 20 years Alderman, and twice Mayor of Warwick. JOHN DADLEY, their 2nd son, had 9 children, the fifth of whom was Mr. WILLIAM BOWES DADLEY, of the Bull Ring, Birmingham; and he alone of the nine left issue. He had 12 daughters and two sons; of the latter, the elder died in infancy, and the younger is the present Mr. W. F. DADLEY, of Birmingham.

E. *Children of EDWARD HOMER, of Birmingham, and West Town, Somersetshire.*

1. By his first wife, SARAH CHANCE.

    SARAH, b. Dec. 10th 1775, d. at Rugby Apr. 4th 1863.

    "1814 November 3. My niece Sarah Homer was married to the Reverend William Homer of Appleby near Atherstone, Leicestershire, at St. Martin's Church, Birmingham, by Revd. Cooke."

    [MS. note of Wm. Chance sen.]

    The Rev. William Homer was the 15th child of Revd. Henry Homer, Rector of Birdingbury (C), and was therefore first cousin to Edward Homer, Sarah's father.

2. By his second wife, MARY LUCAS.

    EDWARD, b. 1779, died in infancy.[1]

    ELIZABETH, unmarried.

    "W. & S. Chance were Sponsors with Mary Saunders to E. & M. Homer's child who was christened at St. Philip's Church, Birmingham, and registered, name Elizabeth, July 19. 1781."

    [MS. note of Wm. Chance sen.]

---

[1] The late Miss Homer thought that there were two of this name who died in infancy, and that a tablet was erected to their memory "against the outside wall of St. Philip's," Birmingham.

JAMES EDWARD, of Brockley Court, afterwards of Wraxall, Som., Manufacturer. B. Feb. 3rd 1783, d. Dec. 15th 1856. Married Harriet, dau. of Thomas Gee, of Bristol, Merchant. She was b. Nov. 29th 1789, and d. Jan. 3rd 1859.

Issue: Thomas Edward, died young.
    Henry, married Caroline Parkinson.
    Charles Gee, married his cousin Frances Matilda Gee.
    Thomas Edward, married (1) Annie Price, (2) Rosetta Andrews.
    Harriet Gee, of Clifton, unmarried, d. 13 Nov. 1891.
    Louisa, married Jonathan Gray.
    Emily, married George Adams.
    Frances Maria, 2nd wife of her cousin John Homer Chance.

MARIA, b. Jan. 1st 1786, d. Nov. 28th 1858. Married successively John and Frederick Charles, sons of William Burton, of Clifden, Co. Clare. The latter died of an accident near Boulogne in 1847.

LOUISA, b. Nov. 3rd 1787, d. Dec. 24th 1873.

> "W. Chance was Sponsor with Elizabeth Lockier (represented by Mary Saunders) and Mrs. Mole to E. & M. Homer's child, who was christened at St. Philip's Church, Birmingham, and registered, name Louisa, Feb. 7 1788."
>
> [MS. note of Wm. Chance sen.]

She married her cousin Robert Lucas Chance (see p. 79).

PEDIGREE No. 5.—HOMER OF ETTINGSHALL AND SUTTON COLDFIELD.

D. The Revd. THOMAS DADLEY, who married as his 2nd wife KATHERINE HOMER, (B), was Master of Temple Balsall Hospital, and Vicar of Budbrook, Warw., and a son of WILLIAM DADLEY, 20 years Alderman, and twice Mayor of Warwick. JOHN DADLEY, their 2nd son, had 9 children, the fifth of whom was Mr. WILLIAM BOWES DADLEY, of the Bull Ring, Birmingham; and he alone of the nine left issue. He had 12 daughters and two sons; of the latter, the elder died in infancy, and the younger is the present Mr. W. F. DADLEY, of Birmingham.

E. *Children of EDWARD HOMER, of Birmingham, and West Town, Somersetshire.*

---

1. By his first wife, SARAH CHANCE.

SARAH, b. Dec. 16th 1775, d. at Rugby Apr. 4th 1863.

"1814 November 3. My niece Sarah Homer was married to the Reverend William Homer of Appleby near Atherstone, Leicestershire, at St. Martin's Church, Birmingham, by Revd. Cooke."

[MS. note of Wm. Chance sen.]

The Rev. William Homer was the 15th child of Revd. Henry Homer, Rector of Birdingbury (C), and was therefore first cousin to Edward Homer, Sarah's father.

2. By his second wife, MARY LUCAS.

EDWARD, b. 1779, died in infancy.[1]

ELIZABETH, unmarried.

"W. & S. Chance were Sponsors with Mary Saunders to E. & M. Homer's child who was christened at St. Philip's Church, Birmingham, and registered, name Elizabeth, July 19. 1781."

[MS. note of Wm. Chance sen.]

---

[1] The late Miss Homer thought that there were two of this name who died in infancy, and that a tablet was erected to their memory "against the outside wall of St. Philip's," Birmingham.

PEDIGREE No. 6.—BRACEBRIDGE OF KINGSBURY AND ATHERSTONE.

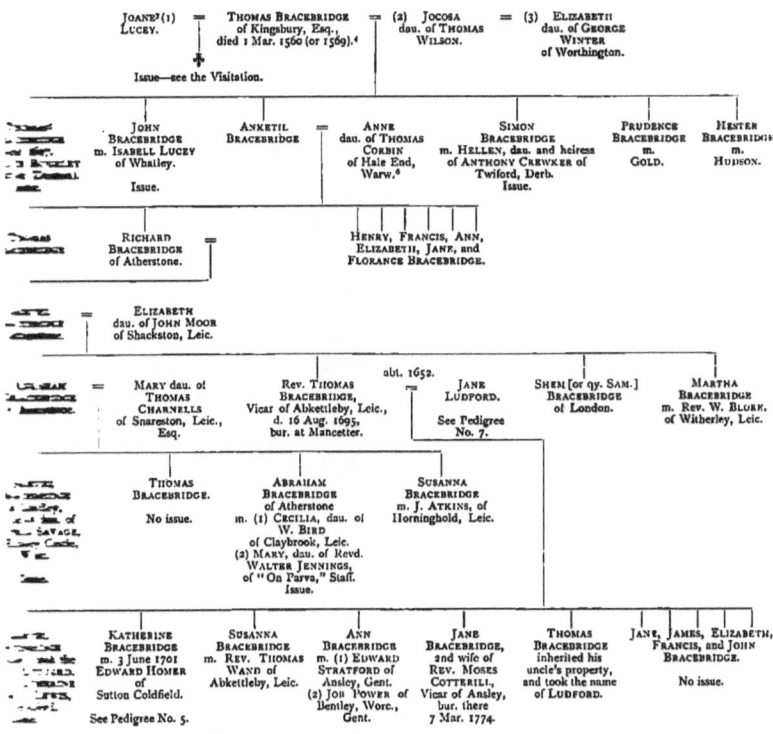

[3] So the Visitation: but Dugdale gives Johanna, dau. of George Catesby, of Lapworth, Esq., as the first wife.
[4] 2 Eliz. (1560) in the Visitation: but Dugdale gives 11 Eliz. (1569).
[5] "Through his great improvidence he came to die miserably." (Dugdale.)
[6] In the Visitation "Holland."

Pedigree No. 7. LUDFORD of Ansley.

(Authorities—Same as for the Bracebridge Pedigree.)

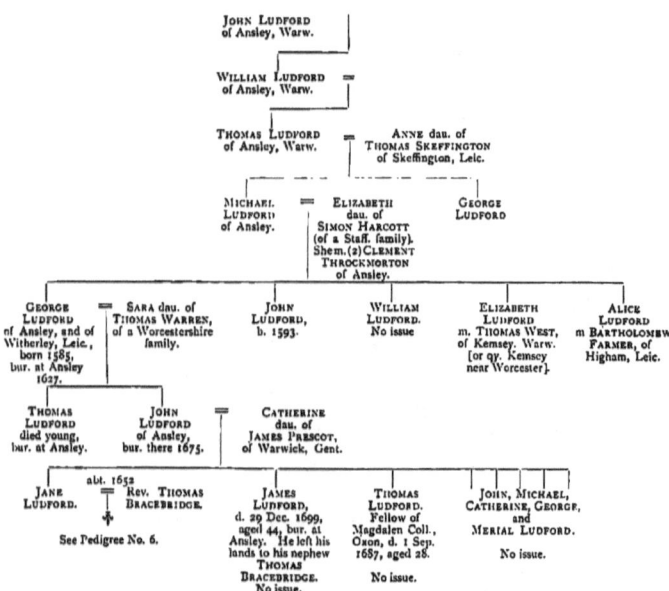

APPENDICES.

A.—Extracts from Parish Registers.
B.—Marriage Bonds.
C.—Tombstone Inscriptions.
D.—Lists of Wills and Administrations.
E.—Extracts from Subsidy Rolls.
F.—Chances of Worcestershire.
G.—A Chance Family in Hampshire.
H.—Early Notices of Chances, other than of Worcestershire.

Appendix A.

EXTRACTS FROM PARISH REGISTERS.[1]

1. CHANCE.

a. From the Parish Registers of Bromsgrove, 1591-1750.[2]

(*List supposed to be complete, cp.* pp. 24, 25.)

1591.	Oct.	17.	bapt.	Nicholas son of Richard Chaunce.
1591.	Oct.	24.	bapt.	Jhon son of Roger Chaunce.
1592.	June	25.	bur.	Rob't Chaunce.
1593.	June	20.	bapt.	Thomas son of Willia' Chaunce.
1593.	Dec.	27.	mar.	Margret Chance and Thomas Maye.
1594-5.	Feb.	2.	bapt.	Jhon son of Richard Chance.
1595.	Oct.	5.	bapt.	Willia' son of Willia' Chance.
1595.	Oct.	23.	mar.	Edward Chance and Lucy Woodward.
1595.	Nov.	17.	bapt.	Richard son of Roger Chance.
1595-6.	Feb.	26.	bur.	Willia' son of Henrie Chance.
1596-7.	Jan.	9.	bur.	two sons of William Chance, unbaptized.
1596-7.	Feb.	3.	mar.	Elizabeth Chaunce and Willia' Fownes.
1597.	Apr.	17.	bur.	Elizabeth wife of Richard Chance of Shepcoote.
1597.	Dec.	24.	bur.	Richard Chaunce.
1597-8.	Feb.	17.	bur.	Jhon son of Richard Chaunce.
1599.	June	9.	bur.	Margret wife of Roger Chaunce.
1599.	July	18.	mar.	Willia' Chaunce and Anne Butler.
1599.	Sep.	21.	bur.	William son of Nicholas Chaunce.
1599.	Dec.	1.	mar.	Roger Chaunce and Anne Butler.

[1] These are not copies of the Register entries, but abbreviations of them; the first one, for instance, running in the original, "The 17th daie of October was baptyzed Nicholas the sone of Richard Chaunce." The original spellings, however, of the names are preserved, except that in the Latin portions the equivalents are given.

[2] Note that up to about 1752, the year was commonly taken to commence on March 25th. Thus the date which the Registers have as 2nd Feb. 1594, we should call 2nd Feb. 1595; and so in any year for all dates from Jan. 1st to March 24th inclusive.

APPENDIX A.—EXTRACTS FROM PARISH REGISTERS.

1599.	Dec.	15.	bapt.	Willia' son of Willia' Chaunce.
1600.	May	25.	mar.	Margret Chaunce and Henrie Lewes.
1600.	June	1.	mar.	Thomas Chaunce and Mary Bradlay.
1600.	Oct.	26.	mar.	Alice Chaunce and Thomas Lewes.
1600-1.	Feb.	3.	bur.	Roger son of Roger Chance.
1601.	Apr.	1.	bur.	Philippe wife of Jhon Chaunce.
1601.	Apr.	6.	bur.	An'e wife of Willia' Chaunce.
1601.	July	1.	mar.	Elizabeth Chaunce and Robart Brooke.
1601.	Nov.	9.	mar.	John Chaunce and Elizabeth Higgo.
1601.	Dec.	4.	bur.	son of Thomas Chaunce, unbaptized.
1601-2.	Jan.	10.	bapt.	Benet daughter of Willia' Chaunce, de Sheplay.
1602.	Oct.	13.	mar.	Jane Chaunce and George Bache.
1602-3.	Feb.	24.	bapt.	Marye daughter of Thomas Chaunce.
1603.	Sep.	11.	bapt.	Willia' son of Willia' Chaunce, de Sheplay.
1603-4.	Feb.	12.	bapt.	Willia' son of Jhon Chaunce, of Worcester.
1604.	June	27.	bur.	Anne wife of Roger Chaunce.
1604.	Oct.	18.	mar.	Roger Chaunce and Elinour Lillie.
1604-5.	Mar.	9.	bapt.	Jhon son of Jhon Chaunce, of Tymberhonger.
1605.	Apr.	14.	bapt.	Mary daughter of Willia' Chaunce, of Sheplay.
1605.	May	1.	mar.	Alice Chaunce and Willia' Oxford.
1606.	July	2.	bapt.	Anne daughter of Thomas Chaunce, de Catshill.
1606.	Dec.	3.	bapt.	Gilbert son of Will'm Chaunce.
1606-7.	Jan.	15.	mar.	Sybil Chaunce and Thomas Saunders.
1606-7.	Jan.	17.	mar.	Mary Chaunce and George Jackson.
1606-7.	Jan.	20.	mar.	Elizabeth Chaunce and Robert Richardes.
1609.	Nov.	19.	bapt.	Richard son of Thomas Chaunce.
1610.	Mar.	29.	bur.	Jane Chaunce, widow.
1610.	May	3.	bur.	Richard Chaunce.
1610.	Aug.	4.	bapt.	Ellinor daughter of John Chaunce.
1610.	Sep.	3.	mar.	Anne Chaunce and Thomas Kettlesby.
1610-11.	Jan.	15.	bapt.	Will'm son of John Chaunce.
1610-11.	Jan.	22.	bapt.	Will'm son of John Chaunce.
1611.	Aug.	18.	bapt.	Elizabeth daughter of Will'm Chaunce.
1611.	Nov.	28.	mar.	Will'm Chaunce and Elizabeth Tilsley.
1612.	July	13.	mar.	Mary Chaunce and Rafe Townsend.
1612.	Sep.	9.	bapt.	Jane daughter of John Chaunce.
1613.	May	15.	bapt.	Henry son of Willia' Chaunce, de Sheplay.
1613.	June	27.	bapt.	Henry son of John Chaunce, de Tymberhonger.
1613.	Nov.	10.	bapt.	Richard son of Thomas Chaunce, blacksmith.
1613-4.	Feb.	1.	bapt.	Anne daughter of Willia' Chance.
1614.	May	11.	bapt.	Anne daughter of Huge Chaunce.
1614.	July	27.	mar.	Willia' Chaunce, gent., and Jane Lillie.
1614.	Dec.	9.	bapt.	Elizabeth daughter of Jhon Chaunce, tanner.
1614.	Dec.	10.	bur.	Elinour wife of Roger Chaunce,
1614.	Dec.	18.	bapt.	Gyles son of Willia' Chaunce, de Sheplay.

APPENDIX A.—EXTRACTS FROM PARISH REGISTERS. 107

1614-5.	Jan.	17.	bur.	Jhon Chaunce, de Burnheath.
1615.	Aug.	6.	mar.	Elinoure Chaunce and Jhon Tyndon.
1615.	Sep.	21.	bapt.	Elizabeth daughter of William Chaunce, glover.
1615.	Nov.	30.	bur.	Elizabeth daughter of William Chaunce, glover.
1615-6.	Mar.	4.	bur.	Thomas Chaunce, blacksmith.
1616.	Apr.	26.	bapt.	Thomas son of Thomas Chaunce, blacksmith.
1616.	June	8.	bapt.	Mary daughter of William Chaunce, de Sheplay.
1616-7.	Feb.	16.	bapt.	Nicholas son of Jhon Chaunce, de Catshill.

The following entries were made in Latin:—

1618.	Sep.	30.	bapt.	Joan daughter of Hugh Chaunce.
1619.	July	21.	bapt.	John son of John Chaunce.
1620.	May	21.	bapt.	John son of Hugh Chaunce.
1620.	June	9.	bur.	Elizabeth Chaunce.
1620.	Oct.	12.	bapt.	Jane daughter of John Chaunce.
1620-1.	Mar.	12.	bapt.	Elizabeth daughter of William Chaunce.
1622.	May	1.	bapt.	Margaret daughter of John Chaunce.
1622.	May	11.	bur.	William Chaunce, gent.
1622.	June	22.	bapt.	Alice daughter of Hugh Chaunce.
1623.	Apr.	25.	bapt.	Anne daughter of Thomas Chaunce.
1623.	May	23.	bur.	Elizabeth daughter of William Chaunce.
1623.	Sep.	19.	bapt.	Mary daughter of Henry Chaunce.
1623-4.	Jan.	10.	bur.	Elizabeth Chaunce, widow.
1623-4.	Feb.	28.	bapt.	Thomas son of John Chaunce.
1624.	July	22.	bur.	Mary Chaunce, of Catshill.
1624.	Sep.	22.	bur.	Henry Chaunce.
1625.	Apr.	16.	bapt.	Hugh son of Hugh Chaunce.
1625.	May	28.	bapt.	Anne daughter of John Chaunce.
1625.	Nov.	5.	bur.	Hugh son of Hugh Chaunce.
1625-6.	Feb.	8.	mar.	Margaret Chaunce and John Harrison.
1626.	Sep.	29.	bapt.	Henry son of Hugh Chaunce.
1626.	Dec.	17.	bapt.	Margaret daughter of John Chaunce.
1626-7.	Jan.	21.	bapt.	Henry son of Thomas Chaunce.
1626-7.	Feb.	1.	mar.	Benet Chaunce and Martin Blick.
1626-7.	Feb.	2.	mar.	Thomas Chaunce and Ursula Tylt.
1626-7.	Feb.	18.	bapt.	Anthony son of John Chaunce, tanner.
1626-7.	Mar.	14.	bapt.	Elizabeth daughter of Henry Chaunce.
1627.	June	17.	mar.	William Chaunce and Alice Mence.
1628.	Nov.	26.	bapt.	William son of John Chaunce, of Woodrowe.
1628.	Dec.	12.	bapt.	Joan daughter of William Chaunce, of Byrcott.
1628-9.	Feb.	24.	bur.	son of Thomas Chaunce, mason, unbaptized.
1629.	May	30.	bapt.	Mary daughter of Thomas Chaunce.
1629.	Dec.	26.	bur.	Joan daughter of Thomas Chaunce.
1629-30.	Jan.	13.	bur.	Elizabeth daughter of Henry Chaunce.
1629-30.	Jan.	17.	bapt.	Hugh son of Hugh Chaunce.
1630-1.	Feb.	24.	bapt.	William son of William Chaunce.

APPENDIX A.—EXTRACTS FROM PARISH REGISTERS.

1630-1.	Feb.	27.	bapt.	Mary daughter of William Chaunce.
1630-1.	Mar.	9.	bur.	William son of William Chaunce.
1632.	Apr.	22.	bapt.	Margaret daughter of William Chaunce.
1633.	Aug.	22.	bur.	Anne wife of John Chaunce.
1633.	Sep.	12.	bur.	Anne Chaunce, widow.
1633.	Oct.	12.	bapt.	Thomas son of William Chaunce.
1633-4.	Mar.	18.	bur.	Benet Chaunce, widow.
1634.	June	27.	bur.	Henry son of John Chaunce.
1634.	July	12.	bapt.	Elizabeth daughter of Henry Chaunce.
1634.	July	19.	bur.	Elinor daughter of John Chaunce, of Tymberhonger.
1634.	Nov.	19.	bur.	John son of Thomas Chaunce.
1634-5.	Feb.	10.	bapt.	Nathaniel son of John Chaunce.
1635.	Oct.	1.	bapt.	Edward son of William and Elizabeth Chaunce.
1635-6.	Feb.	2.	mar.	Anne Chaunce and William Biggs.
1636.	July	14.	bur.	daughter of Henry Chaunce, unbaptized.
1636-7.	Jan.	24.	mar.	Richard Chaunce and Margaret Badger.
1636-7.	Feb.	5.	bapt.	Jonathan son of Thomas and Lucy Chaunce.
1636-7.	Feb.	24.	bapt.	Gamaliel son of John and Anne Chaunce.
1637.	Apr.	11.	bur.	son of William Chaunce, unbaptized.
1637.	Nov.	2.	mar.	Elizabeth Chaunce and John Ganderton.
1637-8.	Feb.	6.	mar.	William Chaunce and Elizabeth Wilde.
1638.	Apr.	11.	mar.	William Chaunce and Katharine Ogden.
1638.	Apr.	24.	bapt.	Anne daughter of Richard and Margaret Chaunce.
1638.	May	3.	bapt.	Henry son of William and Alice Chaunce.
1638.	June		mar.	Giles Chaunce and Elizabeth Parr.
1638.	Aug.	29.	bur.	Ursula wife of Thomas Chaunce.
1638.	Sep.	18.	mar.	Elizabeth Chaunce and Richard Potter.
1638.	Oct.	18.	mar.	Thomas Chaunce and Jane Higgins.
1638-9.	Mar.	6.	bapt.	Hannah daughter of John (?) and Jane (?) Chaunce.
1638-9.	Mar.		bapt.	Mary daughter of William and Katherine Chaunce.
1638-9.	Mar.		bapt.	J daughter of Giles and Elizabeth Chaunce.
1639.	Sep.	14.	bapt.	Thomas son of Thomas and Jane Chaunce.
1639.	Sep.	22.	bapt.	John son of William and Elizabeth Chaunce.
1639-40.	Feb.	13.	mar.	John Chaunce and Martha Hopkins.
1639-40.	Mar.	11.	bur.	Mary wife of Nicholas Chaunce.
1640.	Apr.	16.	bapt.	William son of William and Elizabeth Chaunce.
1640.	May	14.	bapt.	Mary daughter of Richard and Margaret Chaunce.
1640.	July	2.	mar.	Jane Chaunce and John Wakeman.
1640.	Aug.	11.	bur.	Nicholas Chaunce.
1640.	Oct.		bapt.	Anne daughter of Giles and Elizabeth Chaunce.
1640.	Dec.	17.	bapt.	Elizabeth daughter of William Chaunce.

English is now resumed. The greater part of the years 1641 to 1652 are wanting.

1647-8.	Feb.		mar.	Anne Chaunce and William
1647-8.	Feb.		bur.	William Chaunce of Yarnhill.
1652.	Apr.	14.	bapt.	Ann and Aquila daughters of Hendery Chance.

APPENDIX A.—EXTRACTS FROM PARISH REGISTERS.

1653-4.	Feb.	28.	bur.	Anne daughter of Tho: Chance.
1654.	Sep.	19.	born	Henry son of Henry and Elinor Chance.
1655.	May	23.	born	Henry son of Richard and Margret Chance.
1655-6.	Jan.	2.	born	Anne daughter of Nicholas Chance.
1655-6.	Feb.	27.	born	Samuel son of William and Katherine Chance.
1655-6.	Mar.	9.	banns	published the third time between Thomas Milward the younger of the Welch House, Harborne, and Margret Chance.
1655-6.	Mar.	18.	banns	published the third time between William son of John Chance, of Sheply, yeoman, and Elizabeth Porkes of Fairfield, widow; married 19th June following.
1656.	Sep.	7.	banns	published the third time between John Chance, husbandman, and Elizabeth , both of Sidemore (Bromsgrove); married Sept. 18th.
1656.	Nov.	26.	bur.	Thomas son of John Chance, de Catshill.
1656-7.	Feb.	3.	banns	published the third time between William Chance and Elizabeth Brunt, both of Beoly.
1657.	Nov.	10.	bur.	Henry Chance, of Burcot, ropier.
1657-8.	Jan.	10.	bur.	Mrs. Chance, of Woodcot, widdowe.
1658.	Apr.	17.	born	Nicholas son of Nicholas Chance, Catshill.
1658.	July	24.	bur.	Richard Chance, olim blacksmith.
1658-9.	Feb.	10.	born	son of William Chance, of Fock. [i.e. Fockbury.]
1659-60.	Feb.	17.	bur.	Thomas Chance, of the Stonehouse.
1659-60.	Feb.	29.	bapt.	John son of Anthony and Eliz: Chance.
1659-60.	Mar.	15.	born	25. bur. an infant of Wm. and Cath: Chance.
1660.	Dec.	20.	bapt.	Thomas son of Nicholas Chance.
1660-1.	Feb.	20.	bur.	Elizabeth wife of John Chance, of Catshill.
[1661.	June	11.	born	Thomas son of Henry Cance.]
1662.	Oct.	28.	mar.	Nathaniel Chaunce and Mary Freeman.
1662-3.	Jan.	17.	bur.	William son of Anthony Chaunce.
1662-3.	Jan.	29.	bapt.	Mary daughter of Henry Chaunce.
1662-3.	Feb.	12.	mar.	Ann Chaunce and Richard Brettell.
1664.	May	18.	bapt.	Anthony son of Anthony Chance.
1664.	Dec.	6.	bur.	William Chanis.
1664-5.	Jan.	19.	bapt.	Hannah daughter of Jonathan Chance.
1665.	May	21.	mar.	John Chance and Ann Woodward.
1665.	July	5.	bapt.	Joyce daughter of Henry Chance.
1666.	Apr.	17.	bapt.	William son of John Chance.
1666.	Dec.	16.	bur.	Tho. son of Rich. Chance.
1666-7.	Jan.	11.	bapt.	Hanna daughter of Anthony Chance.
1666-7.	Feb.	28.	bur.	Wm. Chance, of Sheply.
1667.	June	2.	mar.	Anne Chance and Jonathan Atwell.
1667.	July	14.	bapt.	Lucy daughter of Hen: Chance.
1667.	Oct.	7.	bur.	John Chance, warden.
1667.	Oct.	10.	bapt.	William son of John Chance.
1667.	Dec.	16.	bur.	Jonathan Chance.
1667-8.	Feb.	8.	bapt.	Elizabeth daughter of John Chance.

APPENDIX A.—EXTRACTS FROM PARISH REGISTERS.

1667-8.	Feb.	8.	bur.	Anne wife of John Chance.
1667-8.	Feb.	19.	bur.	Lucy daughter of Henry Chance.
1668.	July	18.	bur.	Mary daughter of Richard Chance.
1669.	Nov.	29.	bur.	Mary Chaunce, wid^e.
1669-70.	Jan.	3.	bur.	John Chaunce, of Shepley.
1669-70.	Jan.	17.	bur.	the widow Chaunce, of Shepley.
1669-70.	Feb.	17.	bur.	Elinor Chaunce, wid.
1670.	Aug.	3.	bur.	Thomas son of Nicholas Chaunce.
1670.	Aug.		bur.	of Henry Chaunce.
1670-1.	Mar.	5.	bapt.	Sarah daughter of Nathaniel Chance.
1671.	Mar.	26.	bur.	John son of John Chaunce.
1671-2.	Mar.	21.	bur.	Joane Chance, vid.'
1674.	May	2.	bur.	Elizabeth Chaunce, widow.
1674.	Dec.	1.	bur.	Ormill son of Nicholas Chaunce.
1674-5.	Feb.	11.	mar.	Ann Chaunce and Robert Sitch.
1675.	Nov.	22.	bur.	Mrs. Jane Chaunce, widow.
1675-6.	Mar.	6.	bur.	Jacob son of Nathaniel Chaunce.
1676.	Sep.	30.	mar.	Ann Chaunce and Ralph Persall.
1676.	Oct.	21.	mar.	Elizabeth Chaunce and Thomas Hall.
1677.	July	10.	bur.	Margaret wife of Richard Chaunce.
1678.	Nov.	2.	mar.	Joane Chance and Will'm Saunders.
1679.	Sep.	1.	bapt.	son of Will'm Chaunce.
1679-80.	Feb.	17.	bur.	Elizabeth Chaunce, widow.
1680.	May	1.	bapt.	John son of John Chaunce, de Catsel.
1680-1.	Mar.	9.	bapt.	John son of John Chaunce, de Catsel.
1681.	July	19.	mar.	Nicholas Chaunce and Lidiah Dewce.
1682.	Apr.	5.	bur.	John son of John Chaunce, de Catshill.
1682.	May	11.	bapt.	Elizabeth daughter of Nicholas Chaunce.
1682.	July	2.	bur.	Nicholas Chaunce, Alderman.
1682.	Oct.	23.	bur.	Mary wife of John Chaunce, de Shepley.
1682.	Dec.	12.	bur.	Mary daughter of Nicholas Chaunce.
1683.	Aug.	2.	bapt.	Mary daughter of John Chaunce.
1683.	Sep.	2.	bapt.	Joyce daughter of John Chaunce.
1683.	Oct.	6.	mar.	John Chaunce and Rebecka Blick.
1683-4.	Mar.	5.	bur.	William Chance.
1684.	Dec.	30.	bur.	John son of John Chaunce, de Shoply.
1684-5.	Jan.	2.	bapt.	of Nicholas Chance.
1684-5.	Feb.	26.	bur.	George son of Will'm Chance.
1684-5.	Mar.	22.	bur.	John son of Will'm Chance.
1685-6.	Feb.	2.	bapt.	Ann daughter of John Chance, taner.
1685-6.	Mar.	8.	bur.	Ann daughter of John Chance.
1686-7.	Jan.	21.	bapt.	of Nicholas Chance, de Catshill.
1686-7.	Mar.	16.	bapt.	Will'm son of John Chance, de Catshill.
1687.	Apr.	24.	bapt.	Joseph son of John Chance.
1688.	Mar.	28.	mar.	Elizabeth Chance and Job Eckles.
1688.	Aug.	3.	bur.	Elizabeth daughter of Nicholas Chance.

APPENDIX A.—EXTRACTS FROM PARISH REGISTERS.

1689.	Apr.	23.	bapt.	John son of John Chance, de Catshill.
1689.	Nov.	6.	bapt.	Edward son of Will'm Chance (or Chancey?).
1690.	Apr.	23.	bapt.	John son of John Chance.
1690.	July	24.	bapt.	Elizabeth daughter of Nicholas Chance.
1690.	Aug.	1.	bur.	Will'm Chance.
1691.	Aug.	13.	bur.	Joyce daughter of John Chance.
1692.	Apr.	1.	bapt.	Colib son of Nathanel Chance.
1692.	July	8.	bapt.	Ann daughter of Will'm Chance, de Catsol.
1692.	Sep.	15.	bapt.	Joane daughter of Nicholas Chance.
[1692.	Nov.	30.	bapt.	Samuel son of Jerimy Chance.]
1694.	May	12.	mar.	Sarah Chance and Johnathan Holmes.
1695.	July	31.	bapt.	Mary daughter of Anthony Chance.
1695.	Oct.	7.	mar.	John Chance and Joyce Cole, by banns.
1695.	Nov.	27.	bur.	John son of John Chance.
1695.	Dec.	25.	bur.	Elizabeth Chance.
1695-6.	Jan.	9.	mar.	Christopher Chance of Inkborrow and Sarah Yates of Hanbury, by a lycence.
1696.	Apr.	15.	bapt.	Sarah daughter of William Chance.
1696.	Apr.	28.	bur.	Nathanael Chance.
1696.	May	1.	bur.	Sarah daughter of William Chance.
1696.	Sep.	24.	bapt.	John son of Nicholas Chance.
1696.	Nov.	5.	mar.	Jane Chance and Richard Weaver, by banns.
1696.	Dec.	14.	bur.	daughter of Wm Chance.
1697.	July	4.	bur.	Joyce wife of John Chance, of Chadwitch.
1697.	July	29.	bapt.	Thomas son of John Chance, of Catshill.
1697.	Aug.	18.	bapt.	John son of Anthony Chance jun', of the Town.
1697.	Oct.	6.	mar.	Ann Chance and Henry Lilly, both of Bromsgrove, by banns.
1698.	July	24.	bapt.	Elizabeth daughter of John and Joyce Chance.
1698.	Sep.	22.	born	a child of William Chance, of Shepley.
1698.	Oct.	6.	bapt.	Hannah daughter of William and Frances Chance.
1699.	June	4.	mar.	Mary Chance and John Juggins, of Bromsgrove, by bans.
1700.	May	20.	bur.	John Chance.
1700.	June	5.	bapt.	William son of Anthony and Mary Chance.
1700-1.	Feb.	13.	bapt.	William son of John Chance, of Bornheath.
1700-1.	Feb.	14.	bur.	the said William Chance.
1701.	Oct.	16.	bur.	John Chance, of Rocking Lane.
1702.	Nov.	2.	bur.	William Chance.
1703.	Aug.	18.	bur.	Jone Chance, widoe, of Bornheath.
1703.	Aug.	31.	bapt.	Rebeckah daughter of Anthony and Mary Chance.
1703.	Oct.	12.	mar.	Sarah Chance and William Sanders, by banns.
1703.	Dec.	23.	bur.	John Chance, of Bournheath, naylor.
1704-5.	Mar.	17.	bur.	William son of Anthony Chanch.
1705.	Mar.	30.	bur.	Anne wife of Henry Chance.
1706.	May	19.	mar.	Barnet Chance and Mary Mole, by banns.
1706.	Aug.	4.	mar.	Mary Chance and Thomas Clarke, the latter of Inkbarrow.

APPENDIX A.—EXTRACTS FROM PARISH REGISTERS.

1706.	Oct.	3.	mar.	Sarah Chance, of Bromsgrove, and John Gosnell, of Kidderminster, by lycence.
1706.	Dec.	11.	bapt.	Anthony son of Anthony Chance.
1707.	June	23.	bapt.	Sarah daughter of John and Sheusanna Chance.
1708.	Apr.	18.	bur.	Mary daughter of Anthony and Mary Chance.
1708.	Sep.	20.	mar.	Joyes Chance and Richard Buxtons, both of Bromsgrove, by banns.
1709.	Apr.	4.	bur.	Nicholas Chance, of Bornhearth.
1709.	Apr.	8.	bur.	Elizabeth wife of Anthony Chance, of Bornhearth.
1709.	Apr.	19.	bur.	John Chance of Catshill.
1710.	Oct.	12.	bapt.	William son of John Chance.
1710-1.	Mar.	20.	bur.	Henry Chance.
1711.	Aug.	12.	bapt.	Mary daughter of Barnet and Mary Chance.
1711.	Aug.	21.	bur.	Anthony Chance sen^r, of Bornheath.
1711.	Nov.	26.	bur.	Thomas Chance.
1711.	Nov.	29.	bur.	John Chance.
1711-2.	Jan.	2.	bur.	William Chance sen^r.
1712.	Aug.	24.	bur.	Anne Chance, widow.
1712-3.	Mar.	18.	bur.	Mary Chance, widow.
1713.	Aug.	26.	bapt.	Elizabeth daughter of Caleb and Jane Chance.
1713.	Dec.	13.	born	William son of John and Sarah Chance.
1714.	Apr.	2.	bapt.	Elizabeth daughter of Bernett and Mary Chance.
1716.	Apr.	2.	mar.	Edward Chance, of Chadsley Corbett, and Mary Bridges, of Bromsgrove, by lycence.
1716.	Sep.	17.	mar.	William Chance and Anne Sale, both of Bromsgrove, by banns.
1716.	Dec.	21.	bur.	Ann wife of William Chance.
1717.	Apr.	2.	bur.	Anthony Chance.
1718.	Apr.	8.	bur.	Richard Chance, of Stoke Prior.
1718.	Apr.	25.	mar.	William Chance and Hannah Heamus, both of Bromsgrove, by banns.
1718.	Oct.	4.	bur.	Joseph son of John Chance.
1718.	Nov.	17.	bur.	Hannah daughter of John Chance.
1718-9.	Jan.	7.	bur.	John son of William Chance.
1718-9.	Mar.	5.	mar.	Elizabeth Chance and Richard Blick, by banns.
1719.	July	28.	mar.	Jane Chance, of Bromsgrove, and John Perks, of Bell Broughton, by lycence.
1719.	Sep.	24.	bur.	Joane Chance, widow.
1719.	Dec.	23.	bapt.	John son of William and Hannah Chance.
1719.	Dec.	25.	bur.	John son of William and Hannah Chance.
1719.	Dec.	30.	bur.	the widow Chance.
(uncertain year)	April	4.	bur.	Jo: son of Jo: Chance.
1719-20.	Feb.	6.	bur.	Thomas son of John Chance.
1720.	Sep.	10.	bur.	Lidia Chance, widow.
1720.	Nov.	10.	bur.	Hannah daughter of Benj^a and Hannah Chance.
1720-1.	Feb.	3.	bapt.	Elizabeth daughter of Willm and Hannah Chance.
1721.	Aug.	10.	bur.	Elizabeth Chance, widow, provectâ aetate.
1721.	Sep.	6.	bapt.	Will'm son of Barney and Chance.

APPENDIX A.—EXTRACTS FROM PARISH REGISTERS.

1722-3.	Feb.	.	mar.	Ann Chance of Bromsgrove, and John Willkes, of Bellbroughton, by lycence.
1723.	Sep.	14.	bur.	Elizabeth wife of William Chance.
1723.	Oct.	3.	bur.	William Chanc of Shepley.
1723.	Dec.	9.	bapt.	Hannah daughter of William and Elizabeth Chance.
1724.	May	17.	bapt.	Bearnett son of Barnett Chance.
1724.	Sep.	8.	bur.	John Chance of Bournheath.
1724.	Oct.	8.	bapt.	Ann daughter of John and Ann Chance.
1725.	Mar.	31.	mar.	Mary Chance and John Crowfoot, both of Bromsgrove, by banns.
1725.	May	1.	bapt.	William son of William Chance.
1725.	May	17.	bur.	William son of Barnett Chance.
1725.	May	31.	bur.	Barnard son of Barnard Chance.
1725.	Nov.	30.	mar.	Hannah Chance, of Bromsgrove, and William Abbott, of Stoke Prior. by lycence.
1725-6.	Jan.	23.	bapt.	William son of Mr. Thomas and Sarah Chance.
1726-7.	Jan.	8.	bapt.	Ann daughter of William and Hannah Chance.
1727.	Aug.	25.	bapt.	Elizabeth daughter of Mr. Thomas and Sarah Chance.
1727.	Oct.	4.	bapt.	John son of William and Chance.
1727.	Nov.	14.	mar.	William Chance and Catherina Buxton, both of Bromsgrove, by ban :
1727-8.	Mar.	23.	bur.	Ann daughter of William and Hannah Chance.
1729.	May	30.	bapt.	Mary daughter of William and Mary Chance.
1729.	Dec.	27.	bapt.	Thomas son of William Chance Jun :
1731-2.	Feb.	18.	mar.	John Chance of Claines and Febe Tolley of Ombersley, by lycence.
1732.	Apr.	26.	bapt.	Eliz: daughter of William Chance.
1732.	June	20.	bur.	John Chance.
1732.	Nov.	9.	mar.	John Chance and Sarah Lett, both of Allchurch, by lycence.
1732.	Dec.	28.	mar.	Mary Chance and Will: Bate, both of Bromsgrove, by ban :
1734.	Sep.	25.	bapt.	Phebe daughter of William and Elizabeth Chance.
1734.	Dec.	23.	bur.	Elizabeth Chance, widow.
1735.	June	18.	bur.	Elizabeth daughter of Bernerd Chance.
1735.	Aug.	20.	mar.	Elizabeth Chance, of Bromsgrove, and John Brown, solder, by ban :
1736.	Apr.	16.	bur.	William Chance.
[1736.	Sep.	17.	bur.	Aron Chonce.]
1737.	Aug.	27.	bur.	Jane wife of Calib Chance.
1737.	Sep.	21.	bur.	Mary wife of Burnard Chance.
1737.	Nov.	2.	mar.	Catherine Chance, of Bromsgrove, and Thomas Brittel, sojernor, by ban :
1737.	Nov.	16.	bapt.	Mary daughter of William and Elizabeth Chance.
1738.	June	20.	mar.	John Chance, of Oddingley, and Sarah Tibbut, of Elmbridg, by lycence.
1739.	Dec.	27.	bur.	William Chance.
1740.	Apr.	2.	bur.	Calib Chance.
1740.	July	30.	bapt.	Joseph son of William and Elizabeth Chance.
1740-1.	Feb.	9.	mar.	Mr. Willm Chance and Mrs. Hannah Smith, both of Bromsgrove.
1740-1.	Feb.	28.	bur.	Ann Chance, wid: of Catshil.
1741.	Apr.	1.	bapt.	Mary daughter of William and Obedeance Chance.
1742.	Sep.	16.	bur.	Frances Chance, wid :

F

APPENDIX A.—EXTRACTS FROM PARISH REGISTERS.

1742-3.	Jan.	1.	bapt.	Benjamin son of William and Elizabeth Chance.
1742-3.	Mar.	15.	bur.	Hannah wife of Mr. William Chance.
1742-3.	Mar.	24.	bur.	William Chance, of Shepley.
1743.	Oct.	24.	mar.	John Chance and Hannah Hunt, both of Bromsgrove, by lycence.
1744-5.	Feb.	4.	bur.	Mary daughter of John Chance.
1744-5.	Mar.	6.	bapt.	William son of William and Obediane Chance.
1744-5.	Mar.	22.	bur.	Joseph Chance.
1745-6.	Feb.	5.	bur.	Hannah wife of John Chance.
1745-6.	Feb.	9.	bapt.	Lucey Slater daughter of Hannah Chance, a base born.
1746.	Aug.	22.	bur.	Hannah daughter of John Chance.
1746.	Oct.	3.	bur.	Hannah daughter of the wid: Chance.
1746.	Oct.	15.	mar.	John Chance and Mary Tilt, both of Bromsgrove, by lycenc.
1746.	Nov.	1.	bapt.	John son of William and Obediene Chance.
1746-7.	Jan.	5.	bapt.	William son of William and Mary Chance.
1747.	Mar.	31.	bur.	Lucey Slater Chance.
1747.	May	27.	mar.	Benjamin Chance and Mary Fowley, both of Bromsgrove, by ly:
1747.	Oct.	12.	born	Sarah daughter of John and Mary Chance.
1749.	May	16.	born	William son of John and Mary Chance.
1749-50.	Feb.	15.	bur.	John Chance.
1749-50.	Mar.	17.	bapt.	Elizabeth daughter of William and Mary Chance.
1750.	June.	17.	bur.	Mr. Thomas Chance.

Churchwardens:—1622. Thomas Chance.
                  1623. Henry Chance.
                  1626-1628. William Chance.
                  1662. Richard Chance.

b. FROM THE PARISH REGISTERS OF BELBROUGHTON.

| 1656. | Apr. | 18. | mar. | William Chance and Elizabeth Perkes. |
| 1660. | Oct. | 4. | bapt. | William son of William and Elizabeth Chance. |

c. FROM THE PARISH REGISTERS OF BROOME, NEAR STOURBRIDGE.

| 1722. | Oct. | 20. | mar. | William Chance of Bromsgrove and Elizabeth Cole of Broome. |

d. FROM THE PARISH REGISTERS OF BROMSGROVE.

| 1773. | Mar. | 3. | mar. | Sarah Chance, of Bromsgrove, Spinster, and Edward Homer of St. Martin's, Birmingham, Bachelor, by License. |

                                      Witnesses:—Wm Chance Junr and John Southall).

2. BELL.

FROM THE PARISH REGISTERS OF BROMSGROVE.

1755. Sep. 9. Mar. George Bell and Mary Chance, both of Bromsgrove, by License. (Witnesses to this marriage were Joshua and Dorcas Tilt, the father and sister, to wit, of Mary Chance.)

1757. Feb. 11. Born Eliz. ⎫
1760. June 11. Born John ⎬ children of George Bell, of Bromsgrove, Cordwainer, and Mary his wife.
1762. Jan. 2. Born Joshua ⎭

3. TILT.

a. **FROM THE PARISH REGISTERS OF BROMSGROVE.**

(A selection from a large number of entries in the name.)

1590-1. Mar. 7. Bapt. Anne daughter of Henrie Tylte.
1592-3. Mar. 11. Bapt. Richard son of Henrie Tylte.
1594. July 25. Bapt. Venus[1] dau. of Henrie Tylte.
1596. Sep. 29. Bapt. Jhon son of Henrie Tylt.
(There were other Henrie Tyltes at Bromsgrove at this time. One of them was buried 8th Apr. 1597.)
1612. Aug. 3. Bapt. Wyllyam and Henry sons of Wyll'm Tylt.
1612. Aug. 21. Bur. Wyll'm and Henry sons of Wyll'm Tylt.
1613. Sep. 17. Bapt. Elinoure daughter of Willia' Tylte.
1615-6. Jan. 14. Bapt. Willia' son of Willia' Tylte.
1635. Apr. 2. Bur. William Tilt, miller.
1656. Nov. 13. Born Anna daughter of William and Alice Tilt.
1658. July 5. Born Elizabeth daughter of W^m and Alice Tilt.
1658. Dec. 10. Bur. Elizabeth daughter of William and Alice Tilt.
1665-6. Mar. 2. Bapt. Deborah daughter of Willia' Tilt.
1670-1. Mar. 11. Bur. Abell son of Will'm Tillt.
1680. Nov. 8. Bur. Will'm Tillt.
1687. Sep. 30. Born Mary daughter of Caleb Tilt.
1689. Oct. 26. Bur. Will'm son of Calib Tilt.
1690. Sep. 13. Born John son of Caleb Tilt.
1694-5. Mar. 14. Bur. William and Alice children of Calib Tillt.
1716. Aug. 7. Mar. John Tillt and Elizabeth Rose, both of Bromsgrove, by lycence.

[1] She was baptized 25 July 1594. I cannot help thinking that she was the same as Anphilis Tylte (p. 85), who was born in this year.

APPENDIX A.—EXTRACTS FROM PARISH REGISTERS.

1716.	Oct.	16.	Mar.	Mary Tilt of Bromsgrove and John Lord of Stratford (Warw.), by lycence.
1723.	July	1.	Bur.	Sarah daughter of Josuah Tilt.
1726.	July	29.	Bur.	Ann daughter of Josuah Tilt.
1727.	May	29.	Bur.	John son of Joshua Tilt.
1727.	July	28.	Bur.	Caleb Tillt.
1729-30.	Jan.	12.	Bur.	Theado : daughter of Joshua Tilt.
1731.	May	12.	Bur.	John Tilt.
1733.	July	26.	Bur.	Dorcas Tillt wid.

b. From the Parish Registers of Oldswinford (Stourbridge).

1721-2.	Mar.	15.	Mar.	Joshua Tilt and Theodosia Waldron.

4. LUCAS.

a. From the Parish Registers of Rowington.

1638.	Dec.	30.	Bapt.	Clement son of William and Rebbekah Lucas.
1667.	Aug.	13.	Bapt.	Elizabeth daughter of Clement and Dorothy Lucas.
1679.	Apr.	14.	Bur.	William Lucas.
1692.	May	22.	Bapt.	Elizabeth daughter of Clem^t Lucas Ju.
1693.	Sep.	4.	Bapt.	Clement son of Clement Lucas, Ju.
1695.	Aug.	15.	Bapt.	William son of Clem^t Lucas Ju.
1696.	Dec.	20.	Bapt.	John son of Clem^t Lucas Ju.
1702.	Aug.	15.	Bur.	Clem^t Lucas.

b. From the Parish Registers of Hanbury, 1691—1760.

(*List supposed to be complete.*)

1700.	Mar.	30.	Bapt.	Thomas son of Clement Lucus.
1701-2.	Jan.	1.	Bapt.	Joseph son of Clement Lucus.
1703.	Oct.	28.	Bapt.	Margret daughter of Clement Lucus.
1705.	Mar.	28.	Bapt.	Robert son of Clement Lucus.
				(In 1705 and 1706 Clement Lucus was churchwarden.)
1716.	July	5.	Bur.	Benjamin son of Clement Lucus.
1726.	June	10.	Bapt.	Clement son of Clement Lucas Junr.
1728-9.	Jan.	22.	Bapt.	Will. son of Clem^t Lucas Junr.
1730.	July	11.	Bur.	Eliz. wife of Mr. Clement Lucas Senr.
1731.	July	15.	Bur.	Mr. Will. Lucas.

APPENDIX A.—EXTRACTS FROM PARISH REGISTERS. 117

1731-2.	Feb.	23.	Bapt.	John son of Clemment Lucast Ju'.
1734.	June	23.	Bapt.	Margaret daughter of Clement and Anne Lucas.
1736.	Nov.	1.	Bapt.	Robert son of Clement and Anne Lucas.
1738.	Nov.	23.	Bur.	Anne wife of Clement Lucas Jun'.
1739.	June	20.	Mar.	Robert Lucas of Bristol and Elizabeth Butler of Hanbury.
1740-1.	Feb.	16.	Mar.	Clement Lucas Junior and Anne Penrice relict of Robert Penrice.
1741.	Apr.	3.	Bur.	Anne wife of Clement Lucas Junr.
1741.	May	4.	Mar.	Dorothy Lucas and Francis Richards.
				(One of this name was bur. 15 Jan. 1745-6.)
1743.	May	2.	Mar.	Elizabeth Lucas and John Toovey.
1748.	May	12.	Bapt.	Mary daughter of Clement and Mary Lucas of Tardebig.
1749-50.	Feb.	15.	Bur.	John son of Clement Lucas of the Pumphouse.
1753.	Nov.	21.	Bur.	Sarah wife of Clement Lucas.
1754.	Aug.	11.	Bapt.	Elizth daughter of Clement and Mary Lucas.
1754.	June	1.	Bur.	Elizth daughter of Clem^t and Mary Lucas.
				(An apparent confusion in these two entries. They occur in this order in the Register.)
1757.	Sep.	3.	Bur.	Mr. Clement Lucas.
1758.	Jan.	22.	Mar.	Margaret Lucas and William Felton.
				(One of this name was bur. 22 Apr. 1759).

c. FROM THE PARISH REGISTERS OF HADZOR.

1722.	July	2.	Bapt.	Dorothy daughter of Clement and Ann Lucas.

5. TIBBATTS.

FROM THE PARISH REGISTERS OF ROWINGTON.

1663.	May	10.	Bapt.	Elizabeth daughter of Jo: Tibbatts Ju.
1665.	June	6.	Bapt.	Elizabeth daughter of Jo: Tibbatt.
1669.	Nov.	5.	Bapt.	Elizabeth dau. of John and Mary Tibbatts.
				(The entries in the name average at this time more than one per year. Any of these three entries may record the baptism of Elizabeth, wife of Clement Lucas.)

APPENDIX A.—EXTRACTS FROM PARISH REGISTERS.

6. VERNON (ROBERT) AND BUTLER.

a. FROM THE PARISH REGISTERS OF HANBURY.

1609.	June	25.	Bapt.	Ann daughter of Robert Vernon.
1611.	Dec.	8.	Bapt.	Elizabeth daughter of Robert Vernon.
1614-5.	Jan.	1.	Bapt.	Elinor daughter of Robert Vernon.
1616.	Oct.	20.	Bapt.	Sarah daughter of Robert Vernon.
1619-20.	Feb.	6.	Bapt.	Robert son of Robert Vernon.
1622.	Nov.	1.	Bapt.	Alice daughter of Robert Vernon.
1625.	Apr.	3.	Bapt.	Edward son of Robert Vernon.
1644.	June	6.	Bapt.	Alice daughter of Robert Vernon.
1646.	May	21.	Bapt.	Robert son of Robert Vernon.
1648.	Dec.	9.	Bapt.	Ann daughter of Robert Vernon.
1674.	Apr.	30.	Mar.	Robert Vernon and Elizabeth Smith of Stoke Prior.
1674-5.	Feb.	1.	Bapt.	Robert son of Robert Vernon Ju.
1674-5.	Feb.	5.	Bur.	Robert son of Robert Vernon Ju.
1676.	Apr.	25.	Bur.	Sarah daughter of Robert Vernon Ju. of Hadzor.
1681.	Aug.	31.	Bur.	Robert Vernon sen.
1683.	May	10.	Bapt.	Frances daughter of Robert Vernon.
1684.	Oct.	16.	Bapt.	Susannah daughter of Robert Vernon.
1687.	July	28.	Bapt.	Robert son of Robert Vernon.
1689-90.	Mar.	20.	Bapt.	William son of Robert Vernon.
1691-2.	Feb.	4.	Bapt.	Jane daughter of Robert Vernon.
1694.	May	6.	Bapt.	Thomas son of Robert Vernon.
1699.	Nov.	25.	Bur.	Ann daughter of Robert Vernon.
1700.	July	12.	Bur.	Jane daughter of Robert Vernon.

b. FROM THE PARISH REGISTERS OF HADZOR.

1676.	Apr.	13.	Bapt.	Elizabeth and Sarah twin daughters of Robert Vernon.
1677-8.	Jan.	15.	Bapt.	Alice daughter of Robert Vernon.
1680.	May	5.	Bapt.	Ann daughter of Robert & Elizabeth Vernon.
1681.	Oct.	22.	Bapt.	Sarah daughter of Rob : & Eliz : Vernon.

c. FROM THE PARISH REGISTERS OF BROMSGROVE.

1714.	June	22.	Mar.	John Butler and Elizabeth Vernon.
				(That these belonged to Hanbury is shown by their Marriage Bond—Appendix B 5.)

d. FROM THE PARISH REGISTERS OF HANBURY.

1715.	May	26.	Bapt.	Eliz. daughter of John Butler.
1716.	Nov.	11.	Bapt.	Mary daughter of John Butler.
1717-8.	Feb.	20.	Bapt.	Frances daughter of John Butler.

7. HOMER.

a. FROM THE PARISH REGISTERS OF SEDGLEY—1558-1607.

(List supposed to be complete between these dates.)

1560.	June	9.	Bur.	Elizabeth Holmer.
1560-1.	Jan.	20.	Chri.	William Holmer.
1561.	Sep.	8.	Mar.	Katherine Holmer and John Johnson.
1562.	Mar.	27.	Chri.	Thomas Holmer.
1562.	Apr.	11.	Chri.	Isbell Holmer.
1562.	Aug.	16.	Bur.	Margery Holmer.
1562-3.	Jan.	2.	Bur.	Henry Holmer.
1563.	June	4.	Chri.	Agnes Holmer.
1563-4.	Mar.	8.	Chri.	William Holmer.
1564.	Apr.	3.	Bur.	William Holmer.
1564.	Oct.	16.	Mar.	Adam Holmer and Margarett Marlid.
1564.	Oct.	18.	Bur.	Richard Holmer.
1564.	Dec.	7.	Chri.	Ellin Holmer.
1564-5.	Mar.	8.	Chri.	Ann Holmer.
1564-5.	Mar.	20.	Bur.	Willi^m Holmer.
1567.	Oct.	16.	Chri.	Katherin Holmer.
1567-8.	Jan.	4.	Chri.	Phillip Holmer.
1568.	Aug.	3.	Chri.	Thomas Holmer.
1568-9.	Jan.	20	Chri.	Margery Holmer.
1569.	Aug.		Bur.	Phillip Holmer.
1569-70.	Jan.	5.	Chri.	Thomas Holmer.
1570.	June	20.	Chri.	Margarett Holmer.
1570.	July	25.	Chri.	Elizabeth and Ann Holmer.
1571.	Apr.	16.	Bur.	Elizabeth Holmer.
1571.	Aug.	27.	Chri.	Richard Holmer.
1571.	Nov.	5.	Chri.	John Holmer.
1571-2.	Mar.	6.	Bur.	Richard Holmer.
1572-3.	Feb.	21.	Bur.	John Holmer.
1573.	Apr.	22.	Chri.	Joone Holmer.
1573.	Sep.	11.	Chri.	Francis Holmer.
1573.	Oct.	12.	Chri.	Ann Holmer.
1573-4.	Jan.	11.	Bur.	Agnes Holmer.
1574.	Oct.	31.	Chri.	Agnes Holmer.
1574-5.	Jan.	11.	Chri.	Joone Holmer.
1576.	Apr.	22.	Bur.	Thrustan Holmer.
1576.	May	31.	Chri. and bur.	John Holmer.
1579.	May	16.	Mar.	Mary Holmer and Thomas Rogers.

APPENDIX A.—EXTRACTS FROM PARISH REGISTERS.

1580.	Apr.	24.	Mar.	Elizabeth Holmer and John Marsh.
1580.	Oct.	16.	Chri.	Ann or Anne daughter of William Holmer, of Colseley, yeoman.
1582.	June	6.	Chri.	Elizabeth daughter of Richard Holmer naylor.
1583.	June	19.	Bur.	Henry Holmer of Guernall, householder.
1584.	Apr.	7.	Bur.	Francis daughter of William Holmer yo^m.
1584-5.	Jan.	29.	Chri.	Henry son of Richard Holmer naylor.
1585.	Apr.	22.	Mar.	Anne Holmer and Thomas Turner.
1585.	Apr.	22.	Mar.	Thomas Holmer and Anne Turner.
1585.	May	12.	Chri.	Elizabeth daughter of Thomas Holmer yom'.
1585.	June	20.	Bur.	Elizabeth daughter of Thomas Holmer yom'.
1586.	Aug.	11.	Chri.	John son of John Holmer yo^m.
1587-8.	Jan.	12.	Chri.	Thomas son of Richard Holmer naylor.
1588.	July	8.	Chri.	Anne daughter of Thomas Holmer yo^m.
1590.	Apr.	13.	Chri.	Francis son of Thomas Holmer yom'.
1591.	Apr.	28.	Chri.	John son of Richard Holmer naylor.
1591-2.	Mar.	24.	Bur.	Margery wife of Henry Holmer yom'.
1592.	Apr.	9.	Chri.	Ellin daughter of Thomas Holmer yom'.
1593-4.	Jan.	19.	Chri.	Richard son of Richard Holmer nay.
1593-4.	Jan.	27.	Chri.	Henry son of Thomas Holmer yom'.
1596.	Mar.	29.	Chri.	William son of Thomas Holmer yom'.
1598.	Mar.	30.	Chri.	Edward son of Thomas Holmer yom'.
1600.	June	11.	Chri.	Thomas son of Thomas Holmer naylor and Margery Hickmans.
1601.	Sep.	20.	Bur.	Elizabeth wife of Richard Holmer naylor.
1601.	Dec.	16.	Mar.	Margaret daughter of Eve Holmer, wydow, and Edmund Parker, widower.
1606.	July	6.	Chri.	Margrett daughter of Richard Holmer nay.
1606.	Sep.	4.	Bur.	Richard Holmer of Etting naylor.
1607.	June	13.	Bur.	Margarett daughter of Mary Holmer, wydow.

Some later entries are:—

1628.	June	17.	Mar.	Edward Holmer and Elizabeth Willes.
1629.	Oct.	11.	Bapt.	Anne daughter of Edward Homer yeoman.
1631-2.	Jan.	29.	Chri.	Elizabeth daughter of Edward Holmer.
1634.	Nov.(?)	9.	Bapt.	Edward son of Edward Holmer.
1637.	June	15.	Bapt.	Thomas son of Edward and Elizabeth Holmer.
1638-9.	Mar.	24.	Bapt.	Simon son of Edward and Elizabeth Holmer.
1641.	Apr.	19.	Bur.	Edward son of Francis Holmer.
1641-2.	Jan.	21.	Bapt.	Richard son of Edward and Elizabeth Holmer.
1645.	Sep.	28.	Bapt.	Elysabeth daughter of Will'm and Mary Holmer.
1647.	Apr.	19.	Bapt.	Mary daughter of Will'm and Marye Holmer.
1648.	Dec.	10.	Bapt.	Mary daughter of Will'm and Marye Holmer.
1656.				"The purpose of marriage betwixt Edward Homer sonne of Edward Homer and Ann Guibins daughter of the now Widdow Robbins both of the p'ish of Sedgly was published 3 Sabbaths in June and July 1656 at the appoynted time in the p'ish-church of Sedgly aforesaid no one contradicting it and were married with friends cons: before Justice Stone July 16, 1656."

b. FROM THE PARISH REGISTERS OF WATER OUTON (PRESERVED AT ASTON).

Baptisms of Children of Thomas and Elizabeth Homer.

1674.	July	14.	Edward.	1681-2. Feb. 16.	Mary.
1675.	Nov.	30.	William.	1682-3. Feb. 25.	Rebecca.
1677.	Apr.	1.	Thomas.	1683-4. Mar. 10.	Henry.
1679.	May	18.	John.	1685. May 17.	Richard.
1680.	May	13.	Ann.	1687. June 16.	Dorothy.

1683-4. Jan. 20. Mar. Thomas Homer and Mary Holland.

c. FROM THE PARISH REGISTERS OF CASTLE BROMWICH.

1681. June 7. Bapt. Ann daughter of Thomas Homer.

d. FROM THE PARISH REGISTERS OF SUTTON COLDFIELD.

1725.	May	25.	Bur.	Mrs. Elizabeth Homer, widow.
1726.	Aug.	26.	Bur.	A child of Mr. Edward Homer's, named Jane.
1733.	Nov.	17.	Bur.	Mrs.[1] Elizabeth Homer, daughter of Mr. Edward Homer.
1740.	Apr.	19.	Bur.	A child of Mr. Richard Homer, named Mary.
1744-5.	Mar.	7.	Bur.	Mr. Edward Homer sen.
1745-6.	Jan.	11.	Bur.	Mr. Thomas Homer.
1745-6.	Mar.	12.	Bapt.	A child of Mr. Edward Homer, named William.
1749.			Bapt.	A child of Mr. Edward Homer, named Edward Homer.
1750.			Bur.	Mr. Edward Homer jun.[2]
1757.	Mar.	24.	Bur.	The wife of Edward Homer, Gent., named Jane.
1760.			Bur.	Miss Catherine Mary Homer, spinster.

[1] "Mrs." (Mistress) was formerly a title expressing rank or status, and was applied to spinsters as well as to married women.

[2] Not the Deputy-Steward, as he died in 1763. Perhaps a cousin.

APPENDIX B.

WORCESTERSHIRE MARRIAGE BONDS.[1]

(Preserved in the Bishop's Registry, Worcester.)

1. CHANCE.

NOTE.—This list is supposed to be complete, 1660-1725. Only a few bonds of date earlier than 1660 are preserved. The information is chiefly from the calendars of reference; but, where desirable, I have consulted the actual documents. The ages given in these bonds are approximate only.

1660/1. Feb. 6. { John Chance, of Salwarp, husbandman;
Anne Fidkin, of Hartlebury:
  To be married at Worcester Cathedral.

1661. June 5. { John Chance, of Bromsgrove, tanner, aged 60, widower;
Mary Lawrence, of Broughton Hackett, aged 60, widow:
  To be married at Broughton Hackett, or Upton Snodsbury.
  Bondsman: John Ganderton, of Upton Snodsbury, husbandman.

1663. May 23. { Thomas Chaunce, of St. Andrew's, Worcester, dyer, aged 25, bachelor;
Beatrice Ayleway, of the same, aged 21, parents dead:
  To be married at St. Andrew's, or at the Cathedral.

1664/5. Jan. 18. { Richard Chaunce, of Worcester, aged 25, bachelor;
Joane Nicholls, of Worcester, aged 20, maiden, parents dead:
  To be married at St. Peter's, Worcester.

1665/6. Jan. 20. "Caveat" entered against granting Marriage-license to William Saunders, of Ombersley, bachelor, and Elizabeth Chaunce, of Newland (Salwarp), maiden.

1666. Nov. 22. { William Chaunce, of St. Andrew's, Worcester, aged 23, bachelor;
———— Bound, of St. Clement's, Worcester, aged 30, maiden, dau. of John Bound, of that parish, "walker and clothier"[2]:
  To be married at Powick.
  Bondsman: Thomas Knight, of Worcester.

1667. Apr. 12. { Warner Chaunce, of Worcester, aged 22, bachelor;
Elizabeth Jordan, of All Saints, Worcester, aged 20, maiden, parents dead; her guardian George Oswald of Worcester:
  To be married at All Saints, Worcester.

[1] Cp. p. 64, note 1.   [2] See p. 19, note.

APPENDIX B.—MARRIAGE BONDS.

1668. June 2. { Edward Morgan, of Chaddesley Corbet, husbandman, aged 40, widower;
Katharine Chaunce, of Dodderhill, aged 40, maiden, parents dead:
To be married at Chaddesley Corbet or Dodderhill.

1678. Aug. 31. { Warner Chance, of St. Andrew's, Worcester, widower;
Sarah Brinton, of All Saints, Worcester, maiden.

1678. Nov. 9. { William Chance, of Chaddesley Corbet, aged 32, bachelor;
Anne Barber, of Hartlebury, aged 32, maiden:
To be married at Upton Warren, Rushock, or Doverdale.

1680. Aug. 19. { John Chance jun., of St. Andrew's, Worcester, bachelor;
Mary Allen, of Worcester, aged 25, maiden:
To be married at All Saints, Worcester.

1683. Oct. 6. { John Chance, of Shepley, Bromsgrove, husbandman, widower;
Rebeckah Blick, of Bromsgrove, aged 50, maiden:
Married at Bromsgrove same day.
Bondsman: William Herbert, of Bromsgrove.

1684. Dec. 16. { Thomas Chance, of Himbleton, aged 28, bachelor;
Anne Crumpe, of Deane Dish, Inkberrow, aged 28, maiden:
To be married at Oddingley or Salwarp.

1685/6. Jan. 27. { Richard Chance, of St. Andrew's, Worcester, widower;
Susanna Hill, of Hollow, maiden.

1688. May 5. { Christopher Chance, of St. Andrew's, Worcester, aged 25, bachelor;
Mary Reynolds, of St. Clement's, Worcester, aged 20, maiden.

1690/1. Jan. 13. { John Callowe, of Dormeston, aged 22, bachelor;
Mary Chance, of St. Andrew's, Worcester, aged 19, maiden.

1693/4. Mar. 19. Anthony Chance and Mary Nash. (See p. 27.)

1694. July 7. { John Chance, of Kidderminster, aged 53, widower;
Bridget Clark, of St. Peter's, Droitwich, aged 53, widow:
To be married at Kidderminster Parish Church.
Bondsman: Thomas Yarnold, of Kidderminster.

1695. Apr. 13. { William Chance, of Salwarp, aged 40, widower;
Mary Watmore, of the same, aged 30, maiden:
To be married at Rushock.
Bondsman: George Hay, of Oddingley, yeoman.

1695. Oct. 1. { Richard Moore, of Tardebig, widower;
Catherine Chance, of Bromsgrove, aged 25, maiden:
To be married at Bromsgrove or "Cawfton" Hackett.
Bondsman: John Wallis, of Bromsgrove.

1695/6. Jan. 9. { Christopher Chance, of Inkberrow, husbandman;
Sarah Yates, of Hanbury, aged 24, maiden:
To be married at Bromsgrove or Hanbury.
Bondsman: George Yates, of Hanbury.

1695/6. Feb. 24. { Charles Chance, of Oddingley, husbandman, aged 27, bachelor;
Anne Hay, of the same, aged 22, maiden:
To be married at Oddingley.
Bondsman: Thomas Fincher, of Hanbury, husbandman.

APPENDIX B.—MARRIAGE BONDS.

1697. Dec. 18. { William Chance, of Salwarp, aged 23, bachelor ;
Hannah Dugard, of the same, aged 24, maiden :
To be married at Worcester Cathedral.

1706. May 20. { John Chance, of St. Clement's, Worcester, aged 22, bachelor ;
Sibilla Parnell, of the Cathedral Precincts, aged 23, maiden :
To be married at the Cathedral, or St. Clement's, Worcester, or Kemsey, or Ripple.

1706/7. Jan. 9. { John Chance, of Tardebig, aged 30, bachelor ;
Susanna Hunt, of the same, aged 30, maiden :
To be married at Tardebig, or St. Helen's, Worcester.

1708. Nov. 15. { William Chance, of Moore, Fladbury, aged 34, bachelor ;
Elizabeth Philips, of the same, aged 40, widow :
To be married at All Saints, Evesham.

1710. Nov. 18. { Richard Chance, of Hartlebury, aged 22, bachelor ;
Mary Let, of Wisher, aged 23, maiden :
To be married at Hartlebury.

1710. Nov. 27. { William Chance, of Solihull, aged 37, bachelor ;
Anna Pointer, of Beoley, aged 30, widow :
To be married at Beoley or Chaddesley Corbet.

1711/2. Jan. 5. { Joseph Chance, of St. Andrew's, Droitwich, aged 27, bachelor ;
Ann Bourn, of the same, aged 24, maiden :
To be married at St. Andrew's, Droitwich, or St. Michael's, Bedwardine.

1712/3. Jan. 31. { Benjamin Chance, of Bromsgrove, aged 23, bachelor ;
Hannah Butler, of the same, aged 32, maiden :
To be married at Bromsgrove or Chaddesley Corbet.

1716. Apr. 2. { Edward Chance, of Chaddesley Corbet, aged 25, bachelor ;
Mary Bridges, of Bromsgrove, aged 24, maiden :
Married at Bromsgrove same day.

1716. Sep. 20. { William Chance, of Bromsgrove, aged 26, bachelor ;
Mary Arden, of Upton Warren, widow :
To be married at Dodderhill.

1716. Sep. 25. { John Chance, of St. Clement's, Worcester, aged 30, widower ;
Mary Haynes, of All Saints, Worcester, aged 30, maiden :
To be married at All Saints, St. Clement's, or St. Andrew's; all in Worcester.

1718. Sep. 22. { Richard Chance, of Lower Mitton (Kidderminster), aged 30, widower ;
Martha Addis, of All Saints, Worcester, aged 40, " soluta."
To be married at St. Clement's, Worcester, or St. Oswald's Chapel.

1719. Oct. 1. { John Chance, of Wellford, Glouc., aged 22, bachelor ;
Margaret Price, of Cleeve Prior, aged 21, maiden :
To be married at Cleeve Prior, or St. Swithin's, Worcester.

1721/2. Jan. 25. { Joseph Chance, of Chaddesley Corbet, husbandman, aged 40, widower ;
Elizabeth Hooman, of the same, aged 30, maiden :
To be married at Chaddesley Corbet or Rushock.
Bondsman : John Raybold, of Rushock, husbandman.

APPENDIX B.—MARRIAGE BONDS.

1722. Oct. 16. { William Chance, jun., of Bromsgrove, yeoman, aged 30, bachelor;
Elizabeth Cole, of Broome, aged 25, maiden:
    Married at Broome, Oct. 20th.
    Bondsman: William Chance, sen., of Bromsgrove, yeoman.

1722/3. Feb. 12. { John Chance, of Bromsgrove, yeoman, aged 22, bachelor;
Anne Dewce, of the same, aged 22, maiden:
    To be married at Bromsgrove, Stone, or Mitton Chapel.
    Bondsman: Joseph White, of Kidderminster.

1722/3. Feb. 18. { John Wilkes, of Belbroughton, aged 45, bachelor;
Anne Chance, of Bromsgrove, aged 30, maiden:
    Married at Bromsgrove.
    Bondsman: John Chance, of Bromsgrove.

1725. Apr. 9. { Thomas Chance, of Bromsgrove, Gent., aged 25, bachelor;
Mrs.[3] Sarah Vernon, of the same, aged 28, maiden:
    To be married at Bromsgrove, Shrawley, or Upton Warren.
    Bondsman: Thomas Vernon, of Bromsgrove, Gent.

1725. May 18. { John Barrett, of Great Whitley, yeoman, aged 22, bachelor;
Mary Chance, of Bromsgrove, aged 30, singlewoman:
    To be married at St. Michael's, Bedwardine.

1725. May 19. { Henry Chance, of Claines, wheelwright, aged 27, bachelor;
Jane Lyes, of the same, aged 33, singlewoman:
    To be married at Claines.
    Bondsman: William Watkins, of Whitstones, Claines.

1725. Nov. 30. { William Albot, of Stoke Prior, aged 25, widower;
Hannah Chance, of Bromsgrove, aged 25, maiden:
    Married at Bromsgrove same day.
    Bondsman: William Chance, of Bromsgrove.

1743. Oct. { John Chance, of Bromsgrove, cordwainer;
Hannah Hunt, spinster:
    Married at Bromsgrove, Oct. 24th.
    Bondsman: William Chance, of Bromsgrove, saddler.

1746. Oct. { John Chance, of Bromsgrove, mercer;
Mary Tilt, singlewoman:
    Married at Bromsgrove, Oct. 15th.
    Bondsman: William Chance, of Bromsgrove, saddler.

[3] See p. 121, note 1.

APPENDIX B.—MARRIAGE BONDS.

2. TILT.

1663. Sep. 10. { William Tilt, of Bromsgrove, aged 34, bachelor;
Elizabeth Derling, of the same, aged 25, maiden:
To be married at St. Helen's or St. Peter's, Worcester.
1667. Aug. 3. Henry Tilt and Elizabeth Cole, both of Belbroughton.
1672/3. Feb. 6. Thomas Tilt and Hannah Cookes, both of Bromsgrove.
1674. Aug. 14. { Thomas Tilt, of Bromsgrove, aged 26, widower;
Mary Laurimore, of the same, aged 26, maiden:
To be married at Bromsgrove.
1678. Sep. 14. William Tilt, bachelor, and Sarah Jefferies, maiden, both of Bromsgrove.
1681. May. Thomas Tilt and Anne Lilly, both of Bromsgrove.
1681. June 25. { William Tilt, of Bromsgrove, aged 27, widower;
Rebecca Payton, of Tardebig, aged 25, maiden:
To be married at Bromsgrove, Tardebig, or Upton Warren.
(Rebecka Tilt, widow, was buried at Bromsgrove 12 Feb. 1719-20.)
1697. July 16. { Henry Tilt, of Bromsgrove, aged 25, bachelor;
Mary Brittaine, of the same, aged 25, maiden:
To be married at All Saints, Worcester.
1698. Aug. 11. { William Tilt, of Bromsgrove, aged 29, bachelor;
Anne Cookes, of the same, aged 36, widow:
To be married at Hartlebury or Bromsgrove.
1708. Dec. 3. Henry Tilt, bachelor, and Catherine Elvins, widow, both of Bromsgrove:
To be married at Bromsgrove.
1710. Sep. 11. { John Tilt, of Bromsgrove, aged 30, bachelor;
Mary Cotterill, of the same, aged 22, maiden:
To be married at Worcester Cathedral, or Bromsgrove.
1716. Aug. 6. { John Tilt, of Bromsgrove, aged 25, bachelor;
Elizabeth Rose, of the same, aged 23, maiden:
Married at Bromsgrove Aug. 7th.
1720. Nov. 21. { William Tilt, of Bromsgrove, aged 21, bachelor;
Elizabeth Perkins, of the same, aged 23, maiden:
Married at Bromsgrove Nov. 22nd.
1721/2. Mar. 10. { Joshuah Tilt, of Bromsgrove, yeoman, aged 25, widower;
Theodosia Waldron, of Oldswinford, aged 27, widow:
Married at Oldswinford, Mar. 15th.
Bondsman: John Tilt, of Bromsgrove, yeoman.
1722. Mar. 30. { Joseph Lees, of Bromsgrove, yeoman, aged 50, widower;
Sarah Tilt, of the same, aged 55, widow:
Bondsman: Thomas Wright, of Bromsgrove.

I have only found two other Marriage-bonds in the name: one for Henry Tilt, of Whitstones (Claines); the other for William Tilt, of Beaudley, Herefordshire.

3. LUCAS. (A SELECTION.)

1691. May 22. { Clement Lucas, of Rowington, aged 23 (or 28 ?), bachelor;
Elizabeth Tibbits, of the same, aged 27, maiden:
　　To be married at St. Nicholas', Warwick.
　　Bondsmen: John Tibbats of Rowington, and Thomas Slye, innholder, of Warwick.

1721. Apr. 6. { Clement Lucas, of Hadzor, yeoman, aged 27, bachelor;
Anne Lilly, of Dodderhill, aged 20, singlewoman:
　　To be married at Hadzor, Dodderhill, or St. Michael's, Bedwardine.
　　Bondsman: Robert Wakeman, of St. Michael's, Bedwardine.

1722. Dec. 6. { Thomas Lucas, of Hanbury, aged 24, bachelor;
Anne Olives, of Dodderhill, aged 19, spinster:
　　To be married at St. Martin's, Worcester.
　　Bondsman: Charles Olives (or Oliffs), of Dodderhill.

1724. May 12. { Samuel Lucas, of Hanbury, aged 23, bachelor;
Anne Thompson, of St. Nicholas', Droitwich, aged 22, spinster:
　　To be married at Worcester Cathedral, or at St. Peter's, Worcester.
　　Bondsman: William Boraston, of Rock, yeoman.

1739. June 14. { Robert Lucas, of St. Wiburg [St. Werburgh's], Bristol, aged 34, bachelor;
Elizabeth Butler, of Hanbury, aged 24, spinster:
　　Married at Hanbury, June 20th.
　　Bondsman: Samuel Lucas, of Claines.

4. TIBBATTS.

1676. Apr. 18. { Robert Tibbats, of Rowington, aged 28, bachelor;
Alice Tibbats, of the same, aged 23, maiden:
　　To be married at Rowington or Preston Baggott.

1682. May 27. { John Tibbotts, of Arrow, aged 24, bachelor;
Jane Willis, of Inkberrow, aged 21, maiden:
　　To be married at Inkberrow, or at All Saints, Evesham.
　　Bondsman: Robert Willis, of Peopleton, yeoman.

1695. Nov. 27. { Samuel Tibbits, of Rowington, aged 25, bachelor;
Sarah Green, of Old Stratford, aged 22, maiden:
　　To be married at St. Nicholas', Warwick.
　　Bondsman: Rowland Green, of Rowington, husbandman.

1696/7. Feb. 2. { Samuel Tibbets, of Tanworth, aged 30, bachelor;
Anne Bradnock, of the same, aged 24, maiden:
To be married at St. Nicholas, Worcester (or Warwick?).

1708. Nov. 18. { Clement Tibbatts, of Rowington, aged 28, bachelor;
Elizabeth Watton, of St. Mary's, Warwick, aged 24, maiden:
To be married at St. Mary's, Warwick.

---

5. BUTLER. (A SELECTION.)

1664-5. Jan. 13. { John Butler, of Feckenham, aged 30, bachelor;
Elizabeth Perks, of the same, aged 21, maiden, parents dead; guardian,
her brother William Perkes, of Feckenham, yeoman.
To be married at Feckenham or Bradley.

1668. May 22. { James Yeate, of Hanbury, aged 24, bachelor;
Elianor Butler, of the same, aged 22, maiden, dau. of Robert Butler, of
Hanbury, husbandman.
To be married at St. Clement's, Worcester.

1669. Aug. 10. { John Butler, of Bromsgrove, aged 26, bachelor;
Mary Hollyman, of the same, aged 26, maiden:
To be married at Alvechurch.

1675. Apr. 3. { Joseph Butler, of Bromsgrove, bachelor;
Susanna Hinckley, of Northfield, maiden:
To be married at Northfield.

1679. May 5. { Robert Butler, of Bromsgrove, aged 31, bachelor;
Mary Lyes, of Claines, aged 31, maiden:
To be married at St. Helen's, Worcester, or at the Cathedral.

1682. Sept. 17. { Gilbert Butler, of Bromsgrove, aged 24, bachelor;
Elizabeth Crab, of the same, aged 28, maiden:
To be married at St. Swithin's or St. Helen's, Worcester.

1714. June 22. { John Butler, of Hanbury, aged 28, bachelor;
Elizabeth Vernon, of the same, aged 30, maiden:
Married at Bromsgrove same day.

6. VERNON (ROBERT).

1674. Apr. 25. { Robert Vernon, of Hanbury, aged 28, bachelor ;
Elizabeth Smith, of Stoke Prior, aged 23, maiden :
Married at Hanbury Apr. 30th.

7. NASH.

1690. Oct. 2. { Jonathan Nash, of Hanbury, aged 21, bachelor ;
Mary Hanbury, of the same, aged 24, maiden :
To be married at Hanbury.
1720. July 26. { Jonathan Nash, of Pirton, aged 22, bachelor ;
Anne Nicholls, of Churchlench, aged 25, maiden :
To be married at Birlingham.
1739. Nov. 1. { Goodwin Nash, of Tarbick [Tardebig], Warw., aged 37, bachelor ;
Alice Miles, of Stratford-on-Avon, aged 26, maiden : ·
To be married at St. Mary's, Warwick.
Bondsman : George Hower, of Warwick.

The name of Nash occurs very frequently among the Marriage-Bonds. I have selected the above three, because it was a Jonathan, son of Goodwin Nash, whom Margaret Lucas married.

Appendix C.

TOMBSTONE INSCRIPTIONS.

1 and 2 see pp. 7, 8.

3. In St. Paul's Churchyard, Birmingham.
(The Inscription all in Capital letters: the words " In Memory of " in Old English letters)

In Memory of
Mary Ann Daughter of
William and Sarah Chance
Who died April 4th 1787
Aged 12 months.
Also William their Son
Who died September 6th 1787
Aged 6 years & 10 months.
Likewise John their Son
Who died May 26th 1792
Aged 8 years.
Also Caroline their
Daughter
Who died February 4th 1818
Aged 19 years.
Likewise
Charlotte Chance
Who died June 2nd 1827
Aged 31 years.

In Memory of
Sarah Wife of
William Chance
Who died September 7th 1809
Aged 53 years.
Also William Chance
Who died March 21st 1828
Aged 78 years.

The inscription was recut and the stone reset on its old site in June 1872. The grave was at the same time newly turfed, and a kerb put round.

[Note of Mr. Edw. Sargant.]

Close by is the tombstone commemorating Elizabeth and William Sargant (p. 59). his parents, and four of his children who died in infancy.

4. From Nash, "History of Worcestershire," s.v. Bromsgrove.

"At the lowest step of the Chancel lieth William Chance died May 3. 1622. Arms of Barnesley. Also Anne his wife, daughter of Christopher Dineley, and her sister Elizabeth. wife of Thomas Russell."

There were three separate stones. The first had the Arms of Barnesley, the others those of Dineley.

For the Barnesleys, see p. 25.

5. From Nash, *ibid.*, s.v. Hadzor (Hadsor).
"Christopher Chawnce lieth here buried A.D. 1625. He was descended from the Bardesleys whose Arms are here."
C. C. really died, as appears from the dates of his will, in Mar. 1623-4 or Apr. 1624.

6. From Nash, *ibid.*, s.v. St. Andrew's, Worcester. (App. p. cxxvii.)
"Mr. Richard Chance, clothier, Jan. 27. 1687 aged 48.
Joan his wife August 12. 1684 aged 43."

7. From Valentine Green, "History of Worcester." (App. p. cxi.)
In St. John's, Bedwardine.
"Beatrix Wife of Thomas Chaunce died 20th Aug. 1676, aged 34. Mr. Thos. Chaunce, late one of the Common Council of the City of Worcester, died 12th Oct. 1691, aged 56."

8. From Nash, *ibid.*, s. v. Bromsgrove.
"In Memory of the Dead.
From the year 1618 to 1739 lieth buried near to this stone 19 bodies of the present family of the Claues o' Cateshill, and on the 15th of March '42 was interred Hannah the wife of William Chanes gent. She was aged 42 years and 5 months."

The word Claues should obviously be Chanes, and was probably misread by Nash; that Chanes stands for Chance appears from the entry in the Parish Register for 15th March 1742-3 (p. 114).

The stone is close to the "Chance Monument" (No. 10—below), and the inscription is now all but illegible. The William Chance mentioned is certainly the person commemorated by the "Chance Monument."

9. Copied from a Stone close by the last by Mr. Edward Sargant (and also by Dr. Frank Chance).
"Here was interred the body of Nicholas Chaunce. He died April ye 1. 1709 aged 48 years. Also Lydia his widow died September 6. 1720 aged 60 years. Here was interred the body of John Chaunce son of the above . . . . . died Septr. ye 6. 1724 aged 28 years."
(There follow four lines of small letters—quite illegible.)
"Here was interred the body of Elizabeth Chaunce. She died on the 27th day of January 1759 aged 70 years."

The persons here commemorated belonged to a younger branch of the Catshill Chances (see p. 27). Elizabeth was an unmarried daughter of Nicholas.

10. The "Chance Monument" in Bromsgrove Churchyard consists of a recumbent figure on a plinth surrounded by a high iron railing. There was formerly a brass plate affixed, which has long been stolen. Nash (s.v. Bromsgrove) has preserved the inscription which was on the plate as follows:—

Erected
To the Memory
of
Wm Chance Gent.
obiit Feb. 5
1768.
Aet. 82.

APPENDIX C.—TOMBSTONE INSCRIPTIONS.

My uncle Mr. William Chance wrote of this Monument in his diary (1856):—
"Monument to William Chance, Gent., who died Feby. 23. 1768, aged 82. A figure covered with drapery. Head reclining on a pillow with tassels. Plain headdress. Arms and hands resting on the breast, feet at the side of the tombstone. Admirably executed by a miller. Palisade of wrought iron bars. All in excellent taste. The brass plate has been stolen."

We do not expect "admirable" sculpture from a miller, but Nash's epithet "clumsy" is too strong. As to the date, Feb. 25. 1768 is probably correct, as the burial took place on the 28th.

William Chance was a leading parishioner of Bromsgrove, and was the last of the Chances of Catshill. His will, proved in London 17 Mar. 1768, contains minute directions to three Trustees for the erection of the Monument. The legatees were his nephews William Chance of Upton-on-Severn, and John Smith. To the former the next inscription (No. 11) relates.

11. On a Stone lying flat at the chancel end of the north aisle of the old Parish Church of Upton-on-Severn.

Underneath in a Vault
lie interred the remains of Sarah
Chance Wife of Thomas Chance of
Bromsgrove and
Daughter of Richard Vernon
of Hanbury in this County
who died September 1777 Aged 85
And Elizabeth Chance her Daughter
who died 1754 Aged 27
Likewise William Chance
Son to the abovenamed Sarah Chance
who died Sepr 3rd 1779 Aged 54
And Barbara his Wife
who died August 1793 Aged 66
Also six of their Children Viz^t
Barbara Chance
died March 1772 Aged 16
John Chance
died March 1784 Aged 27
Letitia Chance
died August 1792 Aged 27
Likewise Elizabeth William & Elizabeth
who died in their Infancy.

Appendix D.

WILLS AND ADMINISTRATIONS.

(Note.—*The usual abbreviation for the latter word is Admon.*)

1. CHANCE.

a. Worcester Probate Registry.

proved				*dated*
1542.	John Chawnse the elder		Bromsgrove	20 Apr. 1542
1542.	John Chawnse the younger		Bromsgrove (Tymberhonger)	10 May 1542
1545.	Isabell Chawnce		Bromsgrove	6 Nov. 1545
1547.	Nicholas Chawnse		Bromsgrove	30 Sep. 1546
1557.	Emelen Chawnse		Kidderminster	Admon.
1558.	Rychard Chawnce		Bromsgrove	1 Sept. 1558
1567.	Hewgh Chawnce		Bromsgrove	12 June 1566
1567.	Nicholas Chawnce		Bromsgrove	Admon.
1569.	Rychard Chaunce	weaver	Worcester (Alsainctes)	1 Feb. 1568-9
1570.	Gilbert Chaunce		Bromsgrove	Admon.
1576.	Richard Chance		Bromsgrove (Borneheath)	30 Dec. 1575
1584.	William Chaunce		Bromsgrove	Admon.
1586.	Elianor Chaunce	widow	Bromsgrove (Shepley)	28 Oct. 1585
1586.	Henrie Chaunce		Bromsgrove (Timberhonger)	7 Dec. 1585
1610.	Richard Chaunce		Bromsgrove	

(Will lost: only the inventory of goods, taken 25 May 1610, preserved.)
In the rest of the Wills I have not preserved the original name-spellings.

1615.	John Chance	yeoman	Bromsgrove (Bournheath)	
1616.	Thomas Chance		Bromsgrove	2 Mar. 1615-6
1618.	John Chance	mason	Bromsgrove (Shepley)	12 Feb. 1617-8
1622.	William Chance	yeoman	Bromsgrove	18 May 1618
1624.	Christopher Chance	gent.	Hadzor	3 Mar. 1623-4
1624.	William Chance	clothier	Worcester	4 May 1624
1624.	Henry Chance	weaver	Bromsgrove	13 Sept. 1624
1633.	Nicholas Chance	husbandman	Kidderminster (Oldington)	13 Dec. 1632

APPENDIX D.—WILLS AND ADMINISTRATIONS.

proved				dated
1639.	Anne Chance	widow	Upton Snodsbury	1 Apr. 1638
1640.	Nicholas Chance	blacksmith	Bromsgrove	11 July 1640
1648.	Gilbert Chance		Chaddesley Corbet	Admon.
1649.	Gilbert Chance	shoemaker	Bromsgrove	2 Dec. 1646
1649.	Thomas Chance	gent.	Hadzor	17 July 1648

For the next decade (the Commonwealth) the Wills are not preserved at Worcester.

1663.	Thomas Chance		Hanbury (Broughton)	Admon.
1670.	John Chance	yeoman	Bromsgrove (Shepley)	17 Sept. 1669
1670.	Eleanor Chance	widow	Bromsgrove (Rosemary Lane)	1 Feb. 1669-70
1670.	John Chance		Bedwardine (St. John's)	Admon.
1671.	Anne Chance	widow	Bromsgrove (Shepley)	Admon.
1676.	William Chance	yeoman	Salwarp (Newland)	13 Jan. 1674-5
1682.	Nicholas Chance	yeoman	Bromsgrove (Catshill)	19 Aug. 1681
1685.	Mary Chance	spinster	Bromsgrove	Admon.
1686.	Richard Chance	yeoman	Bromsgrove (Catshill)	30 June 1686
1688.	Thomas Chance		Worcester (St. Clement's)	Admon.
1689.	Anne Chance	widow	Salwarp (Newland)	24 May 1689
1689.	William Chance		Bromsgrove	Admon.
1691.	Thomas Chance	dyer	Worcester (St. Clement's)	11 Oct. 1691
1702.	John Chance	weaver	Bromsgrove	10 Oct. 1701
1703.	Joan Chance	widow	,, (Catshill)	13 Nov. 1690
1703.	William Chance	yeoman	,, (Fockbury)	3 June 1702
1704.	Joan Chance	widow	Pershore (Abbot's Wood, Holy Cross)	25 June 1704
1705.	William Chance	weaver	Bromsgrove (Bournheath)	3 Jan. 1704-5
1705.	John Chance jun.	innholder	Worcester (St. Clement's)	14 Mar. 1703-4
1705.	John Chance	yeoman	Warndon	19 Feb. 1704-5
1709.	Nicholas Chance	yeoman	Bromsgrove (Bournheath)	28 Mar. 1709
1710.	John Chance		Bromsgrove (Catshill)	9 Apr. 1709
1711.	Anthony Chance	yeoman	Bromsgrove (Bournheath)	8 Nov. 1707
1712.	John Chance	yeoman	Bromsgrove (Bournheath)	21 Nov. 1711
1715.	William Chance sen.		Chaddesley Corbet (Drayton)	1 June 1715
1716.	Elizabeth Chance	spinster	Worcester (St. Nicholas)	7 Nov. 1713
1717.	Mary Chance		Worcester (St. Clement's)	Admon.
1717.	Anthony Chance	skinner (?)	Bromsgrove	5 Mar. 1716-7
1717.	Edward Chance	bachelor	Warndon (Smite)	17 May 1717
1718.	Richard Chance	weaver	Stoke Prior	7 Mar. 1717-8
1720.	Richard Chance		Hartlebury	Admon.
1721.	Henry Chance		Stourbridge	Admon.
1724.	Elizabeth Chance	widow	Worcester (St. Nicholas)	25 Apr. 1723
1725.	John Chance	yeoman	Bromsgrove (Bournheath)	Admon.
1726.	Susanna Chance	widow	Upton-on-Severn	3 Oct. 1721
1726.	William Chance		Oddingley	2 Oct. 1726
1727.	James Chance		Doddenham	Admon.
1729.	Joseph Chance		Chaddesley Corbet (Oakeboul)	11 May 1729
1729.	Henry Chance		Upton-on-Severn	Admon.
1734.	Anne Chance	widow	Oddingley	Admon.

APPENDIX D.—WILLS AND ADMINISTRATIONS.

proved   *dated*

proved	Name		Place	dated
1738.	Margaret Chance	spinster	Warndon	
1740.	William Chance	yeoman	Bromsgrove (Burcott)	25 Sept. 1730
1741.	Richard Chance		Kidderminster (Lower Mitton)	21 Apr. 1741
1743.	Frances Chance	widow	Bromsgrove (Shepley)	13 July 1741
1743.	William Chance	yeoman	Bromsgrove (Shepley)	22 Mar. 1742-3

The above list I believe to be exhaustive. The following are a few of later date, which I have consulted.

1759.	Elizabeth Chance	spinster	Belbroughton	22 Feb. 1743-4
1761.	Benjamin Chance sen.		Bromsgrove	Admon.
1765.	Joseph Chance	dealer in flax	Droitwich	24 Mar. 1762
1769.	William Chance	yeoman	Bromsgrove	4 Oct. 1768
1773.	Benjamin Chance	victualler	Droitwich	13 May 1771
1774.	John Chance	cordwainer	Bromsgrove	20 Feb. 1749-50
1775.	John Chance		Droitwich	Admon.

b. WORCESTERSHIRE WILLS AT SOMERSET HOUSE.

1591.	Nicholas Chaunce	yeoman	Hoblonch	
1606.	William Chaunce	yeoman	Harvington	14 Oct. 1605
1610.	John Chaunce		Hadzor	5 Feb. 1609-10
1652.	Anthony Chance	"trowman"	Worcester	4 Apr. 1652
1656.	Thomas Chaunce	gent.	Hadzor	17 July 1648

Same Will proved at Worcester 1649.

1658.	Henry Chance		Worcester	Admon.
1684.	Christopher Chaunce	clothier	Worcester (St. Andrew's)	26 Feb. 1683-4
1688.	Richarde Chance	clothier	Worcester (St. Andrew's)	12 Apr. 1686
1703.	Susanna Chance		Worcester	Admon.
1706.	John Chance	"trowman"	Worcester (St. Andrew's)	22 Sept. 1706

Besides these there are some 19 other Wills and Administrations in the name of Chance at Somerset House, from the earliest times to 1750 (see Appendix H). The scanty occurrence of the name is quite surprising.

Among the Wills of later date are:—

1768.	William Chance	gent.	Bromsgrove (Catshill)	15 May 1766
1774.	Thomas Chance		Bromsgrove	9 May 1774
1802.	William Chance	gent.	Bromsgrove	31 Mar. 1802
				codicil 24 Apr. 1802

2. BELL.

WORCESTER PROBATE REGISTRY.

proved   *dated*

1779.	Christopher Bell		Bromsgrove	Admon.
1791.	George Bell	cordwainer	Bromsgrove	28 July 1782

APPENDIX D.—WILLS AND ADMINISTRATIONS.

3. TILT.

WORCESTER PROBATE REGISTRY.

proved				dated
1575.	John Tyllett sen.		"Kethermyster"	23 Oct. 1574
1606.	Henry Tylte		Bromsgrove	2 Sept. 1606
1609.	Thomas Tylte	bricklayer	Bromsgrove	21 Nov. 1608
1624.	John Tylt		Bromsgrove	Admon.
1624.	Thomas Tylt		Bromsgrove	Admon.
1626.	Alice Tylt		Bromsgrove	Admon.
1634.	William Tylt	"milleard"	Bromsgrove	10 Nov. 1634
1667.	John Tilt		Worcester (Cathedral Precincts)	
1668.	Henry Tylt	yeoman	Stoke Prior	20 Feb. 1667-8
1672.	Abell Tilt, son of William Tilte,		Bromsgrove	Admon.
1676.	John Tilt		Worcester (St. Helen's)	Admon.
1679.	Henry Hill	yeoman	Bromsgrove & Stoke Prior	16 Dec. 1678
1680.	John Tilt	"millerd"	Kidderminster	18 Dec. 1680
1681.	William Tilt sen.	{"maulster" & alderman}	Bromsgrove town	14 Apr. 1680
1686.	Thomas Tylt	maltster	Bromsgrove	31 Dec. 1685
1686.	Henry Tilt	shoemaker	Bromsgrove	14 Nov. 1685
1699.	William Tilt		Bromsgrove	Admon.
1699.	John Hill	Rector of Upton Warren		8 Aug. 1699
1705.	Henry Tilt	butcher	Bromsgrove	19 Apr. 1705
1705.	John Tilt	yeoman	Stoke Prior	31 Jan. 1692
				codicil 30 June 1705
1706.	Joyce Tilt		Stoke Prior	Admon.
1708.	Thomas Tilt	baker	Bromsgrove	24 Jan. 1705-6
	(brother of the two last)			codicil 31 July 1708
1709.	Henry Tilt		Bromsgrove	
	(His widow Ursula was buried at Bromsgrove 27 July 1716.)			
1714.	Mary Tilt	an old widow	Bromsgrove	27 Oct. 1713
1716.	William Tilt	feltmaker	Bromsgrove	6 May 1709
1716.	Henry Tilt		Bromsgrove	
1716.	John Tylt	yeoman	Bromsgrove	Nov. 1715
1727.	Thomas Tilt		Bromsgrove	Admon.
1727.	Caleb Tilt	gent.	Bromsgrove	18 May 1727
1730.	Charles Tilt		Bromsgrove	
1731.	John Tilt	baker	Bromsgrove	13 Feb. 1730-1
1733.	Dorcas Tilt	widow	Bromsgrove	8 July 1731
1748.	John Tilt		Stoke Prior	
1750.	Caleb Tilt	baker & miller	Bromsgrove	17 July 1750
1759.	John Tilt	"bailief"	Bromsgrove (Bournheath)	17 Sept. 1759

APPENDIX D.—WILLS AND ADMINISTRATIONS.

proved				dated	
1763.	Sarah Tilt	widow	Bromsgrove (Bournheath)	14 Oct.	1761
1766.	Joshua Tilt	skinner	Bromsgrove	27 Oct.	1762
1771.	William Tilt	skinner	Kidderminster	10 Nov.	1770
1780.	Mary Tilt	widow	Kidderminster	30 Nov.	1775
1807.	William Tilt	currier	Stourbridge		

4. LUCAS. (A Selection.)

a. Worcester Probate Registry.

proved				dated	
1638.	Clement Lucas		Stratford	19 Feb.	1637-8
1679.	William Lucas	yeoman	Rowington	8 Apr.	1679
1723.	William Lilly	yeoman	Hanbury	27 Sept.	1723
			(Hanbury Peculiar Court.)		
1757.	Clement Lucas	gent.	Hanbury (Feckenham-park)	30 May	1749
1765.	John Lucas	yeoman	Hanbury	11 Apr.	1765
			(Hanbury Peculiar Court.)		
1777.	Thomas Lucas	gent.	Ipsley, Redditch	9 Mar.	1776
1777.	William Lucas	gent.	Hanbury	30 Jan.	1776
1786.	William Lucas	gent.	Redditch (Tardebig)	16 Aug.	1782

b. At Somerset House.

1776.	Robert Lucas	"hooper"	Bristol (Nicholas St. and Kingsdown)	28 Jan.	1774
1780.	Elizabeth Lucas	(his widow)	Bristol (St. James')	22 June	1779
				codicil 12 Jan.	1780
1784.	Thomas Lucas	"hooper"	Bristol (Lucas' Hall, Marsh St.)	12 Sept.	1780
				two codicils.	
1790.	William Lucas	gent.	Hanbury	10 May	1787
1804.	Clement Lucas	gent.	Hanbury	Feb.	1803
1808.	Elizabeth Lucas	(his widow)	Hanbury	9 Nov.	1807

5. TIBBATTS. (A Selection.)

WORCESTER PROBATE REGISTRY.

proved			dated
1546.	Roberte Tibbot	Tardebig	
1550.	John Tybbatts	Warwick	Admon.
	(father of John Tybbatts of Rowington)		
1580.	Isabel Tybbatts	Rowington	
1603.	Robert Tybbatts	Hatton	
1606.	John Tybbatts	Oldbury	
1620.	Richard Tybbatts	Warwick	
1624.	Alice Tybbatts	Bromsgrove	
1627.	Thomas Tybbatts	Warwick	

I do not know how these last six have the Surname spelt in the Wills.

1664.	Clement Tybbats sen., tanner,	Rowington	2 Nov. 1660
1687.	Thomas Tibbatts	Rowington	1 Oct. 1686
1687.	Thomas Tibbatts	Rowington	Admon.
1699.	John Tibbats yeoman	Rowington	2 May 1694
1707.	Samuel Tibbatts yeoman & baker	Rowington	12 Aug. 1706
1721.	John Tibbatts	Rowington	26 Sept. 1720
1726.	Anne Tibbatts (widow of the last)	Hewell Grange (near Bromsgrove)	25 Nov. 1724
1729.	Ann Tibbatts	Rowington	

6. BUTLER. (A Selection.)

WORCESTER PROBATE REGISTRY.

proved			dated
1558.	John Butler	Feckenham	
1572.	Gilbert Butler	Bromsgrove (Timberhanger)	
1599.	John Butler (or Buttler) gent.	Bromsgrove (Timberhanger)	25 Apr. 1599
1602.	Henry Butler als. Huntington	Feckenham	
1607.	Francis Butler	Feckenham	
1616.	Margerett Butler	Bromsgrove (Timberhanger)	24 Apr. 1616
	(widow of John Butler above)		
1637.	John Butler yeoman	Bromsgrove (Timberhauger)	29 Apr. 1637
1644.	John Butler	Bromsgrove (Timberhanger)	19 Oct. 1644
1661.	William Butler gent.	Bromsgrove (Catshill)	3 Nov. 1660
1681.	Gilbert Butler	Bromsgrove	Admon.

APPENDIX D.—WILLS AND ADMINISTRATIONS.

proved				dated
1684.	Edward Butler		Feckenham	Admon.
1687.	Joseph Butler		Bromsgrove	Admon.
1691.	John Butler	yeoman	Feckenham (Berrow)	5 Apr. 1690
1697.	Richard Butler		Bromsgrove	Admon.
1707.	John Butler	husbandman	Bromsgrove	28 Apr. 1707
1707.	George Butler		Feckenham	
1713.	William Butler		Feckenham	Admon.
1722.	Gilbert Butler	yeoman	Bromsgrove	29 Mar. 1721
1725.	Thomas Butler	yeoman	Feckenham (Berrow)	14 May 1724
1730.	Edward Butler	yeoman	Feckenham & Inkberrow	9 Apr. 1720

7. VERNON. (A Selection.)

WORCESTER PROBATE REGISTRY.

proved				dated
1720.	Robert Vernon	yeoman	Hanbury	14 May 1720
				(Hanbury Peculiar Court)
1723.	Elizabeth Vernon	(his widow)	Hanbury	28 May 1722

8. NASH. (A Selection.)

WORCESTER PROBATE REGISTRY.

proved				dated
1685.	Jonathan Nash		Feckenham	
1725.	John Nash		Hanbury	
1748.	Thomas Nash	yeoman	Stoke Prior	19 Feb. 1746-7
1767.	Jonathan Nash		of Arbor's Gate, Stoke Prior, and Prior's Field, Upton Warren (perhaps the husband of Margaret Lucas.)	7 June 1758
1773.	Goodwin Nash		Binton (Warw.)	Admon.

9. HOMER.

a. LICHFIELD PROBATE REGISTRY.

proved				dated
1681.	Simon Homer	tanner	Walsall	31 Dec. 1680
1700.	William Homer	spurrier	Walsall	31 Mar. 1700
1712.[1]	Thomas Homer	gent.	Sutton Coldfield	8 Mar. 1709-10
1715.[1]	Edward Homer	tanner	Walsall	16 June 1713
1731.[1]	Edward Homer		Ettingshall	27 May 1730
1745.[1]	Edward Homer		Sutton Coldfield	16 Dec. 1742
1807.	William Homer	gent.	Sutton Coldfield	1790

(This Will was left unfinished, the amounts of money and the date not being filled in. Probate was granted after affidavit by two friends.)

[1] These four Wills are sealed with the Homer Arms, Ermine a Fess. (Cp. pp. 44, note, & 62.)

b. AT SOMERSET HOUSE.

1764.	Edward Homer	Sutton Coldfield	11 Mar. 1758

(Mr. Richard Geast of Blyth Hall, who afterwards took the name of Dugdale, was a trustee to this Will, but left it unadministered. The matter came up in 1840, when administration of part of the property was granted to Thomas Eyre Lee, of Birmingham, nominee of another.)

APPENDIX E.

EXTRACTS FROM WORCESTERSHIRE SUBSIDY ROLLS.
(*see* p. 11.)

NAME OF CHANCE.

I HAVE selected the Rolls of those dates at which I could get most complete information, and in each case have combined such Rolls as would cover the whole County of Worcester, including sometimes the City.

1327. Series 200. No. 1. 5000 names.
    Name of Chance (or its equivalent) not found.

1523. Series 200. Nos. 126, 127, 129, 136, 137, 139, 175 (with 135). 4800 names.
    Bromsgrove.   John Chance sen.,   taxed 3s. 4d. ⎫
                     John Chance jun.,   ,,   12d. ⎬ together in the list.
                     Nycoles Chance,   ,,   12d. ⎭
                     Thomas Chance,   ,,   4d. ⎫ together in the list.
                     John Chance servt.,   ,,   4d. ⎭
    Hadzor.   Wyllyam Chaunce,   ,,   18d.
    Stoke Prior.   Joh'es Chance,   ,,   14d., on an assessment of 46s. 8d.

1545. Series 200. Nos. 164, 166. 2800 names.
    Bromsgrove.   Nich'us Chaunce.
    Hadzor.   Joh'es Chaunce.
    Each taxed 3s. 4d. on an assessment of £5 in goods.

1558-9. Series 200. Nos. 188, 189, 190.
    Name of Chance not found.

1586. Series 200. Nos. 196, 197, 198, 199. 2000 names.
    Hadzor.   Christoforus Chaunce taxed 6s. 8d. on an assessment of £5 in land.

1598. Series 201. Nos. 241, 242, 243, 246. 2670 names.

		assessed	*taxed*
Bromsgrove.	Will'm's Chaunce gener.	40s. in land.	8s.
	Joh'es Chaunce	£3 in goods.	8s.
Hadzor.	Christoph'us Chaunce gener.	£3 10s. in land.	14s.
Harvington.	Will'us Chaunce	£4 in goods.	10s. 8d.
Wick Episcopi.	Thomas Chaunce gen.	£8 in goods.	21s. 4d.

APPENDIX E.—EXTRACTS FROM WORCESTERSHIRE SUBSIDY ROLLS.

1640-1. Series 201. Nos. 303, 304, 305 (with 311). 1800 names.

		assessed.	taxed.
Bromsgrove.	John Chance de Catshill	40s. in land.	16s.
	Thomas Chance & Richard his son	30s. ,,	12s.
	John Chance & Will'm his son	20s. ,,	8s.
	Elizabeth Chaunce (?)		
	Ann the wyfe of Rich. Cha'ce, recusant		16s.
Hadzor.	Thomas Chaunce	30s. ,,	12s.
Salwarp.	Will'm Chaunce	20s. ,,	

Nos. 305 & 311 contain the lists as to Bromsgrove, and much is illegible in both.

1662 & 1667. Series 201. Nos. 325, 312. Over 8600 names.

		No. of hearths.	
Bromsgrove.	Henry Chaunce	1	
	John Chaunce	1	
	Widd. Chaunce	1	
	Jonathan Chaunce	2	
	Richard Chaunce	2	occur near each other in the list; the three middle ones together.
	William Chaunce	1	
	Nicholas Chaunce	4	
	Anthony Chaunce	2	"one too many" (1667).
	Widd. Chaunce	2	
	Elinor Chaunce	1	
Hadzor.	Thomas Chaunce	5	gent. "1 too many" (1667).
Salwarp.	William Chaunce	2	Constable of Salwarp.
	John Chaunce	2	"1 too many" (1667).
Alvechurch.	William Chaunce	1	
Beoley.	William Chaunce	1	
Belbroughton.	William Chaunce	1	
Chaddesley Corbet.	Widdow Chaunce	2	"poore—2 too many" (1667).
Himbleton.	William Chaunce	1	
Kidderminster.	Thomas Chaunce	1	"poore"
Bedwardine (St. John's).	John Chaunce	4	shared with John Unett.

These are the Hearthmoney Rolls (p. 11). There may be other mentions of the name in them, as they are in many places illegible.

APPENDIX F.

CHANCES OF WORCESTERSHIRE.[1]

1. CHANCES OF BROMSGROVE.

(See also Part II. Pedigree No. 1 and Appendix A1.)

1. 13th cent. A Bromsgrove Rental of the time of Henry III. does not contain the name of CHANCE. The name most like it is CHENDE, which occurs 3 or 4 times.
   [Record Office, County Bags.]

2. 1351. THOMAS CHAWNS, of Catshill ("de Catsulle"), sold some land in Fockbury in this year.
   [Prattinton MSS.]

3. 14th to 16th cent. (See pp. 22, 23.)

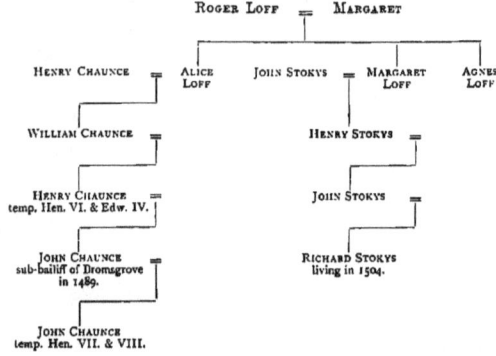

[1] This Appendix consists mainly of fragments of pedigrees, compiled from the contents of the various Wills. To these are added sundry items of information.

144   APPENDIX F.—CHANCES OF WORCESTERSHIRE.

4. 1523. Names in Subsidy Roll, see p. 141.
   1529. JOHN CHAUNCE, Bailiff of Bromsgrove.
                            [Prattinton MSS.]

5. JOHN CHAWNSE = ISABELL
   the elder, of Bromsgrove.   Will dated 6 Nov. 1545,
   Will dated 20 Apr. 1542,   proved at Worc. 23 Aug. 1546
   proved at Worc. 30 Oct. 1542.   (copy of it see p. 65).
   No legatees except the wife.
                          Legatees :
                          EDWARD CHAUNCE, Exec^{r.}
                          MARGARET CHAUNSE
                          ELIZABETH CHAUNSE ;
                          presumably her children.
   (Notices of EDWARD CHANCES, see Nos. 11, 12.)

6. JOHN CHAWNSE the younger = ELIZABETH
   of Timberhanger, Bromsgrove.   survived
   Will dated 10 May 1542,   her husband.
   proved at Worc. 30 Oct. 1542.

   ROGER CHAWNSE.

   A ROGER CHAUNCE, Prebendary, was Vicar of Clent in 1556.
            [Nash. " Hist. of Worcestershire " App. p. xviii.]
   ROGER CHAUNCE witness to a Bromsgrove (Fockbury) Deed—1552.
                                         [Prattinton MSS.]
   RULG'R CHAUNCE mentioned in the Will of Helen Astmore, of Bromsgrove—1556.
      (Possibly a Latin form of ROGER.)
   Another ROGER CHAUNCE below.—No. 20.

7. 1526. WILL'M CHAUNCE and NYCHOLAS BARNYSLEY of Barnysley, gentylma', feoffees
   under the Will of Hugh Lee, of Bromsgrove.

8. NICHOLAS CHAWNSE = ISABELL
   of Bromsgrove.   exec^r. with WILLIAM CHAWNSE,
   Will dated 30 Sept. 1546,   the son presumably, as he is
   proved at Worc. 5 July 1547.   sole reversionary heir.
   (Cp. p. 24.)   A legacy to ANNE LYNALL,
                          on marriage.

9. NICHOLAS   WILLIAM   WILLIAM =   WILLIAM   GILBERT
   CHAUNCE   CHAUNCE   CHAUNCE   CHAUNCE   CHAUNCE
   of Bromsgrove.   of Bromsgrove.   of Bromsgrove.
   Adm'on to his   Adm'on to his son—   Adm'on to his
   brother—Worc.   Worc. 8 Aug. 1584.   brother, and to his
   27 Sept. 1567.   (He was dead some time   uncle, GILBERT
   (Cp. Nos. 11, 13.)   before this ; his estate   BRANDSLEY
                        had been left   (BARNSLEY),
                        unadministered.)   Worc. 10 Apr. 1570.

                          WILLIAM CHAUNCE
                          prob. he who died 1622.
                          (No. 22.)

   1548. WILL'M CHAWNCE a witness to the Will of Thomas Blakeway, of Bromsgrove.
   1548. WYLL'M and JOHANE (Joan) CHAWNCE (not yet of age) legatees under the Will of
   Richard Tybson, of Bromsgrove.

APPENDIX F.—CHANCES OF WORCESTERSHIRE.   145

10. 1554. JOHN CHAUNCE a freeholder of Fockbury.
[Prattinton MSS.]

11. HEUGH CHAUNCE of Bromsgrove. Will dated 12 June 1566, proved at Worc. 1 Feb. 1566-7. = who survived her husband.

NICHOLAS CHAUNCE & WYLLYAM CHAUNCE, Creditors of HEUGH.

Children:
- JHON CHAUNCE unm. in 1566 (probably J. C. of Bournheath, No. 21).
- EDWARDE CHAUNCE unm. in 1566.
  - ROBERT CHAUNCE bur. at Bromsgrove 25 June 1592.

EDWARD CHAUNCE and his son ROBERT were living in 1585 in a house belonging to HENRY CHAUNCE—(cp. No. 15).

12. 1546-1575. Mentions of EDWARD CHANCES in Bromsgrove Wills:
    1546. EDWARD CHAWNSE, witness, Will of John Russall.
    1547. EDWARDE CHAWSE   ,,   ,,   John Bate.
    1554. EDWARD CHAUNCE   ,,   ,,   { Thos. Lynolle.
                                                { Henry Baker.
    1567. EDWARD CHAUNCE   ,,   ,,   John Badger.
    1572. EDWARD CHANCH   ,,   ,,   Rychard Gryffen.
    1573. EDWARD CHANCH   ,,   ,,   John Fownes.
    1575. {EDWARD CHAUNCE   ,,   ,,   John Bridgen.
          {ROBERT CHAUNCE assisted with the Inventory.

13. RYCHARD CHAUNCE of Bromsgrove. Will dated 1 Sept. 1558, proved at Worc. 28 Nov. 1558. = who survived her husband. Her brother, or brother-in-law, was named JHON SMYTHE.

HENRY CHAUNCE and NYCHOLES CHAUNCE are mentioned in the Will, the latter as a kinsman.

Children:
- RICHARD CHAUNCE
- THOMAS CHAUNCE
- WILLIAM CHAUNCE

14. RICHARD CHANCE of Bournheath, Bromsgrove. Will dated 30 Dec. 1575, proved at Worc. 21 June 1576. = ANNE who survived her husband.

JOHN CHANCE als. CHAUNCE overseer to the Will.

- MARY CHAUNCE, in 1575 not yet 16.

15. RICHARD CHAUNCE survived his brother.

HENRY CHAUNCE of Timberhanger, Bromsgrove. Will dated 7 Dec. 1585, proved at Worc. Dec. 1586. =

A HENRY CHAUNCE and ELIZABETH his wife acquired land at Elmley Lovett in 1581.
[Feet of Fines.]

Children:
- WILLIAM CHAUNCE
- MARGARET CHAUNCE
- ELIZABETH CHAUNCE
- JANE CHAUNCE
- ALICE CHAUNCE

T

APPENDIX F.—CHANCES OF WORCESTERSHIRE.

16.
 1597. Apr. 17. ELIZABETH wife of RICHARD CHANCE of Shepcoote (Sheepcoote) buried at Bromsgrove.
 1597. Dec. 24. RICHARD CHAUNCE buried at Bromsgrove.
 1605. RICHARD CHAUNCE a witness to the Will of John Mayne of Bromsgrove.
 1610. May 3. RICHARD CHAUNCE buried at Bromsgrove.

17.
 1568. JOHN CHAUNCE a legatee under the Will of Anne Hill, of Belbroughton.
 1592. JHON CHAUNCE witness to the Will of Thomas Astmoore, of Bromsgrove.
 From the "Feet of Fines"—(p. 12, note 7).
  1592. ELIANOR CHAUNCE, widow, and JOHN CHANCE her son, acquired property in Bromsgrove.
  1593. JOHN CHAUNCE acquired property in Bromsgrove.
  1595. JOHN CHAUNCE acquired property in Belbroughton and Bromsgrove.
  1599. JOHN CHAUNCE and ANN his wife gave up property in Bromsgrove.
 1601. Apr. 1. PHILIPPE wife of JHON CHAUNCE buried at Bromsgrove.

18.
NICHOLAS CHAUNCME of Habbe Lench (Hoblench), Yeoman: holding property in Bromsgrove and Belbroughton. Will proved in London 21 June 1591.
See pp. 14, 15.
 = ELIANOR who survived her husband.

All under 21 at the date of the Will.

JOHN CHAUNCE. | THOMAS CHAUNCE. | NICHOLAS CHAUNCE. | WILLIAM CHAUNCE. | AGNES CHAUNCE. | ALICE CHAUNCE.

Cousins (i.e. prob. nephews):—
THOMAS and WILLIAM CHANCE of Woodcote (Bromsgrove):
CHRISTOPHER and WILLIAM CHANCE of Harvington (No. 19).

19.
WILLIAM CHAUNCE of Harvington, Yeoman. Will dated 14 Oct. 1605, proved in London 18 Oct. 1606.
See p. 14.
 = "ELNOR" who survived her husband.

JOHN CHAUNCE. | WILLIAM CHAUNCE. | Dau. m. JOHN POOLE.

20.
ROGER CHAUNCE survived his three wives.
= (1) MARGRET bur. at Bromsgrove 9 June 1599. (1 Dec. 1599.)
= (2) ANNE BUTLER bur. at Bromsgrove 27 June 1604. (18 Oct. 1604.)
= (3) ELINOUR LILLIE bur. at Bromsgrove 10 Dec. 1614.

ROGER CHAUNCE bur. at Bromsgrove 3 Feb. 1600-1. | JHON CHAUNCE bapt. at Bromsgrove 24 Oct. 1591. | RICHARD CHAUNCE bapt. at Bromsgrove 17 Nov. 1595.

APPENDIX F.—CHANCES OF WORCESTERSHIRE.   147

21.

JOHN CHAUNCE = who survived her husband.
of Bournheath, Bromsgrove, Yeoman;
(prob. son of HEUGH CHAUNCE, No. 11).
Bur. at Bromsgrove 17 Jan. 1614-5.
Will proved at Worcester 1615.

Prob. the J. C. of Bromsgrove assessed in 1598
at £3 in goods, and taxed 8s. (p. 141).

| HUGH CHAUNCE = MARY | ANN CHAUNCE m. HUNTE. | ELINOR CHAUNCE m. WILLIAM AWYER. | MARY CHAUNCE m. 17 Jan. 1606-7 GEORGE JACKSON. | SYBIL CHAUNCE m. 15 Jan. 1606-7 THOMAS SAUNDERS. |

Hugh and his wife gave up land at Bromsgrove in 1622. [Feet of Fines.]

All baptised at Bromsgrove.

| ANNE CHAUNCE bapt. 11 May 1614. | JOAN CHAUNCE bapt. 30 Sep. 1618. | JOHN CHAUNCE bapt. 21 May 1620. | ALICE CHAUNCE bapt. 22 June 1622. | HUGH CHAUNCE bapt. 16 Apr. 1625, bur. at Br'sgrove 5 Nov. 1625. | HENRY CHAUNCE bapt. 29 Sep. 1626. | HUGH CHAUNCE bapt. 17 Jan. 1629-30. |

CHRISTOPHER DINELEY =

22.

WILLIAM CHAUNCE = ANNE DINELEY (qy. bur. at Br, 6 Apr. 1601).   ELIZABETH DINELEY m. THOMAS RUSSELL.
of Bromsgrove, Yeoman and Gent.
(perh. son of WILLIAM CHAUNCE, No. 9).
Will dated 18 May 1618,
proved at Worcester 1622.
Bur. at Bromsgrove 11 May 1622.
See pp. 25, 26.

| JOHN CHAUNCE | WILLIAM CHAUNCE of Worcester, Walker and Clothier. Will dated 4 May 1624, proved at Worc. 1624. | HENRY CHAUNCE of Bromsgrove, Weaver; bur. there 22 Sept. 1624. Will dated 13 Sept. 1624, proved at Worcester 9 Oct. 1624. Wife's name was "LYSSYT." | THOMAS CHAUNCE had a dau. ANNE. Prob. same as T. C. No. 24. | ELIZABETH CHAUNCE m. 3 Feb. 1596-7 WILLIAM FOWNES. 9 children. | CHAUNCE m. JOHN BRAINCH. 5 children. | CHAUNCE m. COTTVE. | CHAUNCE m. PENNS. 6 children. |

JOHN CHAUNCE and four others living in 1624.

NOTE.—1595-6. Feb. 26. WILLIAM son of HENRIE CHANCE buried at Bromsgrove.
1623. HENRY CHANCE, Churchwarden of Bromsgrove.

APPENDIX F.—CHANCES OF WORCESTERSHIRE.

23. 1621. JOHN CHAUNCE and ANN his wife (cp. No. 17) gave up land at Elmley Lovett. [Feet of Fines.]

1633. "Feofermees" of the Manor of Dyers (Bromsgrove):—
JOHN CHAUNCE £3. 13. 4
WILLIAM CHAUNCE 14. 0.
JOHN CHAUNCE £1. 10. 0 [Manorial Records.]

1635. JOHN CHAUNCE of Bromsgrove, Yeoman, was a Defendant in the Chancery Suit of Hall v. Chaunce and others; he had a son WILLIAM. [Record Office—Chancery Proceedings—temp. Chas. I.]

1636. JOHN CHANCE sen. & JOHN CHANCE jun. gave up land in Bromsgrove town, Tymberhonger, Upton Warren, Dodderhill, and Elmley Lovett. [Feet of Fines.]

1636. JOHN CHAUNCE and WILLIAM CHAUNCE gave up land at Snoedes Green, near Elmley Lovett. [Feet of Fines.]

1639. JOHN CHAUNCE and CHRISTIANA his wife and WILLIAM CHAUNCE gave up land in Bromsgrove. [Feet of Fines.]

24.

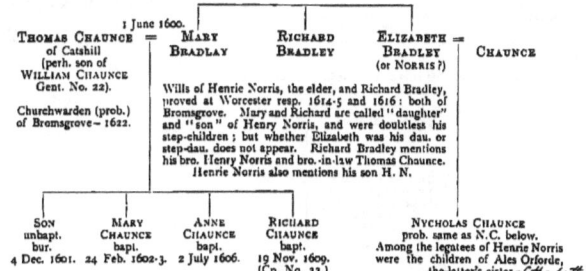

25.

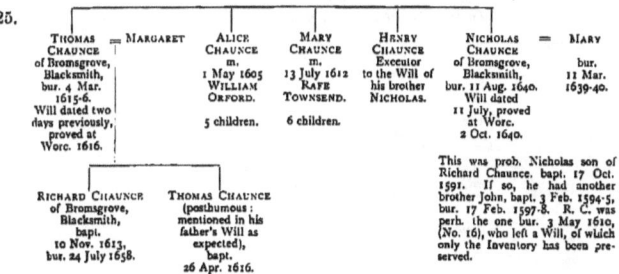

APPENDIX F.—CHANCES OF WORCESTERSHIRE.

26. Shepley. (Cp. p. 74.)

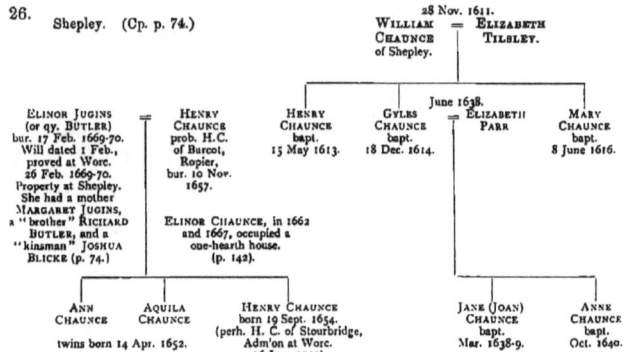

WILLIAM CHAUNCE of Shepley. = 28 Nov. 1611. ELIZABETH TILSLEY.

ELINOR JUGINS (or qy. BUTLER) bur. 17 Feb. 1669-70. Will dated 1 Feb., proved at Worc. 26 Feb. 1669-70. Property at Shepley. She had a mother MARGARET JUGINS, a "brother" RICHARD BUTLER, and a "kinsman" JOSHUA BLICKE (p. 74.) = HENRY CHAUNCE prob. H.C. of Burcot, Ropier, bur. 10 Nov. 1657.

HENRY CHAUNCE bapt. 13 May 1613.

GYLES CHAUNCE bapt. 18 Dec. 1614.

June 1638. ELIZABETH PARR =

MARY CHAUNCE bapt. 8 June 1616.

ELINOR CHAUNCE, in 1662 and 1667, occupied a one-hearth house. (p. 142).

ANN CHAUNCE   AQUILA CHAUNCE
twins born 14 Apr. 1652.

HENRY CHAUNCE born 19 Sept. 1654. (perh. H. C. of Stourbridge, Adm'on at Worc. 16 June 1721).

JANE (JOAN) CHAUNCE bapt. Mar. 1638-9.

ANNE CHAUNCE bapt. Oct. 1640.

Ann was executrix to her mother, and was in 1670 unmarried.

27.

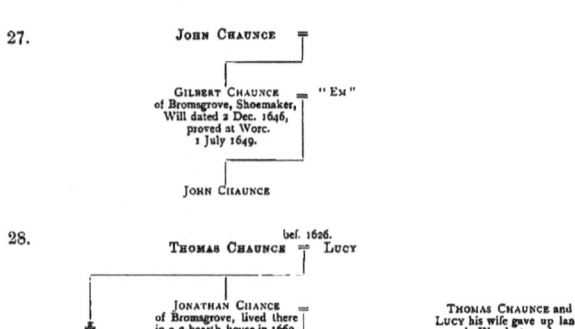

JOHN CHAUNCE =

GILBERT CHAUNCE = "EM" of Bromsgrove, Shoemaker, Will dated 2 Dec. 1646, proved at Worc. 1 July 1649.

JOHN CHAUNCE

28.

THOMAS CHAUNCE = bef. 1626. LUCY

JONATHAN CHANCE of Bromsgrove, lived there in a 2-hearth house in 1662. (p. 142). bapt. 15 Feb. 1636-7. bur. 16 Dec. 1667.

THOMAS CHAUNCE and LUCY his wife gave up land in Woodcote and Bromsgrove in 1626. [Feet of Fines.]

HANNAH CHANCE bapt. 19 Jan. 1664-5.

Notices of other THOMAS CHANCES see Appendix A 1.

APPENDIX F.—CHANCES OF WORCESTERSHIRE.

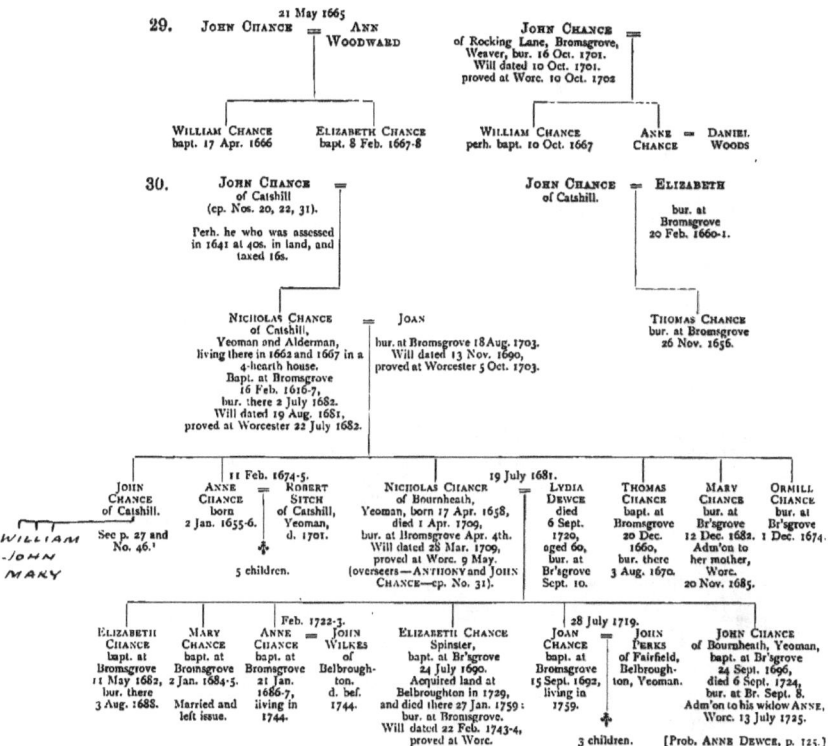

Tombstone Inscription No. 9, Appendix C, refers to this family.

[1] It is impossible to make out from the Bromsgrove Register entries which were the children of this particular JOHN CHANCE, or to say for certain that he was the father of WILLIAM and THOMAS CHANCE (No. 46).

APPENDIX F.—CHANCES OF WORCESTERSHIRE.

31.

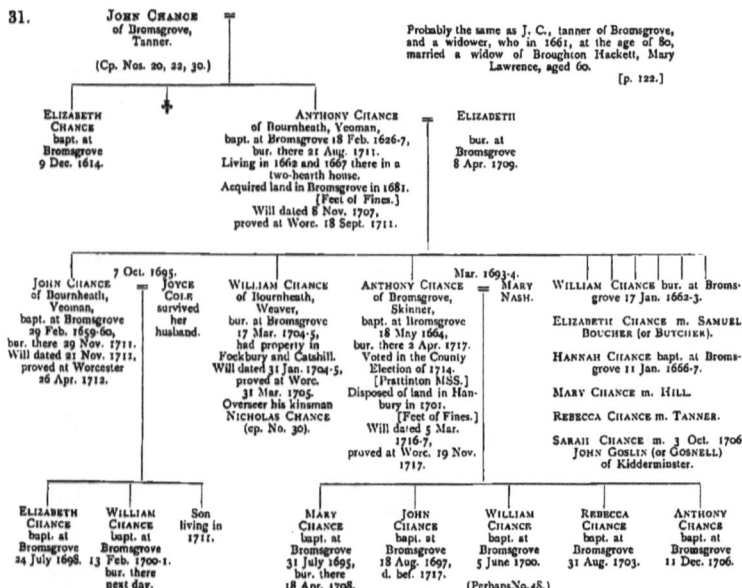

Most probably Anthony Chance the eldest and Nicholas Chance the elder (No. 30) were brothers, because William Chance, son of Anthony, calls Nicholas Chance the younger his kinsman, and the latter calls Anthony (the second) and John Chance his kinsmen, "kinsman" in old wills usually standing for cousin. And Nicholas the elder and Anthony the eldest were both sons of a John Chance.

32.   From the "Feet of Fines":—

1694. JOHN CHANCE acquired land in Catshill, Dudley, Belbroughton, and Bromsgrove.
1723. JOHN CHANCE and ANN his wife gave up land in Fockbury, Catshill, Padstones, and Chadwick, in Bromsgrove parish, and other land in Droitwich.

APPENDIX F.—CHANCES OF WORCESTERSHIRE.

33.

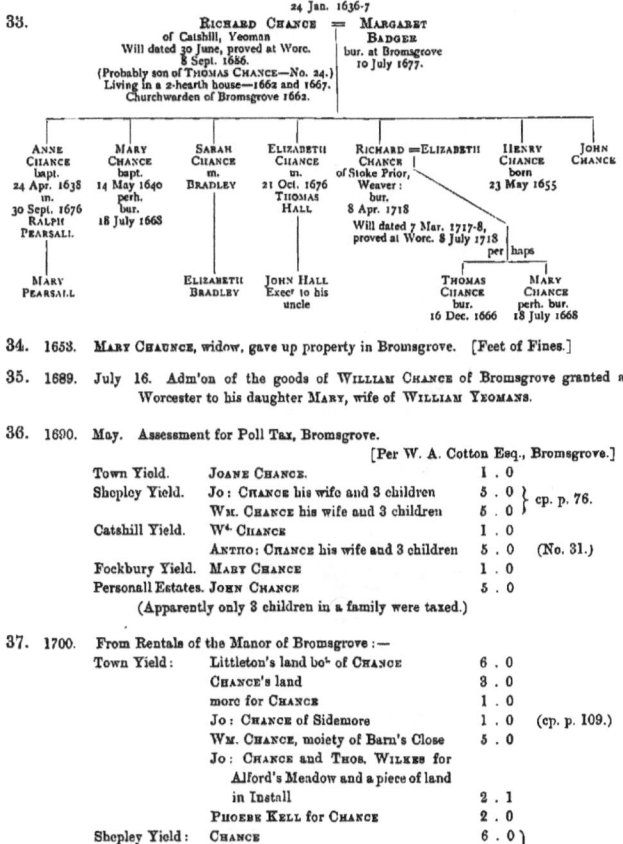

34. 1653. MARY CHAUNCE, widow, gave up property in Bromsgrove. [Feet of Fines.]

35. 1689. July 16. Adm'on of the goods of WILLIAM CHANCE of Bromsgrove granted at Worcester to his daughter MARY, wife of WILLIAM YEOMANS.

36. 1690. May. Assessment for Poll Tax, Bromsgrove.
[Per W. A. Cotton Esq., Bromsgrove.]

Town Yield.	JOANE CHANCE.	1 . 0	
Shepley Yield.	Jo: CHANCE his wife and 3 children	5 . 0	} cp. p. 76.
	WM. CHANCE his wife and 3 children	5 . 0	
Catshill Yield.	W⁴· CHANCE	1 . 0	
	ANTHO: CHANCE his wife and 3 children	5 . 0	(No. 31.)
Fockbury Yield.	MARY CHANCE	1 . 0	
Personall Estates.	JOHN CHANCE	5 . 0	

(Apparently only 3 children in a family were taxed.)

37. 1700. From Rentals of the Manor of Bromsgrove:—

Town Yield:	Littleton's land bo⁴ of CHANCE	6 . 0	
	CHANCE's land	3 . 0	
	more for CHANCE	1 . 0	
	Jo: CHANCE of Sidemore	1 . 0	(cp. p. 109.)
	WM. CHANCE, moiety of Barn's Close	5 . 0	
	Jo: CHANCE and THOS. WILKES for Alford's Meadow and a piece of land in Install	2 . 1	
	PHOEBE KELL for CHANCE	2 . 0	
Shepley Yield:	CHANCE	6 . 0	}
	HY. CHANCE, Hill's	2 . 4 . 0	} (cp. p. 76.)
	WM. CHANCE, Littleton's	6 . 11 . 0	}

APPENDIX F.—CHANCES OF WORCESTERSHIRE.

```
Catshill Yield :  NICHOLAS CHANCE                          2 . 0  ⎫
                  Jo: CHANCE for Hill and Porter's ten¹    1 . 5  ⎪
                  ANTHONY CHANCE                           1 . 3 . 0  ⎬ (Nos. 30, 31, 33.)
                  Mr. LOWE for RICHARD CHANCE              1 . 0 . 0  ⎪
                  Mr. COOKES for CHANCE                    3 . 0  ⎪
                  ANTHONY CHANCE for Hill                  8 . 0  ⎭
Manor of Dyers :  JOHN CHANCE                              1 . 0 . 0
                  WM. CHANCE of Shepley                    4 . 0
                  NICH. CHANCE for CARPENTER               3
```

38. 1703-4. Freeholders of Bromsgrove: value of holdings not less than £10.
    [Grazebrook—"Heraldry of Worcestershire"]

    Shepley Yield.   WILL. CHANCE.
    Catshill Yield. JOHN CHANCE.
                     NICHOLAS CHANCE.
                     ANTHONY CHANCE.

39. WILLIAM CHANCE of Fockbury, Yeoman, bur. at Bromsgrove 2 Nov. 1702, Will dated 3 June 1702, proved at Worc. 8 Mar. 1702-3, left a widow MARY.

40.
```
                        19 May 1706.
              BERNARD CHANCE  =  MARY MOLE
              (als. BARNARD, BARNET,     bur. 21 Sept. 1737.
                    &c.),
    ┌──────────────┬──────────────┬──────────────┬──────────────┐
    MARY          ELIZABETH      WILLIAM CHANCE  BERNARD  ⎫ CHANCE
    CHANCE        CHANCE         bapt. 6 Sept. 1721,  BARNET  ⎬ BARNET
    bapt.         bapt.          bur. 17 May 1725.    bapt. 17 May 1724,
    12 Aug. 1711. 2 Apr. 1714                          bur. 31 May 1725.
                  bur.
                  18 June 1735.
```

41.
```
                            Jan. or Feb. 1712-3.
         BENJAMIN CHANCE, the elder,  =  HANNAH BUTLER
         of Bromsgrove ; born abt. 1690.    of Bromsgrove,
         Adm'on at Worc. 1761.              born abt. 1680.
                    ┌─────────────┬─────────────┐
                    MARY CHANCE        HANNAH CHANCE
                    m. THOS. BRETTELL.  bur. 10 Nov. 1720.
```

42. 1716. Sept. WILLIAM CHANCE, born abt. 1690, m. MARY ARDEN, of Upton Warren, widow.
    In 1718 and 1732 WILLIAM CHANCE sen. and MARY his wife gave up property in Bromsgrove and King's Norton. .[Feet of Fines.]

43. Freeholders of Bromsgrove voting in the County Elections of 1714 and 1741.
    [Prattinton MSS.]
    1714. WILLIAM and ANTHONY CHANCE ; also a CHANCE of Catshill.
    1741. JOHN, THOMAS, and three WILLIAM CHANCES.

APPENDIX F.—CHANCES OF WORCESTERSHIRE.

44. 1741. Tenants of the Manor of Bromsgrove:—
    Town Yield   JOHN CHANCE
    Shepley Yield   WILLIAM CHANCE (p. 78).
    Fockbury Yield { THOMAS CHANCE } Cp. No. 46.
                        { WILLIAM CHANCE }

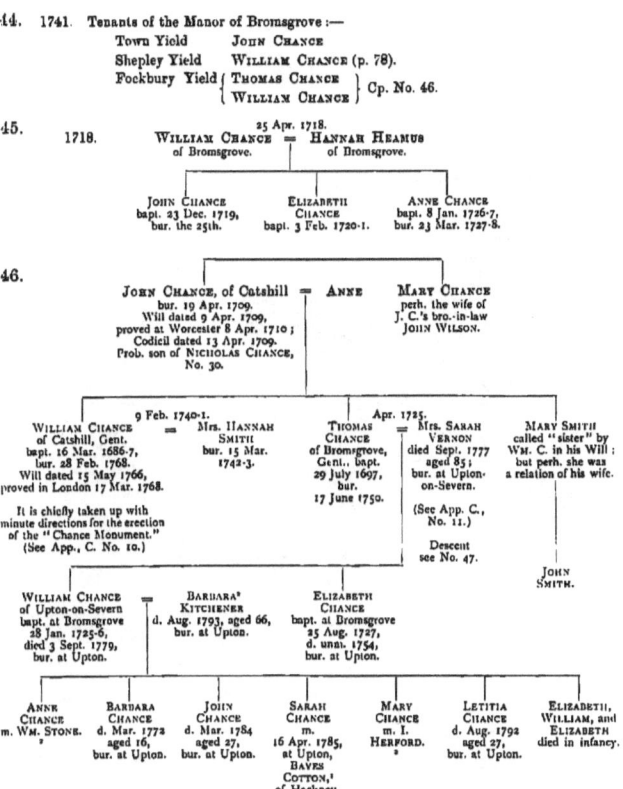

1743. THOMAS CHANCE and SARAH his wife gave up land in Hanbury (perh. part of her marriage-portion) and Alvechurch to THOMAS VERNON, of Hanbury, Gent.
                                                      [Feet of Fines.]

APPENDIX F.—CHANCES OF WORCESTERSHIRE.

47. Descent of SARAH VERNON (No. 46).

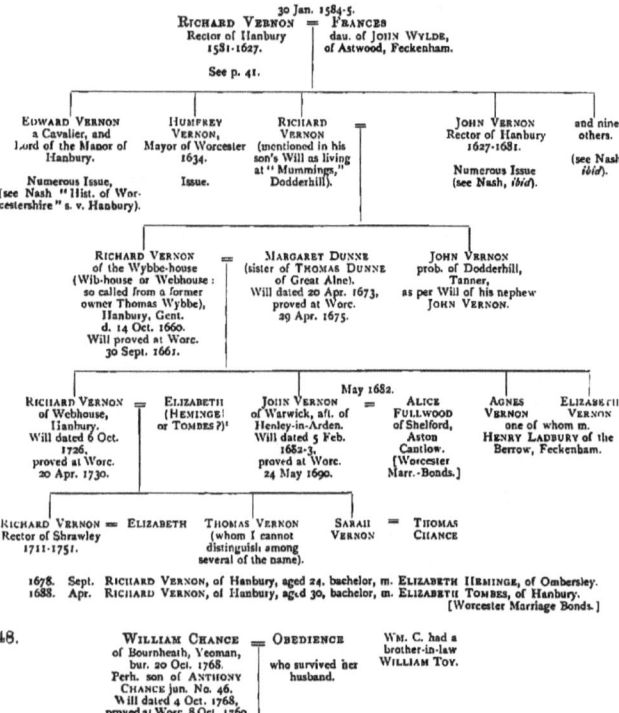

```
                        30 Jan. 1584-5.
             RICHARD VERNON  =  FRANCES
             Rector of Hanbury    dau. of JOHN WYLDE,
             1581-1627.           of Astwood, Feckenham.
                  See p. 41.
```

EDWARD VERNON, a Cavalier, and Lord of the Manor of Hanbury. Numerous Issue. (see Nash "Hist. of Worcestershire" s. v. Hanbury).

HUMPHREY VERNON, Mayor of Worcester 1634. Issue.

RICHARD VERNON (mentioned in his son's Will as living at "Mummings," Dodderhill).

JOHN VERNON Rector of Hanbury 1627-1681. Numerous Issue (see Nash, *ibid*).

and nine others. (see Nash, *ibid*).

RICHARD VERNON of the Wybbe-house (Wib-house or Webhouse: so called from a former owner Thomas Wybbe), Hanbury, Gent. d. 14 Oct. 1660. Will proved at Worc. 30 Sept. 1661.

MARGARET DUNNE (sister of THOMAS DUNNE of Great Alne). Will dated 20 Apr. 1673, proved at Worc. 29 Apr. 1675.

JOHN VERNON prob. of Dodderhill, Tanner, as per Will of his nephew JOHN VERNON.

May 1682.

RICHARD VERNON of Webhouse, Hanbury. Will dated 6 Oct. 1726, proved at Worc. 20 Apr. 1730.

ELIZABETH (HEMINGE! or TOMBES?)[1]

JOHN VERNON of Warwick, aft. of Henley-in-Arden. Will dated 5 Feb. 1682-3, proved at Worc. 24 May 1690.

ALICE FULLWOOD of Shelford, Aston Cantlow. [Worcester Marr.-Bonds.]

AGNES VERNON one of whom m. HENRY LADBURY of the Berrow, Feckenham.

ELIZABETH VERNON

RICHARD VERNON Rector of Shrawley 1711-1751.

ELIZABETH

THOMAS VERNON (whom I cannot distinguish among several of the name).

SARAH VERNON

THOMAS CHANCE

1678. Sept. RICHARD VERNON, of Hanbury, aged 24, bachelor, m. ELIZABETH HEMINGE, of Ombersley.
1688. Apr. RICHARD VERNON, of Hanbury, aged 30, bachelor, m. ELIZABETH TOMBES, of Hanbury.
[Worcester Marriage Bonds.]

48.

WILLIAM CHANCE of Bournheath, Yeoman, bur. 20 Oct. 1768. Perh. son of ANTHONY CHANCE jun. No. 46. Will dated 4 Oct. 1768, proved at Worc. 8 Oct. 1769. Gave up property at Fockbury and Catshill in 1746. [Feet of Fines.]

OBEDIENCE who survived her husband.

WM. C. had a brother-in-law WILLIAM TOY.

MARY CHANCE bapt. 1 Apr. 1741.

WILLIAM CHANCE ba, t. 6 Mar. 1744-5.

JOHN CHANCE bapt. 1 Nov. 1746.

THOMAS CHANCE.

JOB CHANCE.

NICHOLAS CHANCE.

APPENDIX F.—CHANCES OF WORCESTER CITY.

49. 1746. WILLIAM CHANCE and MARY his wife gave up property in Bromsgrove.
[Feet of Fines.]
1746-7. Jan. 5. WILLIAM son of WILLIAM and MARY CHANCE baptized.
1749-50. Mar. 17. ELIZABETH dau. of WILLIAM and MARY CHANCE baptized.

2. CHANCES OF WORCESTER CITY.

50.   RYCHARD CHAUNCE = JOANE
      of All Saints', Weaver.   who survived her
      Will dated 1 Feb. 1568-9,   husband.
      proved at Worc. 21 June 1569.

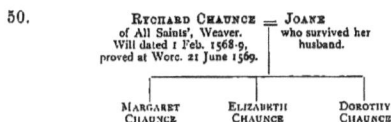

         MARGARET   ELIZABETH   DOROTHY
         CHAUNCE   CHAUNCE   CHAUNCE

Their mother to be in "quyett vest" of their legacies till they should be of age,
and the "Master of the Orphants" not to interfere

51. THOMAS CHANCE, of Worcester, Gent. (see p. 19).

52.   ANTHONY CHANCE = JOAN
      of Worcester, Trowman.   who survived her
      Will dated 4 Apr. 1652,   husband.
      proved in London 19 May 1652.

53.   JOHN CHAUNCE = ELIZABETH   Son =
      of St. John's, Bedwardine
      (see p. 19).
      Adm'on to his nephew at
      Worc. 9 Sept. 1670

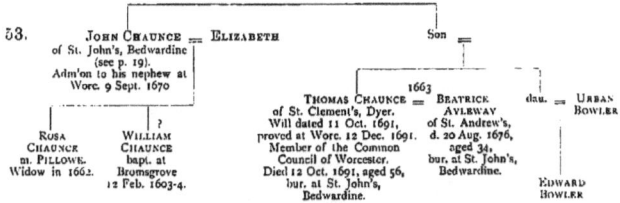

      ROSA   WILLIAM   1663
      CHAUNCE   CHAUNCE   THOMAS CHAUNCE = BEATRICE   dau. = URBAN
      m. PILLOWE. bapt. at   of St. Clement's, Dyer. AYLEWAY   BOWLER
      Widow in 1662. Bromsgrove Will dated 11 Oct. 1691, of St. Andrew's,
                  12 Feb. 1603-4. proved at Worc. 12 Dec. 1691. d. 20 Aug. 1676,
                                  Member of the Common aged 34,
                                  Council of Worcester. bur. at St. John's,
                                  Died 12 Oct. 1691, aged 56, Bedwardine.   EDWARD
                                  bur. at St. John's,   BOWLER
                                  Bedwardine.

54.   CHRISTOPHER CHAUNCE = MARY
      of St. Andrew's, Clothier.   who survived her
      Will dated 26 Feb. 1683-4,   husband.
      proved in London 5 June 1684.

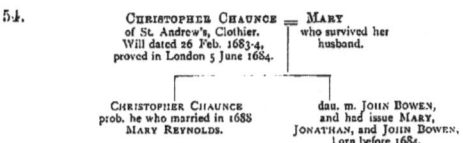

      CHRISTOPHER CHAUNCE   dau. m. JOHN BOWEN,
      prob. he who married in 1688   and had issue MARY,
      MARY REYNOLDS.   JONATHAN, and JOHN BOWEN,
                                     born before 1684.

APPENDIX F.—CHANCES OF WORCESTER CITY.

55. THOMAS CHANCE, of St. Clement's; Adm'on at Worcester, 12 June 1688, to his widow ELIZABETH.

56. JOANE NICHOLLS (1) = RICHARDE CHANCE = (2) SUSANNA HILL
of Worcester,   1665.   of St. Andrew's, Clothier;   1685-6.   of Hollow,
d. 12 Aug. 1684, aged 43;   Warden of the "Walkers and   who survived her husband.
Mont. in St. Andrew's,   Clothiers" in 1682.
Worcester.   Died 27 Jan. 1687-8, aged 48;
Mont. in St. Andrew's.
Will dated 12 Apr. 1686,
proved in London 4 June 1688.

57.   1666.
WILLIAM CHANCE = a dau. of JOHN BOUND
of St. Andrew's;   of St. Clement's, Clothier.
born about 1643.   She was born about 1636.

58.   1667.   1678.
ELIZABETH JORDAN (1) = WARNER CHANCE = (2) SARAH BRINTON
of All Saints';   of St. Andrew's;   of All Saints'.
born about 1647.   born about 1645.

59. JOHN CHANCE Jun. = MARY   JOHN CHANCE Jun.
of St. Clement's, Innholder.   of St. Clement's;   of St. Andrew's,
Will dated 14 Mar. 1703-4,   Adm'on at Worc.   m. in 1680 MARY ALLEN,
proved at Worc. 13 Mar.   4 Mar. 1716-7.   of Worcester,
1704-5.   born abt. 1655.

JOHN CHANCE   JOHN CHANCE   JOHN CHANCE,
(their only son).   of St. Clement's,   of St. Clement's, widower,
m. in 1706 SIBILLA   m. in 1716 MARY HAYNES,
PARNELL, of the   of All Saints'.
Cathedral Precincts.

60. JOHN CHANCE = RACHEL
of St. Andrew's, Trowman.   who survived her
Will dated 22 Sept. 1706,   husband.
proved in London 3 Dec. 1706.

    1690-1.
RICHARD   MARY = JOHN CALLOWE,   SARAH CHANCE
CHANCE.   CHANCE   of Dormeston, son of   m. CRISPE.
b. abt. 1672.   JOHN CALLOWE, of Dormeston,
and MARGARET PHILLIPS,
of Inkberrow.

61. ELIZABETH CHANCE   She had a sister-in-law ELIZABETH CHANCE, and a
of St. Nicholas', Spinster.   nephew JOHN CHANCE. The former was perhaps
Will dated 7 Nov. 1713,   the ELIZABETH CHANCE, widow, of St. Nicholas',
proved at Worc. 12 Dec. 1716.   whose Will, dated 25 Apr. 1723, was proved at
Worcester 6 June 1724. This Will mentions no
relatives.

62. 1741. CHRISTOPHER CHANCE and JOHN CHANCE, both of All Saints', voted in the City Parliamentary election.

3. CHANCES OF HADZOR, SALWARP, ODDINGLEY, AND WARNDON.

63. WYLLYAM CHAUNCE, of Hadysor, assessed in 1523 at £3 in goods, and taxed 1s. 6d., was perhaps the father of
JOH'ES CHAUNCE, of Hadsor, assessed in 1545 at £5 in goods, and taxed 3s. 4d.; and he was perhaps the father of

64.

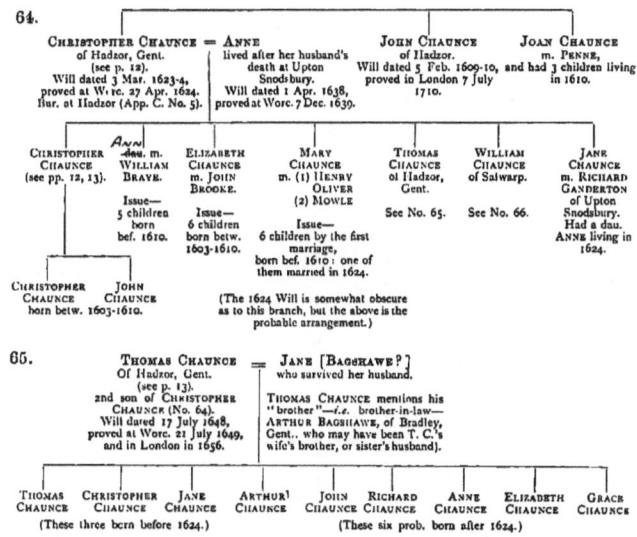

65. THOMAS CHAUNCE = JANE [BAGSHAWE?]
Of Hadzor, Gent. who survived her husband.
(see p. 13).
2nd son of CHRISTOPHER THOMAS CHAUNCE mentions his
CHAUNCE (No. 64). "brother"—i.e. brother-in-law—
Will dated 17 July 1648, ARTHUR BAGSHAWE, of Bradley,
proved at Worc. 21 July 1649, Gent., who may have been T. C.'s
and in London in 1656. wife's brother, or sister's husband).

THOMAS	CHRISTOPHER	JANE	ARTHUR[1]	JOHN	RICHARD	ANNE	ELIZABETH	GRACE
CHAUNCE	CHAUNCE	CHAUNCE	CHAUNCE	CHAUNCE	CHAUNCE	CHAUNCE	CHAUNCE	CHAUNCE
(These three born before 1624.)			(These six prob. born after 1624.)					

The property at Hadzor went to the eldest son THOMAS, and that in Hanbury to the four younger sons. All these nine children were living in 1648.

APPENDIX F.—CHANCES OF HADZOR, SALWARP, ODDINGLEY, AND WARNDON. 159

66. WILLIAM CHAUNCE
Of Newland, Salwarp,
3rd son of CHRISTOPHER
CHAUNCE (No. 64);
assessed in 1641 at 20s.
in land.

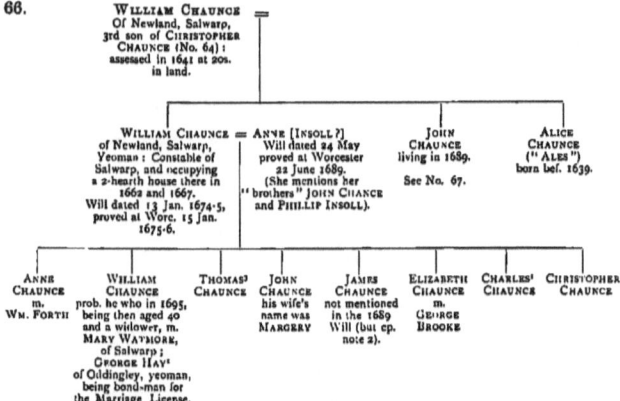

¹ CHARLES CHANCE, of Oddingley, born abt. 1669, m. in 1695-6 ANNE HAY, of Oddingley, then aged 22. He was living in 1726, when he was executor to his nephew WILLIAM CHANCE, of Oddingley (Will dated 2 Oct., proved at Worc. 12 Nov. 1726). His wife was probably the ANNE CHANCE of Oddingley, widow, adm'on of whose goods was granted at Worcester to her son JOHN CHANCE 19 Oct. 1734; and the last was perh. the JOHN CHANCE of Oddingley, who m. at Bromsgrove, 20 June 1738, SARAH TIBBUT of Elmbridge.

² Adm'on of the goods of a JAMES CHANCE, of Doddenham, was granted at Worcester, 15 Apr. 1727, to his widow MARTHA.

³ THOMAS CHANCE, of Himbleton, aged 28, m. in 1684 ANNE CRUMPE of Deane Dish, Inkberrow, aged 28.

⁴ CHRISTOPHER CHANCE, of Inkberrow, husbandman, m. 9 Jan. 1695-6 at Bromsgrove SARAH YATES, of Hanbury, aged 24.

67.

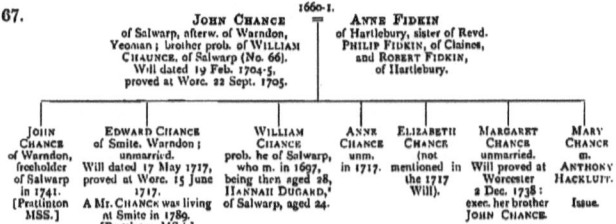

¹ WALTER DUGARDE mentioned, as a kinsman, in the Will of ANNE CHANCE of Salwarp (1689); and GEORGE DUGARD witnessed the Will of WILLIAM CHANCE, of Salwarp (1674-5); (No. 66).

4. OTHER WORCESTERSHIRE CHANCES.

a. STOKE PRIOR.

68. 1523. JOH'ES CHANCE, of Stoke Prior ("Prior's Stoke"), assessed at £2 6s. 8d., and taxed 14d.

b. KIDDERMINSTER.

69. KENELM CHAUNCE of Kidderminster. Ad'mons at Worcester, to the widow 26 Feb. 1556-7, and to the son 24 Aug. 1580. = AGNES who survived her husband.

JOHN CHAUNCE.

Perhaps he, who with MARGARET his wife gave up land at Haberley and Kedermynster to NICHOLAS CHAUNCE (No. 70) in 1601. [Feet of Fines.]

70. NICHOLAS CHAUNCE of Oldington, Kidderminster. Will dated 13 Dec. 1632, proved at Worc. 1 Feb. 1632-3. Gave up the property above-mentioned in 1602. [Feet of Fines.] = ELIZABETH

———— dau. m. HUGH BROOKE, and had 3 children.

71. 1642. THOMAS CHAUNCY Gent., and KATHARINE his wife, gave up land in Kidderminster. [Feet of Fines.]

72. 1662 & 1667. THOMAS CHAUNCE of Kidderminster, a "poore" man, occupied a one-hearth house there.

73. 1694. JOHN CHANCE of Kidderminster, widower, aged 53, m. BRIDGET CLARK of St. Peter's, Droitwich, widow, aged 53.

J. C. was a freeholder of Kidderminster in 1714 and voted in the County Election. [Prattinton MSS.]

He and his wife were parties to transference of land in Kidderminster and elsewhere in 1714 and 1719 [Feet of Fines], so that they both lived to a great age.

74. RICHARD CHANCE of Lower Mitton, Kidderminster. Will dated 21 Apr. 1741, proved at Worc. 1 May 1741. = ELIZABETH[1] who survived her husband. R. C. had an aunt ELIZABETH STOAKE.

RICHARD CHANCE.   MARTHA CHANCE.

[1] She seems to have been his 3rd wife, as we find that RICHARD CHANCE, of Lower Mitton, a widower aged 30, m. in 1718 MARTHA ADDIS, of All Saints', Worcester.

APPENDIX F.—OTHER WORCESTERSHIRE CHANCES.   161

c. ELMLEY LOVETT.

75. 1581. HENRY CHAUNCE and ELIZABETH his wife acquired land in Elmley Lovett.
[Feet of Fines.]
(Cp. other mentions of Elmley Lovett under No. 23.)

d. HANBURY.

76. 1663. Adm'on of the goods of THOMAS CHAUNCE of Broughton, Hanbury, granted at Worcester to ELIANOR, wife of WILLIAM ELVINS, & *relict of T. C.*

77. 1664. JANE CHAUNCE, widow, and others, transferred land in Hanbury and Claines.
[Feet of Fines.]

e. ALVECHURCH AND BEOLEY.

78. 1656-7. WILLIAM CHANCE of Beoley m. at Bromsgrove ELIZABETH BRUNT of the same. In 1662 and 1667 WM. C. occupied a one-hearth house at Beoley.

79. 1667. WILLIAM CHAUNCE occupied a one-hearth house at Alvechurch.

f. DODDERHILL (DROITWICH).

80. 1668. June 2. EDWARD MORGAN of Chaddesley Corbet, husbandman, aged 40, widower, m. KATHARINE CHAUNCE, of Dodderhill.

81. 1741. BERNARD CHANCE, freeholder of Dodderhill, voted in the County Election.
[Prattinton MSS.]

g. CHADDESLEY CORBET.

82. 1648. Adm'on of the goods of GILBERT CHAUNCE of Chaddesley Corbet granted at Worcester to his widow MARGARETT, who was perhaps the widow CHAUNCE mentioned in the Hearthmoney Rolls as occupying a 2-hearth house at Chaddesley Corbet in 1662 and 1667.

G. C. was perhaps the son of WILLIAM CHANCE bapt. at Bromsgrove 3 Dec. 1606.

83.

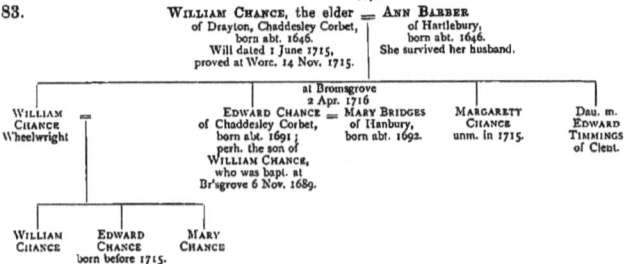

162   APPENDIX F.—OTHER WORCESTERSHIRE CHANCES.

84.   JOHN CHAUNCE =

	1722		
JOSEPH CHANCE of Oakeboul, Chaddesley Corbet, born abt. 1682. Will dated 11 May 1729, proved at Worc. 28 June 1729.	= (2) ELIZABETH HOOMAN, of Chaddesley Corbet, born abt. 1692. She survived her husband.	JOHN CHANCE perh. J. C., freeholder of Chaddesley Corbet in 1741. [Prattinton MSS.]	RICHARD CHANCE

JOSEPH CHANCE had nephews and nieces (born bef. 1729)—
JOHN, JOSEPH, RICHARD, SARAH, and ELIZABETH.

h. HARTLEBURY.

85.   RICHARD CHANCE = JANE
        of Hartlebury.   who survived her
        Adm'on in the Peculiar   husband.
        Court of Hartlebury
        to his widow 21 Oct. 1720.

                1710
        RICHARD CHANCE = MARY LEY
        of Hartlebury,   of Wisher,
        born abt. 1688. b. abt. 1687.

i. SOUTH WORCESTERSHIRE.

86.   CHANCE = JOANE   MILLICENT
              in 1704 widow,   m. TOWERS
              of Abbot's Wood,   and had issue.
              Holy Cross, Pershore.
              Will dated 25 June 1704,
              proved at Worc.
              16 Dec. 1704.

87.   1714. JOHN CHANCE, a freeholder of Eckington, voted in the County Election.
                                                                    [Prattinton MSS.]

88.   1708. WILLIAM CHANCE, of Moore, Fladbury, aged 34, m. ELIZABETH PHILIPS, of
             the same, aged 40, widow.
      1714. WM. C., a freeholder of Fladbury, voted in the County Election.
                                                                    [Prattinton MSS.]

89.   CHANCE . = SUSANA
                        in 1721 widow, of
                        Upton-on-Severn.
                        Will dated 3 Oct. 1721,
                        proved at Worc. 10 Feb, 1725-6.

| HENRY CHANCE of Upton-on-Severn, Adm'on at Worcester 26 July 1729 to his widow JANE.[1] | THOMAS CHANCE. | dau. m. JOHN PIRKINS. Issue. | dau. m. THOMAS AMPHLETT. Issue. | dau. m. WILLIAM TOVEY. Issue. |

1725. HENRY CHANCE of Claines, Wheelwright, aged 27, m. JANE LYES, of the same, aged 33.

APPENDIX G.

CHANCES IN HAMPSHIRE.

A FAMILY of the name of Chance lived in this county in the last century, and claimed descent from the Chances of Bromsgrove. A descendant of theirs, Edward John Chance, was a surgeon, living in London; and he had some acquaintance with, and took interest in the Chances of Birmingham, to whom he supposed himself to be related. His descent was as follows.

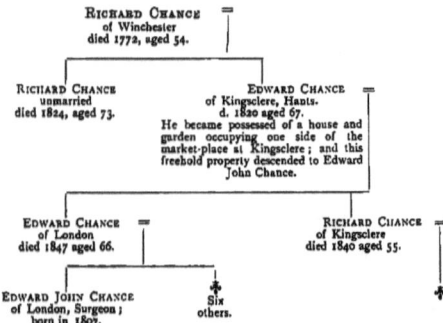

It is a singular thing, that Edward John Chance's father closely resembled in personal appearance Edward Chance of Birmingham, my great-uncle.

[Communication of E. J. C. to Dr. Frank Chance.]

APPENDIX H.

EARLY NOTICES OF CHANCES OTHER THAN OF WORCESTERSHIRE.

CHAWNOS and CHAWNES occur in the Roll of Battle Abbey.

1285. RICHARD CHANCE, when Edward I. made his enquiries into usurpations of lands and manorial rights effected during the troubles of his father's reign, claimed "ab antiquitate" rights to a Court Leet, Assize of Bread and Beer, Gallows, and "Weyf," at Wolford Magna ("Magna Wulward") in Warwickshire, and had his claim allowed. The same RICHARD was lord of the Manor of Wolford Magna in 1316.
[Dugdale—"Hist.: of Warwickshire"—pp. 592-3, and Record Office—Rotuli de Quo Warranto.]

1297. SALOMON DES CHAUNS summoned to the Military Council at Rochester.
[Record Office—Parl'tary Writs.]

1321-2. WILL'MUS CHAUNCE one of the manucaptors (sureties) for the attendance of Philippus le Mareschal, burgher of Lewes, at the Parliament to be held at York.   [*Ibid.*]

1331. RICHARD CHANUS relinquished to Sir John de Ifield (a magnate of Kent and Sussex, and Knight of the Shire for Kent 1330-3) all his claims to lands near Worthing held by his ancestor Thomas de Offington.   [Brit: Mus:—Harl: Charters 76 F 10.]

1398-9. GEORGE CHAUNZ, landholder in Kent. (Probably the name stands for CHAUNCEUS, *i.e.*, CHAUNCEY, a name known in Kent.)   [Record Office—Inq. post Mortem.]

1437. Will of THOMAS CHAUNCES, "Vir venerabilis" and a Burgess of Cambridge, proved in London 13th May 1437. (Probably also a CHAUNCEY, a family well known in the Eastern Counties.)   [Probate Registry—Somerset House.]

1443. JOHN CHAUNCE disposed of property at Gowteby (Godeby) Maureward, in Leicestershire.
[Nichol. "County of Leicester" ii. 195.]

1453. JOHN CHANCE of Berking (Barking), Essex, disposed of property at Shearsby, Leicestershire.
[*Ibid.* iv. 232.]
(As the CHAUNCEYS of Essex were represented about 1450 by JOHN CHAUNCY, it is possible that these two notices relate to him.)

1571. JOHN CHAUNCE, was "servant" to Sir Henry Cheney, Knt., of Harlington, Beds. The latter put him into a copyhold of which one Ralphe Anstry (or Astrye) had been dispossessed; and he consequently brought a suit in Chancery.
[Record Office—Chancery Proceedings—temp. Eliz.—Anstry v. Cheney and Chaunce.]

1626. Apr. 24. EDWARD CHAUNCE of St. Botolph, Bishopsgate, upholder, and ALICE PEIRCE, of St. Ethelburgh, London, widow of DANIEL PEIRCE, at St. Botolph aforesaid.
[Foster—"London Marriage Licenses."]

1627. WILLIAM CHAUNCE, husband of ELIZABETH SMITH, widow of MARTYN SMITH, citizen and haberdasher, of London.
[Record Office—Chancery Proceedings—temp. Chas. I.—Chaunce v. Hexam.]

1633. JACOB CHAUNCE, "Dutchman and workeman in brasse and Copper Workes," brought a suit in Chancery against Richard Ayleway, of Taynton, Glouc., complaining that the latter had failed to carry out the Agreement, on the strength of which plaintiff and one William Shilling had come over from the Netherlands.
[Record Office—*ibid.*—Chaunce v. Ayleway.]

1635. ELLIN CHAUNCE, Emigrant to St. Kitts.
[J. C. Hotten—Lists of Emigrants 1600-1700.]

1690. The case of CHANCE v. ADAMS is reported in Lord Raymond's "Law Cases," Vol. I. p. 77. Adams was a gauger, or exciseman, who was sued by Chance for gauging certain vessels unduly.

APPENDIX H.—EARLY NOTICES OF CHANCES.

WILLS AND ADMINISTRATIONS AT THE PROBATE REGISTRY, SOMERSET HOUSE.

Year	Name	Place	
1649.	JOHN CHANCE.	London.	Adm'on.
1667.	ANTHONY CHANCE.	Glouc.	
1676.	CHRISTOPHER CHANCE.[1]	London.	
1678.	CHARLES CHANCE.		Adm'on.
1685.	JOHN CHANCE.	For. Parts.[2]	
1693.	ANTHONY CHANCE.	Bristol.	Adm'on.
1694.	ANNE CHANCE.	do.	
1694.	ANTHONY CHANCE.	do.	Adm'on.
1703.	THOMAS CHANCE.	For. Parts.	
1713.	ANTHONY CHANCE.	Glouc.	Adm'on.
1714.	NATHANIEL CHANCE.	do.	Adm'on.
1716.	DANIEL CHANCE.	do.	
1717.	WILLIAM CHANCE.	For. Parts.	Adm'on.
1725.	DANIEL CHANCE.	Glouc.	Adm'on.
1728.	ELIZABETH CHANCE.	London.	
1729.	JOHN CHANCE.	Middlesex.	
1729.	SARAH CHANCE. *alias* MARR.	London.	Adm'on.
1731.	WILLIAM CHANCE.[3]	do.	
1732.	THOMAS CHANCE.	Glouc.	&c.

The Wills in this List, and those given in Appendix D, p. 135, are all that I have been able to find at Somerset House of earlier date than 1750.

[1] Father Christopher Chance, wife Sarah, and dau. Sarah.
[2] Foreign Parts usually means at sea. Thus William Chance, administration of whose goods was granted to his sister Elizabeth Jones in 1717, died on board H.M.S. Exeter.
[3] This was a Citizen and Ironmonger, of London. He left a widow Mary, a son Thomas, and a nephew William Drybutter.

INDEX.

Abbott, *see* Albutt
Abkettleby, Leic., 73, 99
Abney, 98
Adams, 53, 90, 97, 165
Adamson, C., 95
Addis, Martha, 124, 160
Administrations, 10, 133-139, 166
Ages of Chances, 60
Albutt (Abbott), William, 78, 113, 125
  Hannah (Chance) his wife, 49, 78, 111, 113, 125
  William and Mary, 49
Allen, Mary, 123, 157
Alvechurch (Allchurch), 11, 26, 113, 128, 142, 154, 161
America, trade with, 56
Amphlett, Thomas, 162
Andrews, 89, 97
Ansley, near Atherstone, 43, 47, 73, 94, 95, 99, 100
Anstry, Ralph, 165
Appleby, Leic., 52, 95, 96
Arden, Mary, 124, 153
Arden, Osbert and Amicia de, 98
Armorial bearings, Barnesley, 25
  Butler, 62
  Chance, 61, 62
  Homer, 44, 45, 62, 93, 140
  Lucas, 62
  Vernon, 41, 62
  disclaimers, 13, 20, 26
Arnos Vale Cemetery, Bristol, 89
Arrow, by Alcester, 127
Ashwell, William, 76
Ashmoore, Astmore, 85, 144, 146
Aston, near Birmingham, 43, 94, 98, 121
Aston Cantlow, Warw., 155
Astrye, Ralph, 165
Astwood, Feckenham, 155
Athelstane, King, 98
Atherstone, Warw., 43, 73, 96, 98, 99
Atkins, J., 99
Attleborough, by Nuneaton, 95
Attwood, 57
Atwell, Jonathan, 109
Awyer, William, 147
Ayleway, 20, 122, 156, 165

Bache, 86, 106
Backwell, Som., 52, 79, 90
Backwell Hill, 53, 73, 90
Badger, 108, 145, 152
Bagshawe, Arthur, 158
Baker, 23, 24, 145
Ball, Nurse, 81
"Baptism" and "Christening," 81
Barber, 86, 123, 161
Bardesley, *see* Barnesley
Barking, Essex, 165

Barnesley (Barndesley, Bardesley, Brandesley), 12, 25, 26, 64, 130, 131, 144
Barnesley Hall, Bromsgrove, 12, 25
Barrett, John, 125
Bartleet, 36
Bate, 24, 113, 145
Bath, 39, 91
Battle Abbey, Roll of, 31, 164
Bawle, William, 65
Beale, 84
Bean, 53, 90
Beaudley, Heref., 126
Bedwardine, Worcester, 10, 11, 19, 20, 124, 125, 127, 131, 134, 142, 156
Belbroughton, Worc., 11, 14, 15, 27-29, 76-78, 112-114, 125, 126, 135, 142, 146, 150, 151
  cp. Fairfield
Bell, George, 8, 9, 33, 50, 73, 86, 115, 135
  Mary (Tilt, then Chance) his wife, 8, 9, 32, 33, 50, 51, 60, 73, 78, 86, 114, 115, 125
  their family, 33, 86, 115
Bennett, 83
Bentley, Warw., 99
Bentley Pauncefote, Worc., 26
Beoley, Worc., 11, 109, 124, 142, 161
Bercroft, 13
Berrow, the, Feckenham, 139, 155
Betton, 91
Biggs, William, 108
Bilston, Staff., 46
Bingham, Thomas, 79
Binton, Warw., 139
Bircott, *see* Burcott
Bird, 99
Birdingbury, Warw., 43, 46, 47, 52, 94-96
Birlingham, Worc., 129
Birmingham, 7-9, 38, 43, 50-53, 55-57, 59, 61, 73, 78-84, 86, 92, 94-96, 130, 140, 163
  Bread St., 7, 51
  Bull Ring, 96
  Cemeteries, 80-82
  Church St., 51
  George St., Edgbaston, 56
  Great Charles St., 56
  Hockley, 95
  Mount St., 56
  Newhall St., 7, 51-53, 56
  Ring Close, 51
  Royal Hotel, 57
  St. Martin's, 79, 80, 96, 114
  St. Mary's, 83
  St. Paul's, 53, 78-81, 90, 130
  St. Philip's, 79-82, 84, 96, 97
  Warstone Lane, 80, 81
Birmingham Political Union, 57
Bishopsgate, London, 165
Blackheath, Battle of, 17

INDEX

Blackroot Pool, Sutton Park, 46
Blackwell-hall, London, 19
Blakeway, Thomas, 144
Blathwayt, 90
Blick, Martin and Bennet (Chaunce) and family, 74, 107
    Joshua, their son, 74, 149
    Rebecca, their dau., 74, 76, 110, 123
    Richard, 112
Blore, Rev. W., 99
Blyth Hall, Warw., 140
Bontemps, M., 55
Boraston, William, 127
Boston, U.S.A., 46
Boucher (Butcher), Samuel, 151
Boulogne, 97
Bound, John, 21, 122, 157
Bourn, Ann, 124
Bournheath, Bromsgrove, 22, 27, 107, 111-113, 133, 134, 136, 137, 145, 147, 150, 151, 155
Bow Church, London, 81, 82
Bowdok, Roger, 23
Bowen, 20, 156
Bower, 19
Bowler, 20, 156
Brace, Francis, 12
Bracebridge family, 43, 73, 98, 99
    Rev. Thomas, 73, 99, 100
    Jane (Ludford) his wife, 73, 99, 100
    Katherine Homer their dau., 73, 94, 99
    spelling of the name, 98
Bracebrigg, Linc., 98
Bradley, Bradley, 148, 152
    Mary, 26, 106, 148
Bradley, Worc., *see* Stock and Bradley
Bradnock, Anne, 128
Brailes, Warw., 35, 64
Brainch, John, 147
Brampton, 82
Brandesley, *see* Barnesley
Braye, William, 158
Bread St., Birmingham, 7, 51
Brettell, Brittel, 109, 113, 153
Brewster, 82
Bridgen, John, 145
Bridges, Mary, 112, 124, 161
Brinton, Sarah, 21, 123, 157
Bristol, 10, 34, 36-38, 51-54, 57, 58, 73, 78, 80, 89-91, 94, 95, 97, 117, 127, 137
    Arnos Vale, 89
    Christchurch, 91
    College, the, 80
    Hot Wells, 95
    Kingsdown, 38, 137
    Limekiln Dock, 38
    Lucas' Hall, Marsh St., 37, 89, 137
    Montpelier, 90
    Nicholas St., 37, 38, 52, 54, 89, 137
    St. Augustine's, 38
    St. James', 137
    St. Mary Redcliffe, 91
    St. Werburgh's, 89-91, 127
Bristol, Bishop of, 80
British Crown Glass Co., 55
Brittaine, Mary, 126
Brittel, *see* Brettell
Brockley Court, Som., 53, 97
Bromall, Joan, 45
Bromsgrove, passim
    Alford's Meadow, 152
    Barnesley Hall, 12, 25
    Barn's Close, 152
    Church, building of, 24
    Crebbmill Farm, 29
    Free School, the, 19

Bromsgrove, Grafton Lodge, 36, 88
    Hill's, Hill and Porter's, 152, 153
    Littleton's, 152
    Rocking Lane, 111, 150
    Rosemary Lane, 134
    Sauntridge, 32
    Slideslow, Slightslow, 33
    Spadesbourne Brook, 32
    cp. Bournheath, Burcott, Catshill, Chadwick, Dyers, Install, Lickey, Padstones, Sheepcote, Shepley, Sidemore, Timberhanger, Woodcote, Woodrowe, Yarnhill
Brooke, 49, 78, 106, 158-160
Broome, near Stourbridge, 78, 114, 125
Broughton, Hanbury, 16, 134, 161
Broughton Hackett, Worc., 122, 151
Brown, John, 113
Brunt, Elizabeth, 109, 161
Budbrooke, Warw., 46, 96
Bullard, Catherine, 86
Bunney, Robert, 58
Burcott, Bromsgrove, 7, 8, 22, 49, 77, 78, 107, 109, 135, 149
Durlestone, 95
Burls, 90
Burne, Rev., 83
Burneford, John, 23
Burton, 97
Bush, Ann, 90
Butcher (Boucher), Samuel, 151
Butler, general. 62, 63, 73, 128, 138, 139
    Samuel, 40, 41
    of Bromsgrove, 40, 74, 105, 124, 128, 138, 139, 146, 149, 153
    Margaret, 74-76, 138
    Anne Chaunce her dau., 74-76, 105
    of Defford, 41
    of Feckenham, 38, 40, 128, 138, 139
    of Hanbury, 40-42, 73, 92, 118, 128
    Elizabeth Lucas, 38, 40, 42, 73, 79, 90, 92, 117, 118, 127, 137
    of Strensham, 41
Buxton, Buxtons, 112, 113

Callowe, John, 123, 157
Cambridge, 47, 56, 164
Canada, conquest of, 58
Cance, 109
Canterbury, Archbp. of, 81, 82
    Province of, 10
Carlisle, 83
Carpenter, 86, 153
Carpet manufacture, 19
Castle Bromwich, Warw., 43, 73, 94, 121
Catesby, 99
Catshill (Catsel), Bromsgrove, 11, 22, 26, 27, 106, 107, 109-113, 131, 132, 134, 135, 138, 142, 143, 148, 150-155
Cave-Browne-Cave, 84
Cemeteries, Arnos Vale, Bristol, 89
    Bath, 91
    Birmingham, 80-82
    Highgate, 81
    Kensal Green, 82
    Southsea. 91
Chaddesley Corbet, Worc., 10, 11, 16, 112, 123, 124, 134, 142, 161, 162
Chadwick, Bromsgrove, 25, 111, 151
Chamberlin, John, 87
Chance, general, 7-21, 49-63, 73-84, 105-114, 122-125, 130-135, 141-166
    spelling of the name, 30, 31
    of Alvechurch, 11, 113, 142, 161
    in Bedfordshire, 165

INDEX.   iii.

Chance of Bedwardine, 10, 11, 19, 20, 131, 134, 142, 156
 of Belbroughton, 11, 27, 135, 142, 150
 of Beoley, 11, 109, 142, 161
 of Birmingham
  general, 33, 38, 51-60, 78-84, 130, 163
  armorial bearings, 61, 62
  William ("No. 4"), 5, 7-9, 32, 34, 38, 43, 50-54, 58-61, 73, 78-80, 82-84, 90, 96, 97, 114, 130
  Sarah (Lucas) his wife, 5, 34, 52, 53, 73, 78, 84, 90, 96, 130
  their children & grandchildren, 53-60, 79-84, 130
  Robert Lucas sen., 38, 52-56, 58, 79, 82, 91, 97
  William ("No. 5"), 55-58, 61, 80, 82, 83
  George, 56-58, 60, 83
  Edward, 51, 58, 81, 82, 163
  Henry, 5, 38, 51, 54, 58, 59, 79, 81
  Maria, 59, 82
  Robert Lucas jun., 36, 82
  Dr. Frank, 5, 82, 131, 154, 163
  James Timmins, 5, 56, 83
  William ("No. 6"), 56, 83, 132
 of Bournheath, Bromsgrove, 22, 27, 107, 111-113, 133, 134, 145, 147, 150, 151, 155
 of Bristol, 10, 166
 of Bromsgrove, 6-11, 14-16, 22-29, 73-78, 105-114, 122-125, 130-135, 141-150
  Isabell (d. 1546), 23, 24, 65, 133, 144
  William (d. 1622), 12, 25, 26, 107, 130, 133, 141, 144, 147
  see also Chance of Bournheath, Catshill, &c.
 of Burcott, see Chance of Shepley
 of Catshill, Bromsgrove, 11, 22, 26, 27, 106-114, 131, 132, 134, 135, 142, 143, 148, 150-154
  William (d. 1768), 27, 131, 132, 135, 154
  Thomas his bro., 27, 132, 154, 155
 of Chaddesley Corbet, 10, 11, 16, 112, 123, 124, 134, 142, 161, 162
 of Chadwick, Bromsgrove, 111
 of Claines, 113, 125, 162
 of Clent, 16, 144
 of Doddenham, 134, 159
 of Dodderhill, 123, 161
 of Droitwich, 124, 135, 161
 of Eckington, 162
 of Elmley Lovett, 15, 148, 161
 in Essex, 165
 of Fladbury, 124, 162
 of Fockbury, Bromsgrove, 22, 109, 134, 145, 152-154
 in Gloucestershire, 10, 124, 166
 of Hadzor, 10-14, 24, 26, 131, 133-135, 141, 142, 158
 of Halesowen, 16
 in Hampshire, 163
 in Hanbury, 10, 16, 134, 161
 of Hartlebury, 15, 124, 134, 162
 of Harvington, 10, 14, 15, 135, 141, 146
 of Himbleton, 11, 123, 142, 159
 of Hoblench, 10, 14, 135, 146
 of Inkberrow, 111, 123, 159
 of Kidderminster, 10, 11, 15, 123, 124, 133, 135, 142, 160
 in Leicestershire, 165
 in London, 10, 163, 165, 166
 in Middlesex, 10, 166
 of Oddingley, 113, 123, 134, 159
 of Pershore, 134, 162
 of Salwarp, 10, 11, 14, 122-124, 134, 142, 158, 159
 of Sheepcote, Bromsgrove, 105, 146

Chance of Shepley and Burcott, Bromsgrove
  general, 7-9, 17, 18, 22, 27-29, 40, 49-51, 66, 73-78, 105-114, 123, 125, 133-135, 149, 152-154
  John (d. 1618), 17, 28, 74, 133
  John (d. 1670), 18, 28, 66, 74-77, 109, 110
  William ("No. 1"), 7-9, 18, 29, 49, 50, 73, 76-78, 111, 114, 125
  William ("No. 2"), 7, 18, 29, 49, 78, 113, 114, 125
  John ("No. 1"), 7, 49-51, 73, 78, 112
  John ("No. 2"), 8, 9, 50, 73, 78, 86, 94, 114, 125
  William ("No. 3"), 7-9, 49-51, 53, 78, 112, 125, 135
  Thomas their bro., 7-9, 50-52, 78, 135
 of Sidemore, Bromsgrove, 109, 152
 of Solihull, 124
 of Stoke Prior, 16, 26, 112, 134, 141, 152, 160
 of the Stonehouse, 109
 of Stourbridge, 134, 149
 of Tardebig, 124
 of Timberhanger, Bromsgrove, 22, 106, 108, 133, 144, 145
 of Upton-on-Severn, 27, 132, 134, 154, 162
 of Upton Snodsbury, 10, 14, 134, 158
 of Warndon, 14, 134, 135, 159
 of Wick, Worcester, 141
 of Winchester, 163
 of Wolford Magna, 164
 of Woodcote, Bromsgrove, 11, 14, 22, 26, 109, 146
 of Woodrowe, Bromsgrove, 107
 of Worcester, 10, 11, 15, 16, 18-21, 106, 122-124, 131, 133-135, 147, 156, 157
  cp. Chance of Bedwardine and of Wick
 of Yarnhill, Bromsgrove, 108
Chance Bros. and Co., 55, 56
Chance, Edward John, 163
Chance and Homer, 7, 8, 51-53, 56
Chance Monument, the, 27, 131, 132, 154
"Chance on Powers," 59
Chance, Wm. and Geo., 56, 58
Chance, Wm., Son, and Co., 56
Chancery Proceedings, 12-15, 19, 20, 45, 148, 165
Chances and Hartleys, 55
Chancey, 111
Chanch
Chanes, Chanis } for Chance, 31
Chanus, Richard, 164
Charnells, 99
Chaunce, see Chance
Chaunces, Thomas, 164
Chauncey, Chauncy, 15, 31, 160, 164, 165
Chaunche for Chance, 31
Chaunse, see Chance
Chauns, Chaunz, 164
Chawnce, le Chawne, Chawns, Chawnse, Chawse, 22, 24, 30, 31, 131, 133, 143, 144
Chawnes, Chawnos, 31, 164
Chelwood, Som., 90
Chende, 143
Cheney, Sir Henry, 165
Cheshire, 41
Cheson or Cheston, Robert, 74
Choisy-le-Roi Glassworks, 55
Chonce for Chance, 31
"Christening" and "Baptism," 81
Christopher, 74
Churchlench, Worc., 129
Claines. Worc., 113, 125-128, 159, 161, 162
Clark, Clarke, 15, 74, 111, 123, 160
Claybrook, Leic., 99
Cleeve Prior, Warw., 124

INDEX

Clent, Worc., 16, 144, 161
Clifden, Co. Clare, 97
Clifton, Bristol, 53, 89, 90, 97
Cloth trade at Worcester } 11, 18, 19, 21, 26
Clothiers' Guild
Clutton, Rev., 80
Coathupe, 52, 54
Cobbold, 95
Cofton (Cawfton) Hackett, Worc., 123
Cole, 111, 126, 151
    Elizabeth Chance, 7, 49, 78, 113, 114, 125
Coleridge, S. T., 54
Coleshill, Warw., 46
College of Arms, 61, 62
Colseley, *see* Coseley
Combe, Dr., 47
Comer, Elizabeth (Nash), 89
Cooke, 38, 81, 91, 96
Cooke and Sons, 54, 58
Cooke, Prince, and Co., 38, 91
Cookes, Cooks, 92, 126, 153
Cooperage firms, 36-38, 52, 89, 90
Cope, 79-83
Corbin, 99
"Cordwainer," meaning of, 50
Cornwallis, Bishop, 81
Coseley (Colseley), Staff., 44, 120
Cotterell, Cotterill, 88, 99, 126
Cotton, Hayes, 154
Cottye, 147
Courthand, 11, 65
Court Rolls (Manorial Records), 22-24, 29, 30, 44, 49, 93, 148, 152-154
"Cousin," meaning of, 14, 44, 64
Covell, John, 53
Coventry, 58, 95
Crab, 24, 40, 128
Cradley, Worc., 45
Crane, 33, 50, 51, 86
Creats, 61, 62
Crewker, 99
Crispe, 157
Croft, Rev. Dr., 80
Crowfoot, John, 113
Crumpe, Anne, 123, 159
Curdworth, Warw., 46
"Cutting off with a shilling," 50

Dadley, 46, 79, 80, 94, 96
Dales, Rev., 81
Deakin, Elizabeth (Nash), 89
Deeple, 85
Defford, Worc., 41
De Peyster, 58, 80
    Cornelia Maria, 58, 80, 83
Derling, 126
De Ste Croix, 90
Dewce, 27, 110, 125, 150
Dineley, 25, 130, 147
Directories, 7, 37, 58
Dixon, Benjamin Homer, 46
Doddenham, Worc., 134, 159
Dodderhill, Worc., 15, 88, 123, 124, 127, 148, 155, 161
Dormeston, Worc., 123, 157
Doverdale, Worc., 123
Downward, 83
Droitwich, Worc., 10, 12-15, 41, 123, 124, 127, 135, 151, 160, 161
Drybutter, William, 166
Dudley, 45, 46, 151
Dugard, 124, 159
Dugdale, Mr. Richard, 140
Dumbarton Glass Works, 54

Duncomb, Joseph, 46
Dunne, 155
Dunton, } Warw., 99
Dutton,
Dyers, Manor of, Bromsgrove, 29, 148, 153
Dypple, *see* Deeple
Dytham Park, Glouc., 90

Eckington, Worc., 162
Eckles, 110
Edgbaston, 36, 56, 58, 88
Edington, Wilts, 84
Elections, Chances &c. voting at, 15, 32, 38, 151, 153, 157, 160-162
Elmbridge, Worc., 113, 159
Elmley Castle, Worc., 99
Elmley Lovett, Worc., 15, 145, 148, 161
Elvins, 126, 161
Emmanuel Coll., Cambridge, 47
Essex, 34. 165
Ettingshall (Etynghold), Sedgley, 43, 44, 46, 62, 93, 94, 120, 140
Evans, 59, 81, 86
Evesham, 124, 127
Exeter, H.M.S., 166

"Factor," meaning of, 51
Fairfield (Forfield), Belbroughton, 76, 77, 109, 150
Farmer, 100
Feckenham, Worc., 38, 40, 128, 138, 139, 155
Feckenham Park, Hanbury, 34, 73, 87, 137
"Feet of Fines," 12, and references
Felton, 80, 88, 94, 117
Fenton, Linc., 62
Ferguson, 83
Fidkin, 122, 159
Fincher, Thomas, 123
Finstal Heath, Stoke Prior, 49, 74
Fladbury, Worc., 124, 162
Fockbury, Bromsgrove, 22, 109, 134, 143-145, 151-155
"Foreign Parts," 166
Forfield, Forefield, *see* Fairfield
Forth, William, 159
Foster, 39, 91
Fowley, Mary, 114
Fownes, 74, 105, 145, 147
Freeman, Mary, 76, 109
Fullwood, Alice, 155

Ganderton, 14, 108, 122, 158
Geast, Mr. Richard, 140
Gee, 38, 53, 91, 97
Glass Manufacture, 38, 52, 54, 55
Glenefy, Co. Tipperary, 83
Gloucester, Gloucestershire, 10, 36, 88, 166
Gnorle, John, 85
Godeby Maureward, Leic., 165
Gold, Prudence, 99
Gorle, John, 85
Gornal, Lower, *see* Guernall
Goslin or Gosnell, John, 112, 151
Gower, 19
Grafton Lodge, Bromsgrove, 36, 88
Granger, Mary (Lucas), 89
Grantham Linc., 81
Gravesend, 56
Gray, Jonathan, 97
Great Alne, Warw., 155
Great Whitley, Worc., 125
Green 87, 127
Greening, Elizabeth, 86

INDEX.

Gryffen, Richard, 145
Guernall, Staff. (prob. for Lower Gornal), 120
Guibins, Ann, 93, 120
Guildford, 99

Haarlem, 58
Habbelench, *see* Hoblench
Haberley, Habberley, Worc., 15, 160
Hackluit, Anthony, 159
Hackney, 154
Hadzor, (Hadsor, Hadysor), Worc., 10-14, 24, 26, 30, 35, 41, 88, 92, 117, 118, 127, 131, 133-135, 141, 142, 158
Hale End, Warw., 99
Halesowen, 16, 45, 46
Hall, 110, 148, 152
Hambden, Som., 53
Hampshire, 163
Hampstead, 91
Hanbury, Worc., 10, 13, 16, 27, 34-38, 40-42, 46, 73, 67-90, 92, 111, 116-118, 123, 127-129, 134, 137, 139, 151-154, 155-158, 159, 161
   Broadmeadow, 41
   Broughton, 16, 134, 161
   Feckenham Park, 34, 73, 87, 137
   Goshull, 13
   Holloway Field, 27
   Moorecroftes, 41
   Pumphouse, the 35, 88, 117
   Webhouse, 155
Hanbury, Mary, 129
Hancox, Elizabeth, 87
Handsworth, 55
Harborne, Worc., 83, 109
Harcott, 100
Hardy, John Croft, 86
Harlington, Beds., 165
Harrington, Countess of, 37
Harris, 33
Harrison, Haryson, 74, 85, 107
Hartlebury, Worc., 15, 122-124, 126, 134, 159, 161, 162
Hartley, 54, 55
Harvington, Worc., 10, 14, 15, 135, 141, 146
Haryson *see* Harrison
Hatton, Warw., 138
Hay, 123, 159
Haynes, Mary, 124, 157
Heamus, Hannah, 112, 154
Hearthmoney, 11, 40, 142
Hellicas, Ames, 57
Heminge, Hemming, 98, 155
Hendon, Middlesex, 38, 90, 91
Henley-in-Arden, Warw., 155
Heralds, Heralds' Office, 61-63
Heralds' Visitations, 13, 20, 25, 26, 98, 99
Herbert, William, 123
Herford, I., 154
"Heriot," 49
Hewell Grange, Worc., 138
Hexam, 165
Hickmans, Margery, 120
Higge, Higges, 23, 106
Higgins, 65, 108
Higham, Leic., 100
Highgate, 38, 54, 55, 81
Hill, 21, 63, 64, 123, 146, 151, 153, 157
   Henry and John, and Alice Till, 33, 85, 136
Hill's, Hill and Porter's, Bromsgrove, 152, 153
Himbleton, Worc., 11, 123, 142, 159
Hinckley, Susanna, 128
Hoblench, Worc., 10, 14, 135, 146
Hockley, Birmingham, 95

Holemer, Holemere, 44, 45
Holland, Mary, 121
Holland, Warw., 99
Hollow, Worc., 21, 123, 157
Hollyman, Mary, 128
Holmer, Holmor, Holmore, 44, 45, 93, 119, 120
Holmes, Jonathan, 76, 111
Holte of Aston, 98
Homer, general, 43-48, 51-54, 62, 63, 73, 93-97, 119-121, 140
   spelling and derivation of the name, 44
   Andrew, 45, 62
   of Appleby, Leic., Rev. William, 52, 95, 96
   of Bilston, Staff., 46
   of Birdingbury, Warw., 43, 46, 47, 52, 93-96
   of Birmingham, *see* Homer of West Town
   of Boston, U.S.A., 46
   of Burlestone, Rev. Henry, 95
   of Coseley, Staff., 120
   of Coventry, Thomas, 195
   in Dorsetshire, 45, 46
   of Ettingshall, *see* Homer of Sedgley
   of Guernall (qy. Lower Gornal), Staff., 120
   of Leamington, Dr. Henry, 95
   in Oxfordshire, 45
   of Sedgley (Ettingshall), Staff., 43-46, 62, 93, 119, 120, 140
   of Solihull, Warw., 95
   in Somersetshire, temp. Jas. I., 46
   modern, *see* Homer of West Town
   in Staffordshire, 45, 46
   ep. Homer of Bilston, Coseley, Sedgley
   of Sutton Coldfield, Warw., 43-48, 62, 73, 94, 121, 140
     Thomas, 43, 44, 46, 73, 93, 94, 120, 121, 140
     Edward (No. 1), 43, 44, 46, 73, 93, 94, 99, 121, 140
     Edward (No. 2), 46, 47, 73, 94, 121, 140
     William, 47, 48, 80, 94, 121, 140
     Edward (No. 3), *see* Homer of West Town
   of Walsall, 44, 93, 140
   of West Town, Som., 45, 52-54, 96
     Edward, form. of Sutton Coldfield and Birmingham, 5, 7, 8, 34, 38, 43, 48, 51-54, 73, 78-82, 90, 94, 96, 97, 114, 121
     Sarah (Chance), his 1st wife, 7, 9, 53, 73, 78, 82, 94, 96, 114
     Mary (Lucas), his 2nd wife, 7, 34, 52, 73, 78, 80, 81, 90, 94, 96, 97
     Sarah, his dau., 51, 52, 82, 95, 96
     Louisa Chance, his dau., 51, 79, 82, 97
     James Edward and family, 38, 53, 54, 82, 97
     Miss H. G., 5, 54, 96, 97
   of Worcester, 45
   in Worcestershire (North), 45, 46
Homere, Thomas de, 45
Homersham, Homerton, Homerwych, 44
Hooman, Elizabeth, 124, 162
Hopkins, Martha, 108
Horace, Variorum Edition of, 47
Horne, Elizabeth, 87
Horninghold, Leic., 99
Hot Blast, the, Crane's Patent, 50
Houghton Hall, Carlisle, 83
Hower, George, 129
"Hudibras," 41
Hudson, Hester, 99
Hughes, 37
Hunt, Hunte, 9, 50, 78, 147
   Hannah Chance, 8, 9, 50, 78, 114, 125
Huntingdon, 82
Huntington als. Butler, 138

INDEX.

Hurst, Chance, and Co., 58
Hutchins, 95

Ifield, Sir John de, 164
India House, the, 47, 95
Inkberrow (Inkbarrow, Inkborrow), Worc., 111, 123, 127, 139, 157, 159
Insoll, 159
Install, Bromsgrove, 152
Inventories attached to Wills, 17, 18, 28, 65-68, 133
Ipsley, Redditch, 37, 89, 137
Ireland, 34
Islington, 59

Jackson, George, 106, 147
Jamaica, 51
James, 37, 80, 81
Jefferies, Sarah, 126
Jennings, 99
Jersey, 90
Johnson, 53, 119
Johnsons, Percival, 19, 20
Jones, 13, 166
Jordan, Elizabeth, 21, 122, 157
Juggins, Jugina, 111, 149

Kell, Phœbe, 152
Kemsey, 100, 124
Kennedy, Rev. Ran, 53, 82
Kensal Green Cemetery, 82
Kent, 164
Kesteven, 83
Kettlesby, Thomas, 106
Kidderminster, 10, 11, 15, 19, 32, 33, 45, 86, 112, 123-125, 133, 135-137, 142, 151, 160
Kidson, William, 85
Kimberley, Gilbert, 88
"Kin," meaning of, 14, 27, 44, 64, 151
Kingsbury, Warw., 98, 99
Kingsclere, Hants, 163
Kingsdown, Bristol, 38, 137
King's Norton, Worc., 59, 153
Kitchener, Barbara, 154
Knight, Thomas, 122
Knighthood, Distraint of, 13
Kyre Park, Worc., 28

Ladbury, Henry, 155
Lapworth, Warw., 99
Lardner, 80
Latimer, Bishop, 16, 17
Laurence, 80, 81
Laurimore, Mary, 126
Lawrence, 95, 122, 151
Leamington, Warw., 59, 81, 95
Ledsam, 83
Lee, Eyre, 79, 140
  Hugh, 24, 26, 144
Lees, Joseph, 126
Leicestershire, 52, 98, 165
Leigh, Lord, 47
Let, Lett, 113, 124, 162
Lewes, Sussex, 164
Lewis, Lewis, 99, 106
Lichfield, 63, 140
Lickey, the, Bromsgrove, 25
Lillie, Lilly, 75, 100, 111, 126, 146
  William, of Hanbury, and family, 35, 88, 137
  Anne Lucas, his dau., 35, 88, 127
Lincoln, Bishop of, 81

Lincolnshire, 98
Lincoln's Inn, 58
Lindley, Leic., 98, 99
Littleton's land, Bromsgrove, 152
Liverpool, 154
Lloyd, Sarah (Lucas), 89
Lockier, 38, 79, 91, 97
Loff, 22, 23, 143
London, 10, 38, 54, 55, 59, 81, 82, 84, 95, 99, 135, 163, 165, 166
  Bishopsgate, 165
  Bow Church, 81, 82
  Coleman St. Buildings, 58
  Islington, 59
  Lincoln's Inn, 58
  Lothbury, 59
  Russell Square, 84
  St. Botolph's, 165
  St. Ethelburgh's, 165
  St. Pancras, 82
  St. Paul's Churchyard, 58
  St. Paul's Wharf, 54
  Skinner St., Snow Hill, 55
  Upper Gower St., 54
  Upper Thames St., 54
Lord, John, 85, 116
Lowe, 29, 153
Lower Mitton, Kidderminster, 15, 124, 135, 160
Lucas, general, 34-39, 51-53, 62, 63, 73, 67-91, 116, 117, 127, 137
  distribution and derivation of the name, 34, 35
  of Brailes, 35, 64, 65
  of Bristol, 34, 36-39, 51, 52, 73, 89-91, 116, 117, 127, 137
    Robert, 34, 36-40, 42, 52, 73, 87, 89, 90, 92, 94, 116, 117, 127, 137
    Elizabeth (Butler) his wife, 36, 38, 40, 42, 73, 79, 90, 92, 117, 127, 137
    Their daus. (Lockier, Nash, Pater) 37-39, 79, 80, 89, 91, 97
    Mary, their dau., see Homer of West Town
    Sarah, their dau., see Chance of Birmingham
    John Robert, 38, 43, 52, 53, 62, 73, 90
  of Claines, 127
  of Fenton, Linc., 62
  of Hanbury, 34-38, 73, 87-89, 116, 117, 127, 137
  of Redditch, 89, 137
  of Rouslench, 35
  of Rowington, 34, 35, 73, 87, 116, 127, 137
  of Stratford, 35, 137
  of Tardebig, 36, 117, 137
Lucas' Hall, Bristol, 37, 89, 137
Lucey, 99
Ludford of Ansley, 43, 73, 99, 100
Luxmore, Dr., 80
Lyes, 125, 128, 162
Lynall, Lynolle, 24, 144, 145

Macadam, 47
Macomb, General, 58
Madan, Rev., 81
Magdalen Coll., Oxford, 47, 100
Male and Rock, 51
Mancetter, Atherstone, 99
Manley, 39, 81
  Ann (Lucas) 39, 79, 80, 91
Manorial Courts and Customs, 12, 22-24, 44, 49, 93
  cp. Court Rolls
Mare, 166
Mareschal, Philippus le, 164
Margate, 53

INDEX.

Marlid, Margaret, 119
Marriage Bonds and Licenses, 8, 9, 34, 35, 64, 122-129
Marriages, Civil, in 1656, 77, 120
Marsh, John, 120
"Master of the Orphants," 156
Maulden, Beds., 91
Maule, Rev., 82
Mautravers, John, 45
Mayc, Thomas, 105
Mayne, John, 146
Mence, Alice, 107, 152
Mercer, 84
Mercia, Kings of, 98
Metchley, Harborne, 83
Middlesex, 10, 166
Miles, Alice, 129
Milward, Milwarde, 77, 109
Minworth, Warw., 46
"Mistress," meaning of, 121
Mitton, *see* Lower Mitton
Mitton Chapel, 125
Mole (cp. Mowle), 97, 111, 153
Moor, Moore, 99, 123
Morgan, 88, 123, 161
Motices, 61, 62
Mowle (cp. Mole), 158

Nailsea, Som., 38, 52-56
Naples, 39, 91
Nash, general, 37, 38, 89, 129, 139
  Margaret (Lucas) 34, 37, 87, 89, 116, 129, 139
  Jonathan, of Bristol (No. 2), 37, 38, 84, 89
  Anne and Theodosia, his daus., 37, 84
  Thompson, 5, 37
  Mary, 27, 123, 151
Neath, near Swansea, 55
Netherlands, the, 165
New Inn Hall, Handsworth, 55
Newland, Salwarp, 14, 122, 134, 159
New Year's Day, old style, 9, 105
New York, 58, 80
Nicholls, 21, 122, 129
Norris, 148
Northfield, Worc., 19, 128
Northfleet House, Gravesend, 56

Oddingley, Worc., 113, 123, 134, 159
Offington, Thomas de, 164
Ogden, Katharine, 108
Oldbury, 57, 138
Oldington, Kidderminster, 15, 133, 160
Old Stratford, 127
Oldswinford, Stourbridge, 32, 86, 116, 126
Oliver, Henry, 158
Olives (Oliffs), 127
Ombersley, Worc., 113, 122, 155
Onion, 37, 89
"On Parva," Staff., 99
Orford, William, 106, 148
Oswald, George, 122
Oxford, 47, 100
Oxfordshire, 45, 47

Pachet (*i.e.* Paget), William, 23
Padstones, Bromsgrove, 29, 151
Palmer, 55
Parker, Edmund, 120
Parkinson, Caroline, 97
Parnell, Sibilla, 124, 157
Parr, Dr. Samuel, 47
  Elizabeth, 108, 149

Partridge, Margaret (Lucas), 89
Pater, 39, 80, 91
Payton, Rebecca, 126
Pearsall (Persall), 110, 152
  of Willsbridge, Glouc., 37, 89
Peculiar Probate Court—Hanbury, 35, 88, 137, 139
                    Hartlebury, 162
Pedigrees, 71-100, 143-163
Peel, Sir Robert, 57
Peirce, 165
Penne, Penns, 147, 158
Penrice, 35, 88, 117
Peopleton, Worc., 127
Perkes, Perks, 28, 29, 76, 77, 109, 112, 114, 128, 150
Perkins, Pirkins, 126, 162
Persall, *see* Pearsall
Pershore, Worc., 134, 162
Peyton, 82
Philips, Phillips, 124, 157, 162
Phillott, Susan, 91
"Philpot's Ordinary," 62
Pillowe, Rosa, 20, 156
Pirkins, *see* Perkins
Pirton, Worc., 129
Pitt, Pitts (cp. Pytts), 45, 94
Plattsburg, Battle of, 58
Pointer, Anna, 124
Poll Tax Assessment, Bromsgrove, 152
Poole, John, 146
Potter, Richard, 108
Power, Robert, 84
  of Bentley, 99
Powick, Worc., 122
Prescot, 100
Preston Baggott, Warw., 127
"Pretty Polly Saunders," *see* Saunders
Price, 97, 124
Prince, 38, 91
Princep, 94
Pritchett, 39, 76, 91
Probate Registries, 5, 8, 10, 63, *see also* Wills
Property, transfer of, 12
Pulter, John, 23
Pytts, Sir Edward, 28

Queen, the, visit to Birmingham, 57

Raybold, John, 124
Redditch (Ryddyche), Worc., 14, 15, 37, 89, 137
Redfern, 84
Rees, 55
Registers, Parish, general, 5, 6, 64, 77, 105-121
  of Belbroughton, 77, 114
  of Bromsgrove, 8, 9, 24, 25, 30, 31 75
                    77, 105-116, 118, 131
  of Broome, 114
  of Castle Bromwich, 94, 121
  of Hadzor, 117, 118
  of Hanbury, 34, 41, 116-118
  of Oldswinford, 32, 116
  of Rowington, 34, 35, 116, 117
  of Sedgley, 43-46, 119, 120
  of Sutton Coldfield, 94, 121
  of Water Orton, 43, 121
Reynolds, Mary, 123, 156
Richards, Richardes, 88, 106, 117
Ripple, Worc., 124
Roadmaking, 47
Robbins, 120
Robertson, 39, 91
Rochester, 164
Rock, Worc., 127

INDEX

Rock, Joseph and Ann, 79, 84
   cp. Male and Rock
Rodbard, 53, 90
Rogers, Thomas, 119
Rose, 8, 25, 85, 115, 126
Rouslench, Worc., 35
Rowington, Warw., 34-36, 73, 87, 88, 116, 117, 127, 128, 137, 138
   Pool Meadow, 36
   Squadge (Squogg) Hills, 36
Rowley Regis, Worc., 45
Rugby, Rugby School, 47, 52, 95, 96
Rugeley, Alice, 99
Rushock, Worc., 123, 124
Russell, Russall, 24, 130, 145, 147

Sacheverell, Henry, 46
Sadler, 43, 73, 94
   Elizabeth Homer, 43, 44, 73, 94, 121
St. Gall, Switzerland, 37
St. Heliers, Jersey, 90
St. Kitts, 165
St. Oswald's Chapel, 124
Sale, Anne, 112
Salwarp, Worc., 10, 11, 14, 122-124, 134, 142, 158, 159
Sanders, *see* Saunders
Sargant, 37, 59, 79, 83, 84, 130
   William, 53, 59, 79, 82, 84, 130
   Elizabeth (Chance) his wife, 54, 59, 79, 81-84, 130
   Edward, 5, 36, 83, 84, 88, 130, 131
Saunders, Sanders, 76, 88, 106, 110, 111, 122, 147
   John, of Grafton Lodge, Bromsgrove, 36, 80, 88
   Mary (Lucas) his wife ("Pretty Polly Saunders"), 36, 79-81, 88, 96, 97
   Elizabeth, their dau., 36, 81, 88
   Abraham, 36
Savage, 99
Scholefield, 57
Schools, Spon Lane and Oldbury, 57
   Bromsgrove Free, 19
Sedgley, Staff., 43-46, 93, 94, 119, 120
Selly, Worc., 19
Shackston, Leic., 99
Shearsby, Leic., 165
Sheepcote (Shepcoote), Bromsgrove, 105, 146
Shepley, Bromsgrove, 7, 9, 17, 18, 22, 23, 27-29, 49, 66, 74-78, 106, 107, 109-111, 113, 114, 123, 133-135, 149, 152-154
Shilling, William, 165
Shipley, Rev., 79
Shrawley, Worc., 125, 155
Sidemore, Bromsgrove, 109, 152
Silvester, 37, 88, 89
Sitch, Robert, 110, 150
Skeffington, 100
Slye, Thomas, 127
Smite, Warndon, 134, 159
Smith, Smyth, Smythe, 88, 113, 132, 145, 154, 165
   Elizabeth Vernon, 41, 63, 73, 92, 118, 129, 139
   Robert, of Edgbaston, 36, 81, 88
Snareston, Leic., 99
Sneedes Green, Elmley Lovett, 15, 148
Solihull, Warw., 95, 124
Somerset House, 8, 10, 63, 135, 137, 140, 164, 166
Somersetshire, 45, 46
Sou'hall, John, 114
Southam, Thomas, 87
Southey, 59
Southsea Cemetery, 91
Spilsbury, Rev. John, 77
Spon Lane, 55-57
Spring Grove, 57

Staffordshire, 43-45, 100
Standlake, Oxon, 47, 95
Stapleton House, Som., 90
Steward, Jane (Nash), 89
Stoake, Elizabeth, 160
Stock, 55
Stock and Bradley, Worc., 36, 128, 158
Stoke Prior, Worc., 16, 26, 33, 34, 37, 41, 49, 73, 74, 78, 92, 112, 113, 118, 125, 129, 134, 136, 139, 141, 152, 160
   Arbor's Gate, 37, 139
   Finstal Heath, 49, 74
Stokes, 22, 23, 143
Stone, Worc., 125
Stone, 120, 154
Stonehouse, the, 109
Stourbridge, 32, 78, 114, 116, 134, 137, 149
Stoure, 74
Stratford, Edward, 99
Stratford, Warw., 35, 85, 87, 116, 127, 129, 137
Strensham, Worc., 41
Subsidy Rolls, 11, 35, 44, 141, 142, and references
Summerfield, 54, 55
Sunderland Glass Works, 55
Sussex, 164
Sutton Bonnington, Notts, 39, 91
Sutton Coldfield, Warw., 43-48, 62, 73, 93, 94, 99, 121, 140
Swansea, 50, 86
Symondes, William, 12

Tailor v. Chaunce, 22, 23
Tanner, Rebecca (Chance), 151
Tanworth, Warw., 128
Tardebig, Worc., 36, 117, 123, 124, 126, 129, 137, 138
Taynton, Glouc., 165
Teignmouth, 95
Temple Balsall, Warw., 46, 96
Tenbury, Worc., 28
Thompson, Anne, 127
Throckmorton, 100
Tibbatts of Rowington, 35, 36, 63, 73, 87, 117, 127, 128, 138
   Elizabeth Lucas, 35, 73, 87, 116, 117, 127
Tibbets, Tibbotts, Tibbut, 113, 127, 128, 138, 159
Tilsley, Elizabeth, 74, 75, 106, 149
Tilt, Tylt, general, 9, 32, 33, 63, 73, 85, 86, 115, 116, 126, 136, 137
   Joshua and Mary, 9, 15, 32, 33, 50, 73, 85, 86, 115, 116, 126, 137
   Mary their dau., *see* Bell
   Hannah Hunt, 50
   Ursula Chaunce, 107, 108
Timberhanger (Tymberhonger), Bromsgrove, 22, 24, 74, 106, 108, 133, 138, 144, 145, 148
Timmings, Edward, 161
Timmins, 56, 58, 80, 83
Tolley, Phoebe, 113
Tombes, Elizabeth, 155
Tombstones and Inscriptions, 5-8, 30, 31, 49, 77, 88, 94, 96, 130-132, and references
Tommys, Richard, 65
Toovey, Tovey, 88, 117, 162
Totnes, Devon, 91
Tovey, *see* Toovey
Towers, Millicent, 162
Townsend, Townshend, 80, 106, 148
Toy, William, 155
Trust, old forms of, 12
Tuncks, Ralph, 45
Turner, 92, 93, 120
Twiford, Derb., 99
Tybson, Richard, 144

INDEX.   ix.

Tyllett, John, 32, 136
Tylt, Tylte, *see* Tilt
Tyndon, John, 107

Unett, John, of Birmingham, 83
    of Bromsgrove, 20, 142
Upton-on-Severn, Worc., 27, 132, 134, 154, 162
Upton Snodsbury, Worc., 10, 14, 122, 134, 158
Upton Warren, Worc., 15, 33, 37, 85, 123-126, 136, 139, 148, 153

Vale, Rev., 81
Vernon, of Hanbury, 27, 40-42, 62, 63, 71, 118, 125, 132, 154, 155
    Ann (Nash), 89
    Richard, 77
    Robert and family, 40-42, 63, 73, 92, 118, 128, 129, 139
Visitations, *see* Heralds' Visitations

Wakeman, 14, 108, 127
Waldron, Theodosia, 86, 116, 126
Walford, Frances (Vernon), 92
"Walkers and Clothiers," 19-21, 122, 157
Wallingford, 45
Wallis, John, 123
Walsall, 44, 45, 140
Wand, Rev. Thomas, 99
Ward, 80, 91
Warndon, Worc., 14, 134, 135, 159
Warren, 100
Wartensce Castle, St. Gall, 37
Warwick, 34, 47, 96, 100, 127-129, 138, 155
    Earls of, 98
Warwickshire, 10, 34, 35, 43, 57, 98, 164
Water Orton, Warw., 43, 46, 94, 121
Watkins, 13, 125
Watmore, Mary, 123, 159
Watton, Elizabeth, 128
Weaver, Richard, 111
"Weavers and Clothiers," 19
Welch, James, 79
Wellford, Glouc., 124
Wellington, Duke of, 57
Wells, Jonah Smith and family, 59, 82, 84
Wells, Som., 39, 91
West, 100
Westbury, Glouc., 91
West Indies, the, 51
Weston School, 59, 79
West Stoke, Som., 53
West Town, Som., 52, 53, 73, 94, 96
Whatley, Warw., 99
Whitacre, Warw., 94
Whitchurch, Salop, 83
White, Joseph, 125
Whitley, Great, Worc., 125
Whitstones, Claines, 125, 126
Wichbold, Worc., 88
Wick, near Bristol, 52
Wick Episcopi, Worcester, 19, 141

Wilde, Elizabeth, 108
Wilkes, John, 113, 125, 150
Willes, Elizabeth, 93, 120
Willington, Dorcas (Tilt), 86
Willis, 127
Willoughby, Warw., 47, 94, 95
Wills, 6, 10, 11, 35, 63-68, 133-140, 166
    cp. Administrations, Inventories
Wilbbridge, Glouc., 37
Wilson, 82, 99, 154
Winchester, 163
Winson Green, Birmingham, 51
Winter, 99
Wisher, qy. Worc., 124, 162
Witham, R., Linc., 98
Witherley, Leic., 99, 100
Wolford Magna, Warw., 164
Wolverhampton, 59, 81
Wolverley, Worc., 23
Woodcock, 79, 82, 84
Woodcote, Bromsgrove, 11, 14, 22, 26, 109, 146, 149
Woodrowe, Bromsgrove, 107
Woods, Daniel, 150
Woodward, 105, 109, 150
Woolley, James, 79
Worcester, 9-11, 15, 16, 18-21, 23, 26, 35, 45, 63, 85, 86, 89, 100, 106, 122-124, 126-128, 131, 133-136, 141, 147, 155-157, 160
    old diocese of, 10
    All Saints', 19, 21, 122-124, 126, 133, 156, 157, 160
    Bishop's Registry, 9
    Cathedral, 65, 122, 124, 126-128, 136, 157
    Newport St., 20
    St. Andrew's, 20, 21, 122-124, 131, 135, 156, 157
    St. Clement's, 20, 21, 122-124, 128, 134, 156, 157
    St. Helen's, 124, 126, 128, 136
    St. Martin's, 127
    St. Nicholas', 128, 134, 157
    St. Peter's, 122, 126, 127
    St. Swithin's, 124, 128
    cp. Bedwardine, Wick Episcopi
Worcestershire, 10, 11, 13, 14, 34, 37, 45, 57, 100, 141, 162
Worthing, Sussex, 164
Worthington, Leic., 99
Wraxall, Som., 53, 54, 82, 90, 97
Wright, 86, 126
Wybbe, Thomas, 155
Wylde, 155

Yardley, near Birmingham, 45, 81
Varnhill, Bromsgrove, 108
Varnold, Thomas, 123
Yates, 111, 123, 159
Yeate, James, 128
Yeomans, William, 152
Yeomen, 11, 16-18, 65
Yniscedwin Ironworks, 50, 86
York, 164
Young, Rev., 53, 79, 80

www.ingramcontent.com/pod-product-compliance
Lightning Source LLC
Chambersburg PA
CBHW020309170426
43202CB00008B/554